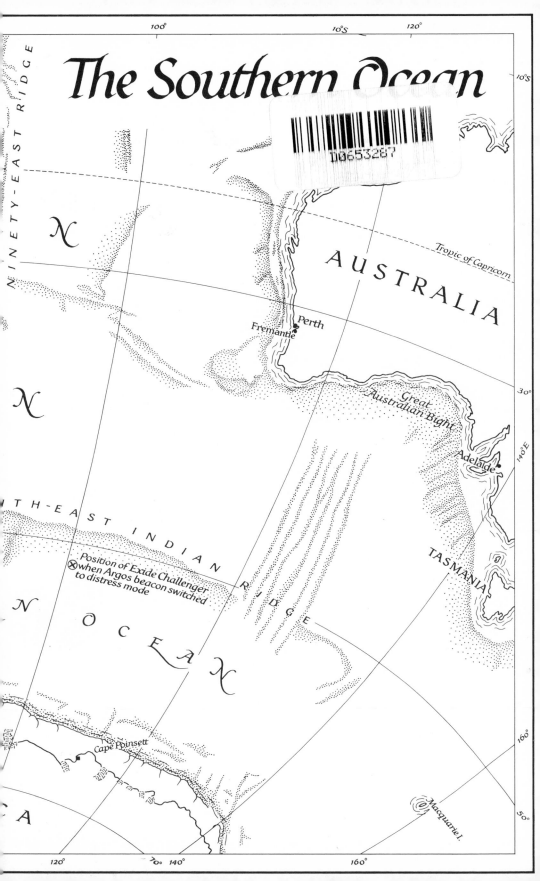

The Southern Ocean

NINETY-EAST RIDGE

Tropic of Capricorn

AUSTRALIA

Perth

Fremantle

Great Australian Bight

Adelaide

⋅TH-EAST INDIAN RIDGE

Position of Exide Challenger
⊗ when Argos beacon switched
to distress mode

TASMANIA

OCEAN

Cape Poinsett

Macquarie I.

SAVED

SAVED

Tony Bullimore

A *Little, Brown* Book

First published in Great Britain in 1997
by Little, Brown and Company

This edition produced for The Book People Ltd,
Hall Wood Avenue, Haydock, St Helens WA11 9UL.

PICTURE CREDITS
Section 1
1-16, 18: Private collection; 17: Popperfoto/Reuter
Section 2
1, 3, 5-9, 10, 12, 14: Popperfoto/Reuter;
2: 92 Wing Photographic Section, RAAF Edinburgh;
4: Associated Press; 11: Rex Features
13: Private collection

A CIP catalogue record for this book
is available from the British Library.

ISBN: 0 316 64150 2

Endpaper map by Alec Herzer

Typeset by Solidus (Bristol) Limited
Printed and bound in Great Britain
by Clays Ltd, St Ives plc

Little, Brown and Company (UK)
Brettenham House
Lancaster Place
London WC2E 7EN

For Lalel

ACKNOWLEDGEMENTS

If I were truly to begin thanking all those people who made this book possible, then the list of names would run into thousands. The mere fact that I can sit here now, typing these words, is a tribute to the courage and perseverence of no single individual, least of all myself. I owe my life to the men and women who took to the air and sea to save me from a very dark and lonely death. I can never repay them, but perhaps in writing their story as well as my own I can bring them greater recognition and lead the applause that each of them deserves.

For giving me back my life, I wish to thank Captain Raydon Gates and the entire ship's company of HMAS *Adelaide*. Among them, I am indebted to Vaughn 'Jock' Heath, Mark 'Knocker' White, Garry 'Gazza' Mason and all the rest of the Petty Officers who looked after me so well in the Mess.

For watching over me from the sky, I wish to thank the brave fliers of 92 Wing at RAAF Edinburgh, Adelaide. Behind the scenes and rarely heralded were the Operations staff in the bunker at 92 Wing, the maintenance crews of 492 Squadron and the 304 Air Base Wing catering staff.

For holding together all the disparate threads of a complex search and rescue, I wish to thank the men and women of the Maritime Rescue Co-ordination Centre in Canberra, Fleet Headquarters in Sydney and Headquarters Air Command.

In the writing of this book, several people gave a great deal of their time in recounting their stories and checking details. In particular I thank Mike Jackson-Calway, Captain Raydon Gates, Chief Petty Officer Pete Wicker, Wing Commander Ian Pearson and Flight Lieutenant Phil Buckley. Thanks also to Michael Robotham for his advice and help with the text; to Jonathan Harris, my agent, for his encouragement; and to Alan Samson, my publisher at Little, Brown.

Without the support and love of family and friends like Steve Mulvany, Yvonne Murray, Anthony Wilson, Wesley and Jane Massam, Alan Rosengren and David Mathieson, I would not have finished this book. They helped me to mend my mind and my body.

Lastly, and most importantly, I wish that I could personally shake hands with the millions of people who prayed and dared to hope that I might be alive. I know that I will never get to meet you all, but I thank you with all my heart.

God bless you all.

Tony Bullimore, May 1997

And now the Storm-Blast came, and he
Was tyrannous and strong:
He struck with his o'ertaking wings,
And chased south along.

With sloping masts and dipping prow,
As who pursued with yell and blow
Still treads the shadow of his foe
And forward bends his head,
The ship drove fast, loud roared the blast,
And southward aye we fled.

And now there came both mist and snow,
And it grew wondrous cold:
And ice, mast-high, came floating by,
As green as emerald.

SAMUEL TAYLOR COLERIDGE
from 'The Rime of the Ancient Mariner'

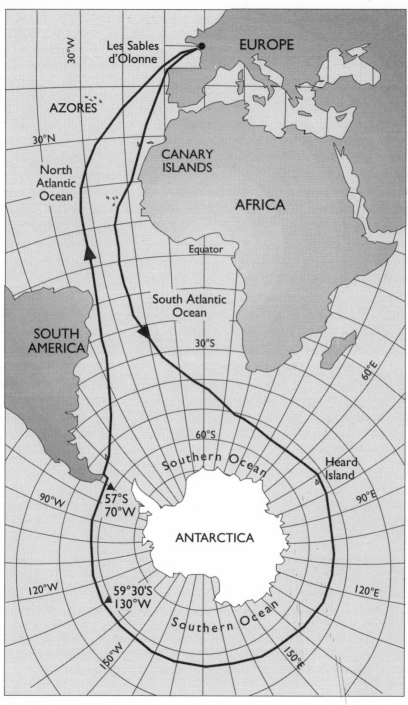

The route of the Vendée Globe race.

1

〰〰〰〰

SOUTHERN OCEAN
Tuesday, 31 December 1996

Heard Island emerges from the morning mist looking wind-swept and prehistoric. My navigation has been spot-on, and I gaze in amazement at my first sight of land in nearly eight weeks. The rocky peaks, streaked with ice and snow, look like ancient pillars holding up the sky, and vegetation clings to the lower reaches like ivy.

Five miles from the island, I alter course to ensure I sail well clear of the coastline and any hidden rocks. There are birds everywhere: kestrels, gulls and albatross which circle and occasionally land in the sea alongside *Exide Challenger*.

I note the time in my log – 'Tuesday 31 December. 0121GMT.' New Year's Eve.

As I skirt the shore, keeping a safe distance, I decide to see if anyone's home. The Admiralty List of Time Signals – a bible for mariners – lists every radio and weather station in the world, giving their frequencies and other details. Opening the book on my chart table, I find the reference to Heard Island and the note, 'Not for public correspondence.' Not open to the public? Well, they can't get too many visitors down here – I'll wish them a Happy New Year. I flip the switch on the SSB (Single Side Band) radio.

'Heard Island, Heard Island, this is *Exide Challenger*, racing yacht *Exide Challenger*, do you copy?'

Silence.

'Heard Island, Heard Island, this is racing yacht *Exide Challenger*, I'm five miles east of you, come in please?'

I try again on two emergency frequencies, 2182 on the SSB and channel 16 on the VHF, but I can't raise anybody. Probably at breakfast, I think, or out on some research trip studying the mating habits of penguins. I think the Australians have a research base or weather station on the island.

For just a brief moment I feel disappointed. Why won't they answer me? Pulling out my binoculars, I scan the shoreline and see a few low huts and what appear to be several small and long-abandoned lighthouses. Very few boats pass this way, apart from the occasional supply vessel sailing to research stations in Antarctica.

As I sail east, away from the island, I keep trying on the SSB and VHF radios. I increase the power from two megs (megahertz) to four megs and then up to eight megs, always on the correct frequencies, but I still can't raise them. Ah, well, it was only a courtesy call.

Fifteen knots of breeze is consistently blowing from the north-west, making it possible for me to sail my chosen course on a broad reach. Apart from the storm a week ago, the Southern Ocean has been kind to me and I've been averaging about 10 knots. Even so, I doubt that's enough to catch the race leaders.

It still upsets me when I think of the problems I've had since leaving Les Sables d'Olonne on the west coast of France in early November. The Vendée Globe is the longest, most challenging yacht race ever conceived, and I know it's impossible to sail non-stop around the world without breaking some equipment and suffering a bit of bad luck. Unfortunately, I've had more than my fair share.

First I had a problem with a fuel line that emptied half my diesel into the engine room. Without sufficient fuel, I would eventually be unable to power the lights, radios, computers, weather fax and navigation instruments. Then the potentiometers came adrift – instruments that give vital information to the automatic pilots – and this forced me to turn back to Les Sables for repairs and to pick up more fuel three days after the race began.

I've never been so frustrated. Every cleat, rivet and padeye on *Exide Challenger* had been checked and re-checked; the sails, winches, pumps, batteries, generator, fuel tanks, beacons, life-raft . . . a million and one things that I had to rely upon during four months at sea.

The mistakes and breakages had put me 1,000 miles behind the fleet, a massive handicap. My only comfort was the knowledge that in the previous Vendée Globe, four years earlier, Philippe Poupon had finished third despite having to turn back soon after the start with keel problems and then losing one of his masts about 1,500 miles from the finish.

Since then I've tried desperately to make up time, but *Exide Challenger* simply can't match the boat speed of the latest breed of ocean greyhounds. The positions on 12 December 1996 put me twelfth in a starting fleet of sixteen, trailing the likes of Christophe Auguin (*Geodis*), Gerry Roufs (*Groupe LG 2*) and Yves Parlier (*Aquitaine Innovations*).

However, long-distance offshore racing isn't just about boat speed. Sailing experience, wind conditions, the right weather routing and problems suffered by other competitors are all part of the equation. Anything can happen over 25,000 miles. It could still go my way, but just finishing the Vendée Globe would be a victory.

The light north-westerly seems likely to continue for a while and *Exide Challenger* feels comfortable. The sixty-foot ketch has two masts, a main and a mizzen, and for the first time since the previous storm, I take all the reefs out, putting up every stitch of canvas. Speed is the name of the game.

I'm 57 degrees south, further than I've ever been, but I want to go down to 60 degrees south. That's my cut-off point. I have to weigh up the benefits of shortening the distance to Cape Horn against the lurking dangers of the Southern Ocean.

Before my big meal of the day, I let 'Bertha' take the helm, punching the button on the autopilot and waiting until I'm sure that she holds her course. After again failing to raise Heard Island, I decide to call home.

'Cape Town Radio, Cape Town Radio, this is *Exide Challenger, Exide Challenger*, Mike Delta Juliet Juliet Seven. Do you copy?'

I try for ten minutes, juggling the frequencies, until I get a reply.

'*Exide Challenger, Exide Challenger*, this is Cape Town Radio, Cape Town Radio, what can we do for you, Tony?'

When I crossed the Equator, I started to use Cape Town radio in South Africa instead of Portishead radio in England. Since then I have become quite friendly with the radio operators in Cape Town and we have organised a scheduled call at 1800 hours GMT every day. This makes life easier, having a time and a specific frequency pre-agreed with the radio station.

'Hello, Harry, can you patch me through to Bristol? I want to wish my wife a Happy New Year.'

'Sure, give us the number again.'

The signal is quite strong, but as the minutes tick by I know it can fade quickly. What's taking so long? I hear Lalel pick up the telephone.

'We have a ship-to-shore call from Tony Bullimore on *Exide Challenger*, will you take the call?'

'Yes!'

The operator comes back to me: 'That's it, you're through.'

'Tony?'

'Lal, how are you?'

'Good, good. I can hardly hear you.'

'Happy New Year!'

'There's a few hours to go yet. What time is it there?'

I glance up at the three clocks above the chart table. 'Local time is just after midnight.'

'I'm just getting dressed to go out.'

'Oh yes, which one of your toy-boys is it this time?'

She laughs. 'They all know you're away, Tony Bullimore.'

'Where are you going?'

'To a dinner and dance at Jury's Hotel with Yvonne, Joyce and Anthony. We got four tickets.' Yvonne is Lalel's niece and Anthony and Joyce are family friends. 'How's it going?' she asks.

'Fine. Great. Weather's good and the boat's on song. I saw Heard Island today. It was nice to see land again.'

I can almost hear her trying to read my voice. She knows I won't tell her if something's wrong.

'So how are you celebrating tonight?'

'I've just made myself a curry. Magnificent it was - diced onion, cayenne pepper, curry powder, tomato ketchup and corned beef. A real belter.'

'You and your curry.'

'Then I polished off the last of the Christmas cake and had a glass of Grand Marnier - it's nearly all gone. I'm feeling quite pleased with myself.'

'How much did you drink?'

'Only a sip.'

'I'm losing you.'

'Sorry. Listen, have a great night and don't drink too much. I'll try to give you a call in a few days.' Lal's voice is breaking up and fading. 'I love you,' I shout, hoping she can still hear me.

I fall asleep in my armchair in front of the chart table. It's a big, comfortable swivel chair that can tilt back almost completely so that I lie flat. If the boat is on a port tack, leaning over, I can spin the chair so that my head is higher than my legs. I don't like the bunk, because you get too comfortable and have trouble getting out. I want to be alert, so I can get on deck quickly and take the helm.

In years gone by, when I raced lightweight multihulls, I was a bit of a purist and would not allow anything on the boat that wasn't really needed. This chair would have had no place on my previous boats *IT82*, *Apricot* or *Spirit of Apricot*. But nevertheless, I have reasoned that if you're going to spend four months at sea, sailing non-stop around the world, a bit of comfort is necessary.

My special chair is both comfortable and functional. I can spin it so I am facing my main chart table and the shelf with my Toshiba laptop computers, printer and satellite comms, or I can spin it again to face another chart table with my weather fax and SSB. A couple of paces from the chair and I'm at the galley, making tea or coffee. It all works really well.

When I'm asleep in the chair, there only has to be the slightest movement of the boat which is out of character and I'm awake. Opening my eyes, I can see the radar, barometer, chart-plotter and other instruments that give a lot of vital details about the speed and direction of the wind.

Glancing up through the large perspex windows in the roof of the doghouse, I can check both the main and mizzen sails. I've sailed more than 35,000 miles in *Exide Challenger* since her launch and I know every creak, groan and whisper. She is my world.

New Year's Day is spectacular. The sun is shining and the barometer is reading about 1010 millibars – relatively high for this part of the world, almost a high-pressure system. The sea mist clears quickly and I eat breakfast sitting in the cockpit. Then I dig into my tobacco pouch, pull out a hefty pinch and drop it into the paper. Rolling it between my fingers, I lick the edge and have my first cigarette of the day.

I wasn't going to take any cigarettes on the voyage because I wanted to give up, but someone suggested that I take 'rollies', claiming I wouldn't smoke as much. Ha! What do they know?

Still heading east-south-east, I steer for a few hours and then go below to tackle the worst chore of the day. My water-maker failed about thirty days into the race – the membrane may have frozen, causing permanent damage – and since then I've been relying on an American-made reverse osmosis water-pump. Known as a 'Survivor', it turns sea-water into drinkable water.

For a while I contemplated pulling into South Africa to make repairs, but under the race rules it would have meant forfeiting any chance of winning, or even qualifying as a finisher. I've tried everything I can think of to fix the problem, but to no avail. After it happened, I pumped out the fresh water tanks and sealed the contents in containers. Then I filled several empty Evian bottles, and worked out that if the Survivor hand-pump failed I had an emergency supply of water that would last ten days.

Since then I've relied on the Survivor water-maker, but to get even a cupful of water means pumping it about a thousand times, which takes ten minutes. I need a minimum of five cups a day. Sitting on the floor near the entrance to the engine-room, I put one tube of the water-maker into the header tank that cools the generator, another into a bucket and a third into a mug. Then I pump a hundred times with my right hand, then switch to my left, and keep doing this until eventually I have a cup of water. I make at least three cups and then put eight hundred pumps straight into the kettle so I can have a celebratory cup of tea. This happens twice a day, morning and afternoon.

If anything, the weather gets even better on Thursday. The sun is strong and warm in a brilliantly blue sky. I open up all the hatches and hang out my oilies to dry, along with three or four pairs of socks on a makeshift line. People used to laugh at my plastic clothes-pegs and call me a washerwoman - normally people tie their socks in a knot to the rigging - but mine dry quicker. Soon *Exide Challenger* looks like an Egyptian barge, but the dampness and musty air are being swept away in the breeze.

Half-filling the kettle, I take out my shaving kit and a little plastic bowl that Lal gave me. Sitting by the galley, I prop up the mirror and shave off two weeks of stubble. Then I add a little cold water, strip out of my long-johns and vest, and wipe down my arms, neck and chest. Then I wet my hair, comb it back and look in the mirror. Suddenly, I remember the aftershave Lal gave me. Normally I never use the stuff at sea, but what the hell, I pour a little in my hands and pat my cheeks.

'There! All dressed up and nowhere to go.'

Up on deck the sun still shines and the air temperature is in the low twenties. Where's the notorious Southern Ocean? I think. It's like a summer's day on Plymouth Sound.

Putting on clean long-johns and canvas shorts, I make a cup of tea, open a packet of chocolate biscuits and sit on deck, dunking them. It's one those rare days when everything comes together and you feel a remarkable affinity with the boat and your surroundings.

I never curse the sea, no matter what she throws at me. I've always shown utter respect because I know the power she has to swallow ships the size of the *Titanic* and break a person's heart. Over the years she's taken a lot of good friends of mine and never given them back.

Yet there are times when everything is magical. I love night sailing under a clear sky, with the stars reflecting on the water. With the boat going nicely through the waves, I sit at the helm and glory at the silence and sheer sense of space. Occasionally, porpoises come alongside the boat and I can hear them chatting to each other. Schools of tiny silver fish whisper just below the surface, and in the darkness manta-like rays leap clear and fall back into the water. I've been in fog at night, so close to whales that I can hear them blowing. I've sailed a racing trimaran up the Saguenay River in Canada, doing 28 knots on water like glass with sheer cliffs on each side. It was like being a bullet going down the barrel of a gun. These are rare moments in an incomparable sport.

At about noon a little bird lands on the deck above the entrance to the doghouse. It's about six inches long, thin and grey, with a touch of colour on its breast. An hour later another one arrives; both are exhausted. They've obviously been blown off course or become lost, and now I'm their only salvation – a tiny floating 'island'. As the wind picks up, they come inside and find a quiet spot to watch me using the water-maker.

'I'll soon have arms like Popeye,' I tell them, as I switch hands and keep pumping.

I get a bowl of water and break up some digestive biscuits and peanuts. One of them seems too exhausted to eat; his tiny chest flutters rapidly as if fighting for breath. I pick him up and put him by the bowl. 'Don't waste this stuff, it's rationed.'

After dinner, they watch me as I write my log and mark my latest position on the chart. Then I make them a little nest out of an old jumper and put it in a corner. They probably won't use it, but it makes me feel better.

The next day they grow more confident and actually fly in and out of the doghouse, circling high over the yacht as if looking for land and then returning. One is definitely healthier than the other. I find myself talking to them while I work, explaining what I'm doing and asking their advice about the weather. There's not a cloud in the sky and the seas are so calm it's almost too good to be true. It makes me uneasy. I'd prefer to be further north, closer to the major shipping lanes, where the winds are normally more favourable. Unfortunately, it's the long way round.

In the southern hemisphere, air masses flooding into a depression spiral clockwise, influenced by the rotation of the earth. They tend to generate winds predominantly from the west. As the depressions move northwards, I should try to move with them, trying to stay on the port side to pick up tail winds. If I stray too far south and get caught on the opposite side, I'll have the wind in my face – along with mountainous seas.

Without my INMARSAT-C I have no way of knowing where the depressions are forming. The satellite communications system failed before I reached the Equator – either the aerial became damaged or there was a fault in the complex electronics. It's a really serious piece of kit, worth about £8,000, that hooks up to my laptop computer. Normally it means I can send and receive messages instantly from anywhere in the world, without any of the atmospheric disturbances radio transmissions experience. I can also use software to receive and analyse the latest weather reports and satellite pictures. (The factory said I should send it back to them, which is very bloody helpful when you're sailing non-stop around the world.)

Since then, I've had no means of getting weather reports apart from my weather fax machine. At set times and on designated frequencies, the information is put on the airwaves. I'm averaging about one clear picture in every ten. Usually it spits out a blank piece of paper covered in fuzzy black lines that are impossible to read.

Now it's all come down to instinct and experience, and for me there's something quite appealing about that. It's like a throwback to the days of yore, when the tall ships would sail from England round the Cape of Good Hope and then on to Australia. They certainly didn't have weather charts or satellite pictures.

When predicting the weather, fishermen and other seafarers have local knowledge and understand weather patterns in their regions. I've crossed the Atlantic about twenty-seven times and know many of the tell-tale signs, what to expect at certain times of the year. But I've never been this far south in the Southern Ocean; this is a totally different beast.

If the seas start building, I can't simply assume a storm is coming because down here the big swells can be pushed for thousands of miles and the storm may never reach me. I might reef the sails, or take them down completely – which is hard work – and then have to put them up again, wasting time and energy. By the same token, if I make the wrong decision, I could get caught in heavy weather with too much sail aloft. It's bloody hard to get them down when the wind is howling and you're running downwind with the sails pinned to the rigging. That's why one of the secrets of single-handed sailing is to be one step ahead of the weather and to know what's going on around you.

My feathered friends have gone; I hope they make it. I haven't seen them since midday, when they watched me strip almost naked and crawl through a hatch in the cockpit to get to the fuel tanks under the doghouse floor. Unfortunately, there is still some diesel fuel sloshing about in this area, which is why I strip off my clothes. But it means having a good wash down after every time I go in there.

Aren't birds supposed to be able to predict the weather? All my instincts tell me that something is brewing, and I keep scanning the horizon for some sign. The wind has picked up a little but there isn't a cloud in the sky. I make up my mind to go a little north-east, having gone as far south as I feel necessary.

'Perth Radio, Perth Radio, this is *Exide Challenger*, racing yacht *Exide Challenger*, do you read me?'

Static.

I keep trying, hoping to get a weather report, then sleep.

A shift in the boat wakes me. I glance up through the windows, check the sails and then study the instruments. It's 6:00 A.M. on Saturday 4 January, and the wind has picked up to a modest 18 knots. When I look at the electronic barometer, I notice a strange thing. For two days it's been glued to 1010 millibars, but now it starts to drop.

Three hours later, the barometer has fallen to 990 millibars. That is amazing, but where's the wind? I tap the display window, press a few buttons and pull out the instruction manual. This had happened to me before, about ten days ago. The barometric pressure fell, indicating much stronger winds, but the winds never arrived.

I watch the wind-speed dial creep up to 23 knots, then 25 knots, and wait to see if it drops back again. No, it seems solid.

It hasn't come in a rush like a squall or a front moving through - just a slow, solid build-up.

'Okay, if it reaches 28 to 30 knots I'll start dropping the reefs in,' I say out loud, in between mouthfuls of cereal.

By 8:00 A.M. I am in my oilies, sea boots and a hat that covers my ears. I wrap a scarf around my neck to stop water leaking down into my thermals. The best gloves in the world for light work on a yacht are gardening gloves that you can pick up for about £1.50.

Up on deck, I first think about what I'm going to do. I never rush unless it's an emergency. I prepare each rope that I'm going to pull, making sure there are no bad tangles and the rope will run free. I'll put one reef in the main and mizzen sails and leave the jib, I decide. The mizzen is easier to put in because I can do it from the cockpit, so I reef the main first.

I point *Exide Challenger* a little more to windward - but not hard on the wind - and then let the main sheet off. The boom swings out to leeward, which allows the mainsail to luff and flutter. Then I scramble forward and crank up the lazy jacks which stop the boom from crashing down on to the deck.

Letting go of the main halyard, I open the rope clutches and get ready to pull in the reefing lines which are on the trailing edge of the sail. The main and mizzen sails each have three reefing points, which can be used to lower them by varying amounts, depending on the wind. Tying off the main, I repeat the process on the mizzen sail. Glancing around the deck, everything seems secure, so I go back down below. The barometer has fallen to 980.

Kettle on, cup of tea, I'm quite pleased with myself. I check the charts and make a little mark to show where I put the reefs in. Keeping one eye on the wind speed, I sip a brew and decide to call Lalel.

'Do you know what time it is? It's two o'clock on Saturday morning.'

'Is it?'

'You know what time it is, Tony Bullimore. What's wrong? What's happened?'

'Nothing, nothing, I just want to hear the sweet sound of your voice.'

'So you wake me up?'

Lal can never stay angry at me for long. She tells me about New Year's Eve and how everyone asked about me; they even drank a toast.

'Have you been round Cape Horn yet?'

'Don't be silly, Lal,' I laugh. 'Have a look at the map, I'm thousands of miles from Cape Horn.'

'Oh, that's all right then. Just you be careful going round the Horn.'

Before the Vendée Globe, I brought home a video of sailing in the Southern Ocean, and it really bothered Lal; it told the story of one yachtsman who went crazy and another who committed suicide. For some reason, Cape Horn stuck in Lal's mind as the place where I'd have problems.

'I'm feeling quite pleased with myself,' I tell her.

'Why's that then?'

'No reason. I just put a reef in the main and mizzen before the wind got up. Looks like I'm in for a blow. Now I'm all cosy with a cup of tea and a biscuit.'

'And a cigarette?'

'That, too.'

I tell her about the two little birds and how I hope they're safe.

'It's a pity *you* can't fly home,' she says, sounding sleepy.

'Won't be long now. I'm almost half-way there. The next call won't be through Cape Town radio; it'll be through Perth.'

Outside, the north-westerly is blowing over 30 knots, and the sea is starting to heave and roll. *Exide Challenger* is disappearing into the troughs, and visibility is down to half a mile. When the wind gets to 35 knots, I'll put in the next reef, I decide. The depression is likely to be somewhere to the south-west of me. One thing's for sure: I don't want the depression to go north-east of me, as I could then end up with nasty head-winds and having to beat directly into the rolling seas.

By 11:00 A.M., I have a gut feeling that it's really going to blow. But how much? Forty-five knots? Fifty? I drop the mainsail completely, wrapping it tightly to the boom with a twelve-metre length of rope, winding it all the way along and back again. 'That main isn't going anywhere,' I think.

Then I put a bridle on the boom, put three reefs in the mizzen and partly roll up the jib, tying off the furling line on a cleat to ensure it does not get loose and let the Solent jib unroll itself, which could cause a lot of damage.

Still the wind keeps coming, stronger all the time, and the sea begins to boil. From the cockpit, I look up and see a dirty grey mass about a mile ahead.

'That's a bloody iceberg,' I think, peering through the gloom. I grab my binoculars from inside and have another look. If anything, it seems to be moving closer. Can icebergs do that? I keep watching, and I swear I can see it building. It seems to stretch across the horizon in an unbroken line, rising higher and higher.

'That's a rogue wave,' I mutter. It's enormous - six, seven, eight storeys high - billions of gallons of water, rolling across the ocean looking for something to slow it down.

Then I see another.

Always in front, never behind, I think, as I drop the mizzen sail and roll up the jib completely. I'm running under bare poles, without a stitch of sail. It takes twenty minutes on deck. The chill factor is way below freezing and it's really biting into me. I roll up the ropes, collect the snatch blocks and make sure no gear is loose or lying about.

The routine is the same inside. I go through the boat, checking everything is lashed down and stowed properly, with nets over the shelves to hold things in place. A bungie cord secures the laptops, my charts are folded and put safely away, along with pencils, the protractor and slide-rule. Everything is under control. If the boat gets knocked down, I'm not going to be injured by anything flying around.

As I reach into a cupboard to where I keep my winch handles, my fingertips brush against something soft and out of place.

'You poor little thing,' I sigh, gently lifting the bundle of feathers into the palm of my hand. The weakest bird had not flown away; it had retreated to the darkness of the cupboard to die. I feel as if I've failed a friend.

'What happened to your mate, then? I hope he made it.'

Carrying the tiny body outside through the companionway entrance, I let it slip over the side of the cockpit, where it disappears into the foaming sea. Such a mighty grave for this little fellow.

I don't have time to think about it any more; the wind is over 50 knots and I'm surfing down fifteen-metre waves under bare poles. I look at the boat speed – 18 knots . . . 20 knots . . . 22 knots – it's like the biggest thrill ride in a theme park except without the built-in safety we all know is there. Roll up for the ride of a lifetime!

The wing masts are the problem. Unlike a sailing boat with a traditional rig, my wing masts have a girth of about three feet, and are cambered like the wings of an aircraft. This means that the masts act as sails and help to power the boat along. It's great for boat speed but, as I discovered in the previous storm, this means I have 'sail area' that cannot be reefed away, it will always be working.

Visibility is down to a hundred metres. Every so often I see another rogue wave, and I begin imagining that if they're in front of me then they must also be behind. I keep glancing around, wishing I had eyes in the back of my head. Clipping on a safety harness, I surf down the swells, steering sharply before I reach the bottom of each trough so the bow doesn't dig into the water. I look round and see a wave on my port side. It's bloody huge, with a face that looks almost vertical. Rearing up, it splits at the top with white water rolling down the front and back.

I look at it in awe, and realise that one of those only has to catch me at the right moment and I'm in serious trouble.

2

SOUTHERN OCEAN
Saturday, 4 January 1997

Late afternoon and I've been at the helm for nearly five hours. The rogue waves must be mighty because the average waves around me are all about sixty feet high. I can hear them coming, rumbling like thunder. They build and build, pushing forward until they peak, and then split at the top, sending water rolling down each side.

The previous storm, ten days ago, lasted eighteen hours. Maybe I can steer through this one if I manage to stay awake and fight off exhaustion. The freezing spray bites at my cheeks and I can feel the cold creeping into my fingers through the wet gloves. I take one hand off the wheel and flex it into a fist, trying to keep the blood circulating. What I'd give for a cup of coffee and a cigarette!

In the twilight, I notice that waves are rolling at me from two different directions, colliding and causing the sea to rise high into the sky. Maybe I have reached the epicentre of the storm, and can now expect a major wind shift.

Walls of water are crashing into each other and sending spray a hundred feet into the air. The sea has turned completely white. I can steer *Exide Challenger* downwind, but she wants to surf down the waves and is hitting speeds of 18–20 knots. The bow digs deep into the troughs and my heart almost stops. Will I pitch-pole this time? The deck groans under the weight of water and then slowly rises again. Unfortunately, Bertha can't hold her on a downwind course. Every time I punch the pilot button and let go of the wheel, a wave knocks the yacht sideways and she wants to luff up to windward. This is crazy.

One of the yacht's design team, Barry Noble, said that *Exide Challenger* would be very strong and capable of holding boat speeds to ensure good daily runs, day after day. I was pleased with this but soon discovered that you can't tackle hurricanes or major storms with wing masts that are continuously driving the boat through the water, even when you want to slow down. Equally, you can't expect to sail through the Southern Ocean with a steady 25 to 30 knots on a broad reach.

A wave crashes ahead of me, sending water rolling over the doghouse, flooding the cockpit. The safety harness keeps me in place as the water runs away through big drainage holes in the stern. I wonder how many hours I can steer for. Sometimes you hear people talk about being on the helm for two or three days in a storm, but that's nonsense - you get absolutely knackered and begin to nod off, and that's when mistakes are made.

A part of me thinks, 'Hell, if I can continue to helm doing 20 knots, that's two hundred miles every ten hours. I can make up some serious mileage.' At the same time, my experience tells me, 'You can only hold the helm for ten or twelve hours in these conditions before you get seriously fatigued.'

Some yachts have a steering position inside the cabin, where you can sit in a comfortable chair, with a mug of tea or coffee and a heater warming your toes. I decided against this because you can't see what's coming or where you're going. Steering by the compass instead of your eyes means you could be steering straight into the wall of a wave or nose-diving into a trough without realising it until it's too late. The entire yacht could pitch-pole. You can have the same problem when using a pilot, too - unless you stay alert and watch the waves.

'C'mon, Bertha, just hold her for a few minutes,' I say, punching the button.

I clamber into the doghouse, shutting the hatch behind me, and put the kettle on. Coffee, sugar and powdered milk are spooned into a mug and I roll myself a cigarette. As the boat begins to lurch dangerously to windward, I dash outside, taking control again.

The whistle screeches on the kettle and I give Bertha another chance. She holds the boat on course just long enough for me to make the coffee and clip on the anti-spill lid. I take a few sips and light the cigarette; wonderful.

The wind speed indicator is nudging 70 knots - surely it can't go any higher? Every so often I look back and see a huge wave building behind me. I come up with the wave and see the whole world before me surfing down into a trough at 26 knots. The entire boat is vibrating with the speed. It's not built to go this fast in these conditions.

How can I slow down? They don't build yachts with hand-brakes. The bow starts to bury and the seas come up to the foremast. Painfully, she rises up again.

She's doing the job, but I'm exhausted; I can't keep this up. I think about using the sea anchor, which is like a small canvas parachute that fills with water and can either be used as a drogue, by towing it from the stern of the boat, or as an anchor, which will almost stop the yacht if used from the bow to hold the boat to windward.

Failing that, I could just point the boat to windward, lash the helm and sit there. It's not going to work. The bloody wing masts make it impossible and I can only run with the wind.

It's near midnight and I haven't eaten since breakfast. This could blow for days, and I need to keep my strength. Somehow, I have to get *Exide Challenger* sailing by herself.

I experiment by steering at various degrees off the wind and then trigger the autopilot. Sometimes it holds for five minutes, or even ten, but then a wave hits the hull and the whole boat shifts to port in the water. Then the wing masts start acting like a sail, generating enormous speed. Bertha tries to get back on course, but the boat suddenly swings to starboard, going too far. I'm zigzagging across the ocean.

Remembering the last storm, I steer sixty to seventy degrees off the wind, going north-east. I hit the button again.

'C'mon, Bertha, you can hold her.'

After an hour and a half she begins to feel comfortable. *Exide Challenger* is doing about 12 to 14 knots, heading north-east. She's taking a hammering, but at least she's not surfing at ridiculous speeds.

Scrambling into the doghouse, I shut the hatch and slump

down on the step by the companionway entrance. I'm shattered. It's a terrific spot because I can brace myself against the violent rocking of the boat and look up through the windows to see the masts. If something goes wrong, I'm only a few steps from the deck.

The galley is next to me and I boil the kettle. Glancing up at the barometer, it's now down to 960. Where am I in this thing, I wonder. How long is it going to last? I tuck my legs up, drop my chin on to my chest and shut my eyes.

Suddenly, the boat heels sideways - hit by a wave. I feel the pressure in my shoulders as they brace against the bulkhead. The masts must almost be touching the water. Slowly she rights herself, pulled upright by the weight of the keel.

I open a can of corned beef and scoop it into a plastic bowl. It would be nice with some chopped onion, but I can't be bothered. Tomato sauce will do. I stir it up and then pull out six Ryvita biscuits - that's my allocation. I spoon the corned beef on to each biscuit, a mouthful at a time - I don't want to spill any.

Then I make myself a cup of tea, roll a cigarette and dunk a few digestives. The boat is leaning at times, as if trying to get knocked over, but at least the big waves are coming from the one direction, west-nor'west.

I slide in a cassette tape and listen to Bob Marley singing 'No Woman No Cry'; he says everything's going to be all right ...

Eyes closed, coffee drained, Bob Marley making me feel mellow ... life's not so bad. The boat heels to leeward again; I brace myself.

Crack!

What was that?

All of a sudden the world turns and I turn with it. It isn't slow motion; it's very, very fast. I keep thinking about the 'crack!'; it sounded like someone snapping a fence-paling across their knee.

I'm sitting on the ceiling of the doghouse, with the floor above me. *Exide Challenger* is upside-down.

'Come on, come on, back you go. Let's get you back the right way up.'

Nothing happens.

Looking down through the windows I can see foam and water surging beneath me. It's like being in a glass-bottomed boat.

Shit! The bloody keel has gone. I can't believe it.

Why didn't I get hurt? I must have instinctively rolled as the boat went over. The lights are still on and the nets have stopped everything tumbling from the shelves and lockers.

Think, Tony, think. What are you going to do? Can you get the boat over?

No keel, no chance. I could have lost the masts, or the rudders and still been okay, but the keel is almighty.

What's happened to the masts?

They've probably snapped on impact. They're designed to be buoyant to help right the boat if she turns turtle. It hasn't happened, so I've lost them.

I have lights. The batteries are held in place by stainless steel bars, but they're now at the top of the boat. Unless I can find a way of swinging the generator around, I won't be able to recharge them.

I roll myself a cigarette and nibble a biscuit. What's next? The boat's not going to sink. It's a foam sandwich design with watertight compartments. With any luck, I can probably stay reasonably dry in the doghouse.

Fresh water could be a real problem, although I have my Survivor water-maker and a few half-litre sachets I was given before the start of the race. Technically I have plenty of food, but most of my stores are in watertight compartments beneath the cockpit floor, which is now underwater. There's no way of getting to the hatches unless I open the companionway entrance and flood the yacht.

Emergency beacons?

I have four of them. Three Argos beacons provided by the race organisers, and my own EPIRB, which operates on a different frequency. One of the Argos beacons has been permanently running from the cockpit, giving race headquarters regular updates of my position.

I have to trigger another beacon in distress mode – but how? The signal won't penetrate the hull, so I have to put it outside. Again, this means opening the companionway entrance and flooding the yacht. Bloody hell, I think – what a mess.

Okay, take a deep breath and let's think about this nice and carefully. There's no rush, I'm not going anywhere. It's 3:00 A.M. and the storm is still blowing. I should wait until daylight; hopefully things might calm down.

In the pit of my stomach, deep down where even the butter-flies are afraid to go, I know that I'm knocking on death's door. It's common sense, really. At more than fifty degrees south, I'm over a thousand miles from the nearest shipping lanes. The only vessels in these waters are likely to be supply ships servicing the research and scientific stations around Antarctica, and there would only be a handful of these each summer. The nearest race competitor, as far as I know, is 800 miles ahead of me. I'm 1,000 miles east of Heard Island, 1,500 miles south-west of Australia and 800 miles north of Antarctica. I'm at the arse-end of the world and couldn't be any further from rescue, even if I tried.

If this were the North Atlantic, I'd have shipping lanes all over the place, going to Africa, America, the Canaries, the Azores and the Caribbean. Instead, I'm in the worst spot I can possibly imagine – east of Heard Island in hostile seas.

Oh, Tony, what a mess.

Half a packet of biscuits and three or four cigarettes later, and still I'm thinking. It's like going to the doctor and being told that your tests have come back. He's not going to prat about; he'll give it to me straight.

'You're going to die, Mr Bullimore, some time in the next few days.'

'Is there any cure?

'No.'

'Is there any way I can give myself more time?'

'Yes, but only by an extra day, maybe two.'

The boat is pitching and rolling so much it's all I can do to stop myself being hurled around the upturned cabin. The nets that once held things on top of the shelves are now sagging under the weight as they hang upside-down. They start to give way. Thankfully, very little water has leaked into the dog-house; just enough to run across the toes of my boots.

Okay, Tony, be realistic, what are your options? If a rescue operation is launched, what form will it take? I'm too far from land to be reached by helicopter, so that's out. The nearest air-craft will be in Australia, but planes can only find me - they can't pick me up.

If I can trigger a distress beacon, they'll try to divert the nearest ships to do a search. From what I can tell, Heard Island is probably deserted and Iles Kerguélen, 380 miles further north-west, has a French community, but I doubt if it has a ship big enough to reach me in time.

What about the shipping lanes? The route across the Indian Ocean from Cape Town to Perth is about a thousand to fifteen hundred miles north of me. Down here, freighters and tankers stick to the safer latitudes, for obvious reasons. I can't imagine any skipper or ship's master wanting to bring a £20 million tanker so deep into the Southern Ocean.

So where does that leave me? I might be lucky and get picked up by a research ship heading for Antarctica, but there's probably only half a dozen all year, so that would be like winning the lottery.

I probably have more chance of drifting to Antarctica. Now there's a thought - don't dismiss anything, Tony. Let's assume I keep drifting south-east, how long would it take me to bump into Antarctica? The wind and waves are probably pushing me along at 1, maybe 2 knots. That's 24 to 48 miles a day. Antarctica is about 800 miles south of here. Even if I could drift directly south, which is impossible, it would take at least sixteen days. I'll die of starvation or the yacht will sink by then.

Think, Tony, think!

I have my toolbox, so maybe I can spin the generator around, as well as the batteries and the gas cooker. Once I reach land, the structural integrity of the air-tight compartments won't matter any more, so I can open the hatches beneath the deck and salvage plenty of food.

I could build myself a shelter, start a fire, and dry my clothes. Then I'll build some skis and a make-shift sleigh that I can drag behind me. I'll wrap my whole body in canvas to counter the wind-chill and trek to the nearest research station. Not all in a day, of course, maybe five or ten miles in a stretch. At night I'll dig an ice-cave and eat plenty of food to stoke the body furnace. Maybe I can take something along to burn.

Get serious, Tony, you're dreaming!

They're going to have to send a ship for me, most likely from Australia. I doubt if they'll bother, but I have to hope. Depending on the weather, it will take a ship three or four days to reach me. Somehow, I have to stay alive that long.

Daylight is coming. Through the window beneath my feet, I see the dark water growing lighter, bathing the doghouse in a green glow. I hear a tapping sound. The boom is hitting the perspex as the yacht plunges into the troughs. I'm not worried. The perspex is twelve millimetres thick and bonded tightly into the deck with rubber, glue and sealant. It's bloody tough; you can hit it with a hammer.

I put it out of my mind and concentrate on how to put an emergency beacon outside.

Traditional yachts (monohulls) aren't built with an escape hatch within the hull in case someone becomes trapped inside an upturned boat. Most of them, like *Exide Challenger*, are designed to be self-righting. The fourteen-foot keel, with a 4.5-ton lead bulb, should drag her upright if she gets knocked over.

The last thing anyone expects is to *lose* the keel. Mine was a piece of engineering genius: made of carbon, with a torpedo-shaped lead weight at the bottom, the keel board wasn't bolted beneath the boat like most keels. This one went up through a slot in the hull, into a keep board below the doghouse floor. Well wrapped-up in carbon and resin, it all fused together to become part of the boat. So why did it break? I don't know. Why do planes suddenly fall out of the sky?

I think the wing masts were probably heeling the boat over, bringing the keel near the surface just as a wave crashed down. It hit the keel just at the right angle with the right resonance – like walking into a punch from Mike Tyson. It found a weakness and 'bang!' – the keel disappeared.

It's all speculation, of course. I'd done 20,000 miles on the boat before the race even started, without a problem. Forget about it; that's all history. All that counts is the here and now.

Green water churns beneath the windows. The boom taps merrily away. I need a rescue and survival strategy, and it has to centre around the distress beacons and someone coming to get me.

First I'll find a way of a getting a beacon outside; maybe I can use my tools to cut a hole in the hull. Then I'll make the boat habitable - I can spin the stove and have hot food, coffee and tea. I have some dry clothes in the 'cuddy' beyond the engine-room - a small room used for storage. The batteries might last two or three days, giving me a little light.

I have some leakage, about six inches of water in the bottom of the boat, not bad at all. I can stay dry and wedge myself in a corner so I don't get chucked around and break any bones. That's the plan; I'm sure it can work.

Tap, tap, tap goes the boom.

3

SOUTHERN OCEAN
Sunday, 5 January 1997

A funnel of water explodes into the hull with such force that it hits the roof above my head. It's like an upside-down waterfall, and for three or four seconds I stare at it blankly, frozen in shock. I hear a faint groan of exclamation and know it must be mine.

Already sea-water swirls around my knees, then my thighs, rising at a tremendous speed. Bloody hell, it's cold!

I know it has to stop at the waterline – that's the law of physics – but there doesn't seem to be much logic about anything that's happening to me. The boom has smashed the window – punching a neat hole about eighteen inches high and three feet long in the deck beneath my feet.

Water surges upwards, now at my chest. It sloshes from side to side in the cabin; I'm in the washing machine from hell. I keep telling myself, 'It's a foam sandwich boat with watertight cells. It's not going to sink.' Tell that to the waves!

The lights have gone; the hull is dark. I'm dead unless I can find my survival suit. Wading through the freezing water, I reach the engine-room, which is still relatively dry. Each of the cabins is separated by a bulkhead with a oval-shaped doorway. The bottom lip of the door is about a foot and a half above the deck.

Beyond the engine room is the cuddy, and in it are four canvas hold-alls on the shelves. I fumble through them in the dark. One contains thermal underwear, vests and socks; another has a spare set of oilies; the third has a small first-aid kit and personal stuff like a razor and shaving cream. The fourth has my survival suit – a nylon shell of lightweight, tightly-woven yarn outside a soft, flexible three-component laminated fabric.

I whip off my oilies and drag on the yellow suit. It's not easy as the boat is rolling and pitching. Zipping it up, I feel warmer instantly. The suit doesn't have hands or feet. At home I have a North Sea survival suit that covers me completely. You're a fool, Tony, for not taking it. It's all a learning curve.

I pour water out of my boots and pull them back on. They offer little protection from the cold, but at least I won't slice my feet open on debris beneath the water.

Okay, number-one priority – activate a distress beacon. One is in a bracket on the bulkhead of the engine-room, another lashed to a shelf nearby and a third beneath the chart table. Two of them are Argos beacons, exactly like the one that has been operating continuously in the cockpit of *Exide Challenger* since the race began.

The beacons have three different operating modes. The normal setting gives your position by continuously sending a simple digital signal via satellite, with a special code to show ownership. Mode two is triggered by pushing a separate button which alters the signal, and is used to test the beacon or, in some circumstances, to indicate a technical difficulty. The third mode is triggered by an alarm/distress switch beneath a screw-top plastic cap.

Unhooking the beacon from the bulkhead wall, I unscrew the cap and flick the switch. A small red light begins flashing slowly. Replacing the cap so it can't accidentally flick off, I plunge into the doghouse. Someone who's six feet six inches tall can stand in the centre of the cabin. I'm only five feet four, and water is nearly up to my chin. I try to keep to the sides, where it isn't so deep.

Exide Challenger seems to be lower at the stern, but it's hard to tell with so much water rolling from side to side. It seems to have stopped at the waterline.

I lash the beacon to a length of rope, take a deep breath and plunge down. Christ, it's cold. It's like having ice-blocks pressed against your eyeballs. I push the beacon through the shattered window and let it go. Rope slips between my fingers and I tug it several times, like a fishing line, trying to feel if the beacon is bobbing on the surface or caught up in broken rigging. There must be masts and ropes everywhere.

I can't be absolutely sure unless I open the companionway entrance and swim outside, but the storm is still raging, and I might not be able to get back. I just have to hope the signal is picked up.

Back in the engine room, I try to get warm. 'The cold will kill you first,' I tell myself.

Now the window has smashed it's a whole new ball-game: a desperate situation has become critical. There's equipment I can't rely upon – including *Exide Challenger*. Water is pouring over the hatch into the engine-room, finding a level at about my knees. I don't think she'll sink, but she's lower in the water than I expect.

I have to get the life-raft prepared – just in case. I don't even know if it's still lashed to the deck or been torn loose. What if someone finds it? They'll say, 'Ah, it's all finished, he's dead,' and call off the search.

Getting my toolbox from the engine-room, I take a hammer, two safety chisels and two spanners. I brace myself against the side of the doghouse to counter the rocking and start trying to chop a hole in the bulkhead above the water line. If I can punch through to the cockpit, maybe I can see the life-raft container without letting more water inside. Please God, let it be there.

Normally, the plastic container sits on four rubber squares on the cockpit sole towards the stern. It's about 36 inches long, 20 inches wide and 10 inches deep. Each side has two padeyes threaded with rope that keep it lashed down. A separate rope inflates the raft.

Bang! Bang! Bang! I keep hitting hard spots in the reinforced carbon of the bulkhead. This stuff is like rock. After an hour I give up and wade back to the engine-room to try to get warm.

Okay, Tony, think about what you want to do. If the raft is

still on deck, it's underwater. I'll have to swim out into the cockpit and cut the ropes. Then I can push it down below the raised flush decking that runs around the cockpit sole and the stanchions (safety rails), before inflating it on the surface.

But I don't want to swim into the open sea, not yet. What if I get tangled in the rigging, or the raft doesn't inflate, or it gets shredded by a wave? What if I can't get back to the doghouse? Come on, Tony, there has to be an answer.

Maybe I can unlash the life-raft, pull the container into the doghouse, tie the ripcord to a long rope and then push it back out again, beneath the cockpit coving and the safety rails, until it clears the hull. Then I can tug on the longer rope and make it inflate. If it works, I won't have to leave the hull.

That's the plan. Let's do it.

Standing at the companionway entrance, I tilt my head back above the sloshing water and take a deep breath. Plunging downwards, the shock of the cold is astonishing and I get the worst ice-cream headache in history. I come up gasping and then go down again, sitting under the water, trying to acclimatise myself.

There's a rope looped under my armpits that I've tied to a rigging wire used to anchor the mizzen mast; this is so I can drag myself back into the cabin if I get into trouble. I don't want the hatch to slam shut, trapping me outside. Bracing my shoulder against the door, I reach for the latch and push hard. At first it won't budge, but then it starts to move as water equalises on both sides.

Submerging, I grasp the door frame near the latch. Suddenly, a surge of water forces the hatch shut with tremendous pressure. My hand slips. A sharp pain. Flesh and bone are no match for plastic and metal.

I hold up my hand and think, 'Good God. Where's my finger?' It's just a stub of jagged bone and blood.

The stab of fire arrives like an after-shock. I squeeze my eyes shut, fighting back hot tears. There are red swirls in the lovely clear sea-water, like a three-dimensional painting. I wonder if I'm going to bleed to death. It's amazing how little pain I feel, my hands have gone so cold.

Holding my hand out of the water, I go back to the cuddy and hunt for my small first-aid kit. I try to wrap the bloody stub in cotton wool and bandages, but within ten minutes the dressing has fallen off into the water. Surprisingly, the bleeding stops after half an hour, and the cold numbs the pain almost completely.

I go back to the companionway entrance and push the door again. I must be stark raving mad, I think, but I've got no choice. I have to get the life-raft.

This time, I push through the hatch, kick off from the bulkhead and see the life-raft about sixteen feet away. By the time I get there, my lungs are empty. I turn back without having cut a rope and burst through the hatch into the doghouse, fighting for air. What happened?

Years ago I could hold my breath for about two and half minutes. Now it's about a minute and a half – that's smoking for you, Tony, although I'm sure it also has something to do with the cold.

Five minutes later, I try again, almost counting down the seconds in my mind. I grip the ropes, braid on braid, and manage to cut two of the dozen lines before retreating inside.

This is bloody hopeless. It's fiercely cold and I must get warm.

The cuddy is still dry and almost pitch black. I notice a narrow shelf along one wall, about eighteen inches wide, with the lip pointing down and the netting still hanging below.

I stand on the lip of the doorway and slide on to the shelf, grinding my ribs against the sharp outer edge until I can almost count the bones as I push forward. Half on to the shelf, I edge my feet up the side of the doorway and then on to the bulkhead, pushing myself further along the shelf.

My shoulders are jammed against the side of the hull, with one arm up and one arm down. There isn't enough room to turn. I'm so tired, I just want to sleep. The sound of water crashing over the hull drowns out any other noise. My eyes won't stay open. So tired, and so cold . . .

4

〰〰〰

'It's all right, son, there's nothing to be afraid of down here.'

The old man took out his handkerchief and wiped his hat and scarf. He smiled at my mother in the half-dark and told her not to fuss.

I lay on a straw mattress on the top bunk of a metal-framed bed. The old man had been in the bunk below when I vomited. I don't remember which Underground station it was, probably somewhere in the East End. We could hear the bombs exploding above us and my grandmother and my aunt were hugging each other. I was only four years old.

I guess you could say that this is my first memory. Not a happy one, mind you, but there wasn't much to be happy about in 1943. My only other memory of that time was when my sister and I were evacuated to the West Country and stayed in a Salvation Army hostel in Montpelier, Bristol. I can remember playing with other children in a small hall, all of us very young and missing our parents.

Towards the end of the war, my sister Diane ('Doody') and I were living with our grandparents in a terraced house in Hainault Avenue, Southend-on-Sea. My mother's family are Sephardic Jews and Doody and I were brought up in the faith. My grandmother worried deeply about events unfolding in Europe, and I remember her holding us close and saying that if the Nazis ever got to England, 'we'll stuff the towel under the door and turn on the gas'. Until I got to school I didn't understand why she said this.

British soldiers were stationed just up the road from Hainault Avenue, mostly ambulance crews, and we were fascinated by them. Grandma had forbidden us to go near them but Doody and I would sneak up through the back alleys, past the Military Police post, and finish up at the large hall that had been turned into a cookhouse.

The soldier in charge was an enormous sergeant who wore a big apron. He'd take us into the kitchen, sit us down at a table and get us each a plate of mashed potato and corned beef, or whatever was on the menu that day.

Southend-on-Sea did not escape the German bombs. It was in the flight corridor for the Luftwaffe and the Doodlebugs so anything that dropped too early or on the return flight risked landing on us. Although I wasn't allowed out at night, especially when the air-raid sirens had sounded, I can still remember seeing the search-lights scanning the dark sky, bouncing off the clouds as they searched for enemy planes.

My mother spent much of the war working in a factory somewhere in the south of England, doing what she could for the war effort. At the same time, my dad was in the army, stationed in the north of England and then, for many years, in the Far East. I don't remember seeing him at all until the whole shooting-match was over.

He came home in 1947, and I can still remember him walking into our house in Southend-on-Sea, wearing his uniform and with a kit-bag slung over his shoulder. He opened his bag and took out some bars of chocolate and other sweets. I sat on the back stairs, looking out over our little garden and eating chocolate, while Mum and Dad sat in the kitchen drinking tea and getting to know each other all over again.

I soon discovered he'd been in the Entertainments National Service Association (ENSA) during the war, entertaining the troops in Malaya, Singapore and India. He called himself 'Bert' Bullimore – his real name was William – and he often worked with his close friend Bunny Reynolds. They had a two-man act called 'The Gale Brothers'.

He kept a scrapbook of all the old photographs and news-paper ads. In it were things like:

HAPPY WORLD CABARET
Tonight presents:
LANI - the first Hawaiian dancer who has travelled
all around the States and has arrived here to demonstrate the
'Hawaiian War Chant' and 'Song of the Islands'.
Never shown before in Singapore.
Also watch out for Bert and Bunny, The Gale Brothers,
on 1st October, 1946.

My dad was a born entertainer, who could sing, dance, tell jokes . . . you name it. He could walk into a silent room, chip off a couple of nice tunes on the piano and have everyone singing, 'Thanks For The Memory' or 'Roll Out The Barrel'.

After the war, he and Bunny did a few nights a week in various music halls and theatres before they split up. Bunny was going to emigrate to Australia and we were going to follow, but he didn't make it further than Singapore. I think he became a policeman.

As a kid, I remember going to see my dad on the stage. I'd stand in the wings behind the curtain, watching him with his straw hat and cane. As the band played the final bars he'd dance off stage, grab a towel, wipe the perspiration off his face, do a quick change and then out he'd go again. It was fabulously exciting.

Soon after the war, he got himself a big-time agent in Shaftesbury Avenue who had a lot of famous names on his books. He pointed Dad at several auditions for West End shows and regional tours. That's when my mother put her foot down and gave him an ultimatum: the war had taken him away from home for seven years, and she didn't want to see it happen again. Family came first, and Dad retired from showbusiness.

He and Mum had a café in Southend called B & K's (Bill and Kitty's) which served sausage, beans and chips, bread and butter and steaming mugs of tea. They did Bed & Breakfast using four rooms upstairs. When they needed a fifth, I ended up sleeping in the shed in the back garden on a make-shift bunk.

There were always loads of strange faces around the house, although some of them grew familiar when they came back year after year. They all loved Mum, and so did I; she made people feel welcome and important.

My dad's family were real Londoners, from the Elephant and Castle, and when they came together there was a carnival atmosphere with sing-songs and revelry into the early hours. Uncle Len used to work down at the Billingsgate Market, and on Fridays he'd bring home plenty of fish for the weekend. Aunt Gladys had a job cleaning one of the local banks. They were an old market-trading family and a lot of them, including my dad, ran stalls at places like Petticoat Lane. Sometimes he went further afield.

When I was nine or ten years old, I used to go with him on weekends, loading up the van and heading off to markets at Peterborough, Kettering or Corby. We'd arrive at seven o'clock, unload all the boxes, set up the trestle tables and then 'put up our flash' (lay out our display). Dad would stroll down to the coffee stall and come back with two big sausage sandwiches and mugs of tea. Then we'd be ready for work.

We were in the chalk game, selling those little plaques that people hang in their sitting-rooms, and statuettes of dogs and horses. Dad would sell them for two shillings a pair and still make a good profit. Not surprisingly his nickname was 'Chalky', and even on a bad trading day, as the rain tumbled down, he could put a smile on the face of anybody who came to his stall.

Dad was one of the best 'pitchers' in the business and he taught me all the tricks of the trade, like 'geeing' the crowd. Holding a statuette aloft, he'd say, 'Ladies and gentlemen, if you tried to buy just one of these in Harrods they'll charge you seven and sixpence. Marks & Spencers will want five shillings, and even if you went to Woolworths you'll pay three and sixpence. But let me tell you, ladies and gentlemen, I'm not just going to give you one ... and I'm not going to give you two.'

He would pause, ready to reel them in. 'Ladies and gentlemen, I'm going to give you three of these. And the first six hands I see raised can have them all for just three bob.' Down near the front row, I'd throw up my hand immediately, along with the other 'gees'. Normally, it was all the motivation needed to get the crowd to start spending.

Although it seemed straightforward, it could be a tough life on the markets. Sometimes it meant getting up in the middle of the night to get to a particular market, and if you didn't have a regular pitch, you'd have to sweet-talk the Toby Man (market inspector) to get a good position. Then you worried about the weather, which could wipe out a day's work if the punters stayed at home.

Making money is something I picked up on very early. I'd barely started school when I used to take my barrow down to the Southend bus station and wait for the coaches of holiday-makers to arrive. Most of them were working-class people who couldn't afford a taxi. I'd wheel their luggage to their Bed & Breakfast and get a threepenny bit.

At Christmas time, I'd blow up balloons, tie them on sticks and sell them outside the supermarkets. I spent a little money on sweets and comic books, but most of it I saved. Every weekend and during school holidays, I'd find a job on the seafront or in the funfairs, always looking for an opportunity.

Back in those days, just after the war, Southend had a reputation as the most drunken resort in England. It attracted loads of dockers from the East End of London who would save up all year and then hire a coach for a day out at the seaside. For a while I became a photographer, taking pictures of the coach parties for Bill Selley, who had a studio in Camberwell. The dockers on their day-trips would gather in the pubs around the East End and I'd wait for them to finish their beers. Then they'd cram crates of beer into the luggage section of the coach and head off on the forty-mile drive to Southend-on-Sea.

Unless there was a spare seat I sat on the floor, nursing my Agfa camera. About halfway there, there'd be a stop by the side of the road so everyone could have a breather and, in some cases, run behind the bushes. This was a good time to get the luggage section open and pass around more beer.

The coach stopped regularly at pubs along the way, like The Halfway House, The Swan and The Fortune of War. That was my big opportunity, because I'd get the dockers to line up alongside the coach so I could take their picture for a souvenir photograph of their day out. On a forty-seater coach it was forty times two and sixpence – a fiver in total. My commission was 30 per cent. The day-trip organiser would give me the money and then hold me by the back of the neck to give me the standard lecture.

'Now, you little bugger, if we don't get these pictures, we're coming looking for you.'

'Yes, sir.'

'And you know what we'll do to you?'

'Yes, sir.'

'Go on then, Tony, piss off.'

I'd wait at the pub for the next coach and take another picture. Normally, I could do about three before I reached Southend. Then I'd hang around the Seaway Coach Park for an hour while more coaches came in. All the organisers knew me, and business became so good that a close friend of mine, Dave Mathieson (people thought we were brothers), got involved and we took on even more pitches.

Bill Selley, who had a wooden leg, would collect the film from us and take it back to London to be printed and posted out. Meanwhile, the dockers would drink all day, get their fish and chips, rent a deck-chair for a sixpence and fall asleep until the pubs opened in the evening. Then they'd have a quick wash in the toilets and go back into the pub until closing time. The coaches were lined up outside, ready to take them home.

If business looked good, I'd skip school for the day. In my family there wasn't a great deal of respect for education or academic advancement, whereas making money was an honourable goal, if not the ultimate vocation.

Like my dad, I found it easy to earn a quid, although I had other ambitions which didn't seem to be compatible: I wanted to become more educated and to write books. I bought my first Olivetti typewriter when I was sixteen and would tap away in the back garden, writing my first novel. Everyone used to giggle and take the piss out of me. What a laugh – Tony writing a book!

At the same time, I had enormous admiration for the great tycoons of British industry; the men creating business and property empires after the war. They made their fortunes and played a major role in rebuilding the country. A part of me wanted to be just like them, and I would study their careers through stories in newspapers and magazines.

When I left school at fifteen, I set up a photographic business and put a dark-room in the back shed behind the B&B. On my first assignment at a wedding, I took pictures of the ceremony and the signing of the register, before dashing home and putting the film in developing fluid. They wanted to see contact sheets at the reception.

I don't know what happened, but the negatives came out blacker than the inside of an oven. I didn't know what to do. The bride's father came round to my house, asking for me.

'You little bugger, I should kill you,' he said, when he finally caught me. 'My daughter's wedding and I haven't got any pictures.'

I'd never been so embarrassed. Eventually, he had to dress her up again and re-enact the ceremony, but someone else took the pictures. I don't blame him.

At seventeen, when I got my driving licence, I bought myself a little van – a 1938 Ford that cost me ten quid from Harry Webb, a dealer in Southend-on-Sea. Not long afterwards, I swapped it with another dealer for a 1930s Rolls Royce, with a glass partition between the front and back seats. It cost me my van plus another five pounds. I slid behind the wheel and turned the key. Nothing. The bloody thing wouldn't start.

The dealer had a reputation as a real hard case, and he refused to listen. We argued for two hours and eventually he gave me back my van but kept the five quid. I should have been furious, but I was actually relieved. It was another lesson learned the hard way.

By then Dave Mathieson and I had started our own door-to-door selling business, B & M Household Supplies, selling blankets, sheets, quilts, eiderdowns, flannelette, twill, knickers and cotton dresses. Two of the greatest selling lines were the Moderno Sorento Spanish Blanket and the Belgium Cotton Carpet. We sold thousands of them.

At times it was bloody hard work, and sometimes it meant knocking on a lot of doors to do enough business to make a profit. Yet within a month we had five people working for us and within a year we had 120 salesmen, four small warehouses around the country, twenty-two A35 Austin vans and a couple of three-ton Bedford vans. I was driving a Humber Super Snipe, one of the great British cars of the day.

Door-to-door selling might seem straightforward, but like market trading it came down to hard work, knowing your product and finding the right pitch. This same philosophy would stand me in good stead years later, when I began doing international business deals.

I used to be able to drive along any street and immediately tell which houses would buy and which houses wouldn't. This was important because a lot of the time we sold on credit – two bob a week – and the collector had to get the repayments to make the deal work. Too many bad payers and the business faltered.

Again there were many tricks of the trade. Sometimes I'd find a corner shop and discover what kind of people lived in the area. I'd get a few promising names and then follow up the leads.

'Good morning, Mrs Jones, we have a special promotion in the area and I've been given your name because you're well-known in the community and respected . . .' Out came the sales patter.

Whether I sold to Mrs Jones or not, I would find out if she had any special friends in the area, or any family, such as a mother, daughter or sister. This often made it easier to sell when I knocked on these doors.

'Hello, Mrs Gibbs, I've just spoken to your daughter Valerie. What a lovely girl. She mentioned you might be interested in a special promotion we're running . . .'

There were different ways to sell to different people. The mothers on council estates, who raised lots of kids, fighting their guts out each day to put food on the table and shoes on their feet, used to love me because I sold on credit and helped make it affordable.

After the war, people were short of everything. They needed carpets, curtains, furniture, linen and new clothes. I was making more money than most people my age, and I remember Dad telling me to keep my feet on the ground. My mother was very proud and a great inspiration. She always believed I would do well in life, and tried to push me in the right direction.

Most Fridays, Dave and I would go out in the West End with a few friends. We'd have a late meal at the London Curry House just off Piccadilly – the hotter the better – and then round midnight book into the all-night Turkish Baths in the basement of the Russell Hotel. It cost seventeen shillings and sixpence, and the facilities included a Turkish bath, hot rooms, swimming pool and an ice-cold plunge.

Afterwards, we'd sit in the lounge, wrapped in towels, eating sandwiches and ordering fruit drinks. The place would normally be full of the same old crowd, which included boxers and boxing promoters who sat around discussing sport, business and politics. Eventually, we would retire to a sleeping area, included in the price, and wake at about 9.00 A.M. to a breakfast of tea, buttered toast and marmalade.

On Saturday nights we'd go clubbing, going to places like the Whisky-A-Go-Go, Ronnie Scott's and the 41 Club, before ending up at the Zambezi Club on Greek Street. Afterwards we'd find a good restaurant that stayed open late. The entire weekend used to cost me between fifteen and twenty pounds.

Life had been tough for my mum and dad, but I was determined to succeed. Making money had become a real passion, and I used to lie awake at night working out business plans. Yet with very little formal education, I realised that I didn't have the knowledge or the communication skills that would allow me to mix with everyone.

I answered an advertisement in the local Southend-on-Sea newspaper, the *Echo*, which read: 'English Language Teaching. Private Tuition.' When I went round, a man called Peter Chilver answered the door and invited me inside. His accent fascinated me.

'If one really wants to reach the top in life,' he said, 'one has to understand and to be understood. I will teach you.'

I started with two lessons a week, and Peter gave me a list of authors to read, such as Dickens, D. H. Lawrence, Huxley, Shaw and F. Scott Fitzgerald. Afterwards, he'd quiz me about how much I understood of the sub-texts and hidden meanings. Then he set about teaching me diphthongs and phonetics, making me repeat words over and over until I could produce exactly the right vowel tone.

After many months, Peter and I parted company, although we remained friends. He had taught me a lot and ignited my desire to learn more. Very few people have influenced my thinking as much as he did, but I came to realise that people would have to accept me for what I am - the son of hard-working parents from London, trying to make his mark in the world.

5

CANBERRA, AUSTRALIA
10:50 P.M., Sunday, 5 January 1997

Mike Jackson-Calway leaned on the heavy swing door and felt
the cool blast from the air-conditioning as he arrived in the
office. Although it was nearly eleven in the evening, the temperature hadn't dropped below 30°C. January could be a cruel
month in Canberra.

The Maritime Rescue Co-ordination Centre (MRCC) at
Belconnen is on the second floor of a squat concrete office
development dominated by walkways and covered car parks.
The various blocks are so grey and uniform that the planners
decided to colour-code them so visitors wouldn't get lost.
MRCC is in the 'Magenta Building'.

It had taken Jackson-Calway less than twenty minutes to
drive to work – the roads were virtually empty so late at night.
Staff at MRCC worked a six-day roster – two days on nights,
two days on mornings and then the afternoon shifts. A ten-
minute change-over is built into every shift, so that operations
can be smoothly passed on to the incoming co-ordinator.

As Jackson-Calway walked into the Ops room, Phil Doyle
looked up and smiled.

'Ah, just the man I want to see.'

'Because you want to go home, I suppose.'

'Absolutely.'

'Have you been busy?'

'Nah, very quiet, but this just came in.' He passed over a single sheet of paper.

It was a telex message from MRCC ETEL, the French Maritime Search and Rescue Centre. A satellite passing on a polar orbit over the Southern Ocean had picked up a 'potential distress alert' from a competitor in the Vendée Globe race.

SUBJ/OVERDUE/ S/V [sailing vessel] 'EXIDE CHALLENGER' (VENDÉE GLOBE RACE)
TXT
1 – WE RECEIVED POTENTIAL DISTRESS ALERT FROM 'ARGOS SYSTEM' CONCERNING
THE S/V EXIDE CHALLENGER (SKIPPER NAME: TONY BULLIMORE)
LAST POSITION KNOWN: 52 03, 8S / 100 30, 5E.

2 – CHARACTERISTICS OF THE VESSEL:
RACE NUMBER: 33 / HULL COLOUR UNDER FLOATING LINE: GREY
LOA [length overall]: 18.28M / MAST COLOUR : WHITE (2 MASTS)
HULL COLOUR: WHITE / LIFE SUIT COLOUR: YELLOW
DECK COLOUR: WHITE
ONE LIFE-RAFT / INMARSAT-C SYSTEM OUT OF ORDER / ONE BLU [Single Side Band
radio] ON BOARD.

3 – IN THE VICINITY AT ABOUT 10 NM [nautical miles], THERE IS LOCATED THE S/V
'AMNESTY INTERNATIONAL' (SKIPPER NAME: THIERRY DUBOIS)
INMARSAT-C NUMBER: 422763210
PC RACE HASN'T MANAGED TO CONTACT THIS S/V
ONE BLU AND VHF [radio] ON BOARD

4 – AT THIS MOMENT, WE ARE WAITING FOR CONFIRMATION OF DISTRESS AS SOON
AS POSSIBLE. REQUEST YOU CONTACT ALL SHIPS IN THE VICINITY.

BEST REGARDS
BT

The telex had been date-stamped and timed at 1115 GMT (Zulu time), yet the 'potential distress alert' had been picked up nearly three hours earlier by an Argos satellite receiving station in Toulouse, France, which notified ETEL.

The Argos system had been established in 1978 under an agreement between the US National Oceanic and Atmospheric Administration (NOAA), the US space agency

NASA and its French equivalent CNES. Using satellites orbiting 1,000km above the North and South Poles, the system can track and locate a transmitter to within 350 metres anywhere in the world. Apart from the obvious benefits to shipping and maritime safety, the system is also used to study wildlife migrations and to monitor icebergs, glaciers, ocean currents, global temperature and atmospheric pressure.

Argos beacons had first been used for ocean racing in May 1979 in the Lorient-Bermuda-Lorient race, and had been an accepted tracking system ever since. By transmitting a codified signal, a beacon not only identified a specific boat but also gave its latitude, longitude, speed and bearing.

Jackson-Calway read the telex again. What did it mean by 'potential distress alert'? Had the yacht signalled distress or hadn't it?

Perhaps a beacon had been triggered accidentally or lost overboard, he thought. After fifteen years with the rescue centre, eleven of them as a senior co-ordinator, he knew how many emergency calls turned out to be false alarms.

'What do you make of this, Mahesh?' he said, handing the telex to the SAR (Search And Rescue) co-ordinator, Mahesh Alimchandani, who sat directly opposite. Jackson-Calway then checked the 'dupe file', which had duplicates of every message that had come into the Ops room during the day. No other alerts or warnings were current.

'He's a long way south, isn't he?' said Mahesh, unable to hide his apprehension.

'Yes.'

They were both thinking about Raphael Dinelli, another lone yachtsman who had been rescued ten days earlier after spending twenty hours clinging to the submerged and sinking hull of his yacht *Algimouss*. The boat sank completely only five minutes after a Royal Australian Air Force (RAAF) plane dropped a life-raft to the stricken sailor.

Another competitor in the Vendée Globe, ex-Royal Marine Pete Goss, had answered Dinelli's mayday call and turned back into the teeth of a ferocious storm. Waves knocked down his yacht *Aqua Quorum* three times, but he fought onwards through the darkness until he reached Dinelli's life-raft and dragged him on board. The Dinelli rescue had been further south than any rescue ever co-ordinated by MRCC Australia, and there wasn't a person involved who didn't believe that the Frenchman was extremely lucky to be alive.

Jackson-Calway leaned back in his chair. 'Right. Let's compose a broadcast to all shipping in the area. I doubt if there's anything within five hundred miles.'

'More like a thousand,' said Mahesh.

The INMARSAT-C message was sent out at 11.27 P.M. from the nearest land-earth station in Perth to the Indian Ocean Region. As with all distress relays to shipping, it was preceded by an alarm signal and then repeated until further notice.

SOUTHERN OCEAN

DISTRESS BEACON DETECTIONS OBTAINED FROM SAILING VESSEL EXIDE CHALLENGER IN POSITION 52 04S 100 30E AT 050830Z [5 January at 0830 Zulu time]. VESSELS WITHIN 200 MILES PLEASE ADVISE THIS STATION VIA PERTH RADIO OR DIRECT TELEX.

An hour and a half later, the Ops room had a telephone call from MRCC ETEL in France. Jackson-Calway could hear only one side of the conversation as Mahesh tucked the phone against his shoulder and jotted down notes.

'Can you confirm those details again? ... Four beacons! ... How far are they apart?'

Mahesh was shaking his head. 'Are you sure? ... Okay, okay, I've got that: "Positional inaccuracies not possible". What assistance do you require? ... Okay ... I'll wait for the fax.'

As he put the phone down, Mahesh spun his chair.

'You're not going to believe this,' he said. 'They've picked up two beacons from *Exide Challenger* eleven miles apart; and two beacons from *Pour Amnesty International*, eighteen miles apart.'

Jackson-Calway said: 'How many in distress?'

'They can't tell me. They're sending the details.'

'Okay, let's wait for the paper.'

A hand-written fax arrived ten minutes later, giving the exact co-ordinates of all four beacons.

The message ended:

AS THE DISTRESS HAS BEEN CONFIRMED BY THE RACE ORGANISATION, REQUEST YOU
ASSUME CO-ORDINATION OF THIS OPERATION.
    BEST REGARDS.
        ETEL.
FOR YOUR INFORMATION: THE CLOSEST RUNNER [race competitor] IS AT A DISTANCE
OF ABOUT 1200NM.

'It's ours,' said Jackson-Calway as he strode to the long chart table along one side of the Ops room. Running his finger down the key, he pulled out the relevant map. With Mahesh at his shoulder, he used parallel rulers to plot the distance, drawing a straight line over the crisp white paper. The map represented thousands of square miles of ocean, broken only by the lines of latitude and longitude.

'I make it 1,400 nautical miles from Perth.'

'Agreed,' said Mahesh. 'Can the Orions fly that far?'

'We'll have to hope so.'

Jackson-Calway picked put the phone to SARO, the aviation search and rescue organisation based in Melbourne. This is going to really impress them, he thought.

'Heads up. We appear to have two yachts in difficulties 2,600 kilometres sou'-sou'-west of Perth. I'm sending a hard copy request.'

It was standard procedure. Wherever possible, civilian aircraft have to be used in Australia for maritime search and rescue operations. Only when the distance is too great, or no civilian aircraft are available, will military resources be used.

In this case there was no question that the only aircraft in Australia that could possible fly such a distance and be of any use when they arrived were the P-3C Orions based at RAAF Edinburgh in Adelaide. It had been an Orion that had managed to find Raphael Dinelli on Boxing Day and drop him a life-raft as his yacht sank beneath his feet. That had been a distance of 1,216 nautical miles south-south-west of Perth. The new emergency was a further 190 nautical miles south.

But what had happened in the Southern Ocean this time? wondered Jackson-Calway. Two of the beacons were apparently positional – set up on board each yacht to operate continuously and give their locations. But what could have caused two skippers to each activate a separate beacon? And why were the beacons drifting so far apart? Something had gone wrong, but what could it be?

He began thinking out loud: 'What if one beacon accidentally fell off the yacht and floated away? The skipper then triggers another, so his real position is still going out. But how could this happen to two yachts at virtually the same time? The chances of that are . . . are . . .'

'Astronomical,' said Mahesh.

'Yes.'

'What if they were hit by the same storm? Maybe they've abandoned their yachts and got into their life-rafts. That could explain the four beacons.'

'Yes. And the drift rates of a life-raft and a boat are going to be different.'

The explanation fitted what few facts they had, but raised a nightmare scenario of having to locate *two* life-rafts in hostile waters and also find a ship capable of picking up any survivors.

'If they're alive, they're closer to Antarctica than they are to us,' said Mahesh, shaking his head. 'God help them.'

At 1:20 A.M. the telephone rang in 'the bunker' of 92 Wing at RAAF Edinburgh. The duty officer, Flight Lieutenant Lindsay Campbell, had spent most of the night dealing with an official request for help in tracking a suspected drug shipment on board a yacht entering Australian waters.

He whistled low between his teeth as he jotted down the phone message: 'Four beacons, two of them separated from their parent vessels - that's four targets but only two possible survivors.'

New positions had come in from the Argos. The satellite passed within range every three hours and would provide them with regular updates. Even so, a life-raft can drift a long way in that time.

Most of the Orion crews were still on Christmas leave and would have to be recalled to the base. At least they'll be home in bed to take the calls, thought Campbell.

At MRCC headquarters, Mike Jackson-Calway had upgraded the distress broadcast to all shipping in the region, hoping to find a merchant ship nearby. He also requested six-hourly weather reports on conditions in the search area since the third of January, as well as 24-hour forecasts in 360-degree notations. This would allow them to calculate drift patterns and plot a search area.

However, trying to forecast the weather so deep in the Southern Ocean is not a straightforward exercise. There are few floating weather stations in the region and no weather satellites orbit directly overhead. Instead, forecasters at the Bureau of Meteorology in Perth had to rely on images from the edges of two other satellite photographs joined together to form one picture. In addition, meteorologists called upon a new generation of satellites, carrying devices called 'scattero-meters' that fire microwave beams to earth to measure wind speed and direction on the ocean surface. All of this infor-mation is programmed into global numerical models run on super-computers that can process the astronomical number of calculations required. Ultimately, the forecasters then pre-dicted the likely weather conditions based on these models rather than direct observations.

The satellite pictures for 5 January showed a huge low-pressure pulse in the region of 52 degrees south. Sometimes called 'a bomb' by meteorologists, these systems are so explos-ive that they seem to hit without warning. Winds shriek in a westerly stream and atmospheric pressure drops so low and so fast that your eardrums almost feel as if they're being sucked out of your head. Some of these storms can be 2,000km across, and with no land-mass to slow them down at this latitude they build and build, generating hurricane-force winds.

Jackson-Calway had a greater problem. No vessel had res-ponded to the mayday call to indicate it was anywhere near the stricken yachts. Yet somehow he had to get a rescue plat-form into the area to pick up possible survivors.

The Royal Australian Navy keep a duty vessel on stand-by at HMAS Stirling in Western Australia. Jackson-Calway called the duty officer at Fleet Headquarters in Sydney at 2:25 A.M. and asked if the navy could give him a surface res-ponse to the emergency. He was in luck. At midnight, a small navy patrol boat had been replaced as duty ship at Stirling by the guided missile frigate HMAS *Adelaide*. If permission were obtained, the warship could be ready to sail within eight hours, with a transit speed of 18 to 24 knots, depending on the weather.

'I take it you understand that no Australian warship has ever been that far south,' said the duty officer.

'You're kidding me.'

'Not at all. I'm not saying we won't go, but I thought I should let you know.'

Jackson-Calway put down the phone and suddenly knew what it felt like to be flying blindfold. Without having any idea of what had actually happened in the Southern Ocean, he had committed an RAAF crew to fly almost to Antarctica on the basis that two yachtsmen might be in trouble. Now he had to ask the Royal Australian Navy to send a ship further south than ever before – so far, in fact, that the frigate might have to be refuelled at sea to get home again.

The first of the P-3C Orions from 92 Wing would leave Adelaide at first light. The flight to Perth was approximately four hours; it would take thirty minutes to refuel and then it would take off again for the search area at 0030 Zulu time.

At 3:33 A.M. in Canberra another option emerged. A Liberian registered tanker, the *Sanko Phoenix*, had responded to the mayday call. It was 728 nautical miles from the stricken yachts, with an ETA of 56 hours. The tanker, bound for Sydney, had 85,000 tonnes of crude oil on board. Under the law of the sea, it would divert to help as long as there was no danger to crew, equipment or cargo. Jackson-Calway decided to wait. He would see what the first Orion discovered before committing any more lives to the search.

It had been five hours since he arrived at work, and he hadn't even managed to make himself a coffee. Dawn would soon be breaking in the Southern Ocean. How much comfort that would bring to Tony Bullimore and Thierry Dubois, he could only wonder at. Were either of them alive to actually see it?

Like most of the SAR co-ordinators, Jackson-Calway was an experienced mariner. Ten months away from possible retirement, the 64-year-old had spent nearly half a century involved with the sea in some capacity.

Born in Chesterfield, Derbyshire, he joined the merchant

navy at the age of fifteen, signing up with the old Elder Dempster West Africa Lines. By the age of twenty-nine, he'd become the master of a merchant ship that steamed between England and Africa. Then he met and married an Australian girl. When their first child was ten months old, they visited relatives in New South Wales. Soon after he accepted a job with the British Phosphate Company at Port Kembla just south of Sydney, as a stevedoring superintendent. That was in May 1963; he spent the next eighteen years with the company.

In many ways, Jackson-Calway exemplified why the MRCC employs people who have experience of the sea and its dangers. The theory is that if people know what it's like to be out there in a storm, they don't lose touch with the plight of survivors and the grim realities of the job. Jackson-Calway had never been able to forget being caught in a gale in the North Sea with an unladen ship heading for a re-fit in Germany. Being 'light ship' and pitching severely, the propeller rose out of the water and spun wildly, causing the main fly wheel to crack. Pieces fell into the engine and it seized up completely.

The ship was off the coast of Amsterdam, near the entrance to the North Sea Canal. The crew put down the anchor, but it wouldn't hold. Soon both anchors were at their maximum length. The only thing holding the ship were the bolts and rivets where the anchor cables were attached to the bottom of the boat.

The master put out a distress call and a lifeboat battled through horrendous seas to reach the ship. As it arrived, Jackson-Calway stood on deck and watched the freighter drift to within 200 feet of the shore. Waves foamed over jagged rocks and the wind cut through him. He waited to hear the sound of metal twisting on rock.

The lifeboat stood by the ship until the storm abated and the crew were safe, but the danger had not passed: two lifeboatmen were washed overboard by a wave and drowned as their boat returned to the canal.

As he drove home at the end of his shift, Jackson-Calway kept wondering if he'd done all that he could for Thierry Dubois and Tony Bullimore. Other questions worried him. Why weren't any of the Argos beacons being picked up in distress mode? Had the survivors made a mistake in triggering them, or were the signals being misinterpreted? And why hadn't either skipper triggered his 406 SARSAT beacon, which could be picked up by receiving stations around the world, including Australia?

The first Orion would be in the search area by late afternoon. HMAS *Adelaide* would leave Perth at about the same time, unless told to do otherwise. All anyone could do now was wait.

6

SOUTHERN OCEAN
Sunday, 5 January 1997

The boat rolls and I tumble off the shelf, landing with a splash instead of a thump. Water? Somehow the cuddy is beginning to fill. Does it mean I'm sinking? I can't see a thing it's so dark; this must be what it's like to be buried alive. Wiping my eyes, I stagger into the engine room.

I pick out a point on the side of the cabin – a shelf with oval stowaway holes underneath. The water line is about two inches underneath the holes, even when it rolls back and forth like a mini-sea. I watch it for a long time but it doesn't seem to move. Maybe it's stopped now, I think. I'll check again later.

The water in the cuddy is up to my knees – high enough to fill my sea boots. I can't feel my toes or fingers unless I consciously try to move them. Wiping my nose, I see a streak of blood on the back of my hand. I must have banged it when I fell. Come on, Tony, you have to be more careful. This isn't a twelve-hour rescue zone – if anyone bothers to send a boat it's likely to take three or four days.

There's equipment and food floating everywhere in the engine-room and doghouse. The netting on the shelves has broken under the weight of equipment and violent movement of the boat. Sodden biscuits, plastic cups, charts, teabags, pencils … everything that had a home when the boat was the right way up is now sloshing all over the place. Hundreds of feet of rope is tangled like spaghetti beneath the water.

How long did I sleep? My wristwatch is somewhere on the bottom, and I'm not diving to find it.

Then I notice a strange thing. Bits and pieces of kit are disappearing. The doghouse is three-quarters full of sea-water, and every time the boat drops into a big trough the level rises. As the boat is carried to the peak of a wave, the water inside is sucked out again through the broken window, carrying more of the boat's supplies and equipment. There goes a Robert Ludlum novel ... my binoculars ... a box of Uncle Ben's rice.

At first it doesn't seem like a big problem, but then I realise that a lot more is happening under the water than I can see. Clocks, instruments, ropes, pantry shelves, even the chart table has gone. The suction is dismantling the boat from the inside.

Where's the toolbox? No, no, no, it can't have gone, surely not ... Wading through the doghouse, I look for the chisels and hammer that I left on top of the upturned stove. They're gone. I can't believe it!

There's even gear missing from the cuddy and engine-room. This is where the dried foods (biscuits, cereals, coffee, tea, sugar and rice) had been stored on *Exide Challenger* because it kept weight down in the bow of the boat. The heavier items like canned food and drinks were towards the stern, in the watertight compartments beneath the cockpit. This is a deliberate design feature because most of the race would be run with prevailing winds.

I edge nearer the broken window and can feel the pressure as the boat rises. The vacuum effect wants to suck me towards the hole. I still can't believe how the interior of the doghouse has been dismantled. The chart table and shelving were made of lightweight material and had no structural role in the yacht - a light boat goes faster. But what about the tool box and the stove and my laptop computers?

All the fittings have gone, bit by bit. How long did I sleep?

Without proper tools, I can forget about converting the boat upside-down. There's no way I can block the hole, the suction is too great. Forget it, Tony, think about the life-raft, you have to get it free.

I go back to the cuddy and find an empty hold-all. I begin

grabbing things that haven't disappeared, fishing them out of the water or from stowaway holes. Two narrow bars of plain chocolate, a Mars bar, three flares, thermal underwear, two strobes, six plastic satchels of water, a can of baked beans, a soggy bandage, a roll of five-millimetre cord and my Survivor water-maker.

The lack of food doesn't worry me – I'm likely to die of hypothermia before I starve to death. Everything goes inside the hold-all except the water-maker, which I tie to the bulk-head near my shelf. Then I seal the hold-all and lash it down in the cuddy. Now if I can get the life-raft free, I have a few things I can put inside. They can supplement the raft's own emergency supplies, which include a knife, torch, fishing line, first-aid kit and a little water.

I can feel my breath condense in the air in front of my unshaven face. I've been standing in sea-water for more than an hour, and the cold is creeping through the survival suit and attacking my exposed skin. A mini-sea rolls back and forth inside the hull. I have to stay warm, but first I'll try for the life-raft again.

At the companionway entrance, I submerge several times to get used to the cold. Then it's down, through the door, kick off the bulkhead and swim towards the life-raft. The buoyancy of the suit pushes me upwards and I bump along the cockpit deck.

This time I manage to cut another two strands on the raft before turning back. My chest wants to explode. Gasping for breath, I go straight to the cuddy and drag myself on to the shelf, bruising my ribs again. I have to get warm.

Wedged in tightly, I lift each leg slightly and feel water drain from my boots. Then I tap my feet against the bulkhead, trying to keep the blood circulating. I clench and unclench my hands, waiting for my body furnace to warm me.

Every time I think the storm has blown itself out, another wave hits the hull and tries to shake me loose. Water is pouring through from above, which suggests that there must be a hole where the keel snapped. At least I'm not going to run out of air.

After about an hour, I check the water-line in the engine-room and find it lapping into the stowaway holes below the shelves. I'm definitely sinking, but only slowly. Maybe I can seal off the cuddy from the engine-room and stop any more water pouring through. There's a carbon and foam sandwich hatch-cover which I normally use to close off the doghouse when it gets cold, so I can run a heater more efficiently. I turn it sideways and try to clamp it across the doorway to the cuddy. Again and again I try, but it doesn't work. I don't get angry or frustrated, I simply put the hatch aside and think about the life-raft.

This time when I dive, I manage to cut four of the ties on the plastic container. There are only three left, but one of them is the rope that inflates the raft and I don't know which it is. This is so bloody horrible, it can't be happening.

Then I have a strange thought as I stand in the doghouse, chest deep in water. If I were in a movie, then this would be about the time that I buried my head in my hands and had a cry. Maybe that's what I should do. I wonder if I can. I squeeze my eyes shut and try to make myself cry by thinking of something sad. Instead I giggle.

'Come on, this is serious, you have to cry,' I tell myself, but it's useless. Instead I try to scream in frustration and despair. I start howling like a banshee, wanting to rail against the sea and whoever else might be listening. But instead of sounding Shakespearean and heroic - like King Lear in the grip of madness, or Othello torn apart by jealousy - I sound pathetic and ridiculous. Why waste my breath and energy?

The shelf in the cuddy is the only way I'll survive the cold, but I need to rig a safety net to stop myself falling off. Most of the netting on the shelves has broken under the weight of equipment and movement of the boat.

Using my knife, I gouge some holes in the 'roof', about half-way along the shelf. The netting is attached to hooks beneath the shelf and I pull a section upwards, tying it to the roof with string. It won't take much weight, but hopefully it will hold me if I doze off and get thrown sideways by a wave.

I cut the corner of a plastic water satchel and drink the contents, about three-quarters of a cup. Then I unwrap a bar of Cadbury's milk chocolate, eat half of it and save the rest for later.

My hands have become those of an old man, full of ghostly

white wrinkles. I press them under my armpits, rocking back and forth. The air is stale and full of diesel fumes that catch at the back of my throat. I need fluid – fresh water, but I can't waste my meagre supplies.

The sound of water is everywhere. It slaps against the side of the hull, sucks through the broken window, leaks through the hole where the keel snapped, trickles, pours, drips, splashes, rolls and swirls into every crack and empty space. Lying on the shelf, my mind starts to wander. Earlier in the voyage, I read a book called *Treasure* – an archaeological thriller about a lost treasure in Ethiopia. It's not particularly good and I can't remember who wrote it, but there's all the usual stuff with good guys, bad guys, ancient curses and booby-traps, that sort of thing. Towards the end of the book, there's an elaborate underground maze that can only be reached by passing through a hole beneath a waterfall. Just like the hole in *Exide Challenger*, water is sucked in and out and the only way to enter or escape the maze is to time your jump and swim through the S-bends. I keep thinking about this, because I wonder if I'm going to be the guy who gets left behind because he can't get through the hole. Life imitating art again.

Years ago I didn't take any books or music with me on voyages. I was a purist who only wanted to see the ocean and hear the sounds of the boat. An American called Walter Green convinced me otherwise. He always carried books, and during one race he lent me one. Since then, I've always carried some. I chose a dozen for the Vendée Globe – nothing heavy like *War and Peace*; just a few good thrillers and detective stories.

These days, I always take music as well. I make up compilation tapes before I leave, and usually end up having really strange combinations, like Bob Marley on the 'A' side and Jimmy Smith on the 'B' side.

I get a lot of time to think, up on my shelf. It's not true that I can't cry. I only have to think of Lal sitting at home in Bristol wondering why she hasn't heard from me and I get all tearful. She won't know about the accident yet – that will probably happen tonight or tomorrow – but she'll sense something is wrong. She always does.

It's probably Sunday morning there. She'll be reading the newspapers in the kitchen and chatting to Yvonne, who'll be getting ready for church. I wonder how Lal's going to manage without me. I know she's going to be sad, but I can't help that. She'll have lots of family and friends around her; her nieces and nephews live nearby; and at least she'll be okay financially. The house is all paid off and there's my life insurance policy, which I've had for years because of my yacht-racing. It's not going to make her rich, but she'll be able to live with some dignity.

On the morning the race started in Les Sables d'Olonne, I made out a will for the first time in my life. It was one of those simple things you pick up in a newsagent for a few pounds. 'I hereby leave all my worldly possessions to ... et cetera, et cetera...' Lal and I had rented a little cottage just outside Les Sables d'Olonne so we could spend some time together. Unfortunately, there were dozens of last-minute chores and checks to be made and we didn't get much time alone. That morning I wrote the will in the bedroom and had Yvonne and an old friend, Jim Doxey, witness my signature.

'What's this?' asked Lal when I slipped it to her.

'It's my will.'

First she looked shocked, and then she started crying. 'Why are you giving me this? You've never had one before. Why now?'

'Well, come on, I should have done it years ago,' I said.

'Yes, but why now? Are you worried that you're not coming back? You've never been worried before...'

'It's not that, I promise.' I put my arms around her.

'Well, why now?' she sobbed. 'I don't want your will. I want you to come back.'

'Shh, I'm just trying to protect you. If anything should happen to me I don't want you left out in the cold.'

We were both weeping as we stood in the bedroom hugging.

'Don't worry. Everything will be all right,' I whispered. 'Remember the "Third Eye"?'

Whenever one of us had problems, we told ourselves we could summon a kind of magical inner strength that would keep us safe. I suppose you could say it works. After all, I've had my share of near-misses and narrow escapes and I'm still here – at least for a little while longer.

Lal was still crying when I left the house for the marina. I hated leaving like that. I should have arranged things earlier and already had a will in place. The logical time to do it would have been in 1989, when I almost drowned off the coast of Dorset, trapped under the safety nets of my capsized trimaran, *Spirit of Apricot.*

Why didn't I do it then? I'm older now, that's one reason, I suppose. And the Vendée Globe is so extreme that it is accepted as the toughest yacht race in the world. In the two previous events – 1989/90 and 1992/93 – twenty-six competitors had started (thirteen each time) and only half that number had ever officially finished. Mercifully, only one competitor had died.

It's easy enough now, lying here on a shelf in the dark, to decide suddenly that I must have had some premonition or inkling of disaster, but that's nonsense – I simply wanted my affairs in place before such a tough race.

A friend of mine once told me: 'Tony, you like to live as close to the edge as possible because you think that one day you might actually be able to look over that edge and see what's there.'

Maybe he's right. Perhaps that's why I wanted to do the Vendée Globe.

Ever since I was a boy, I'd tried to find my limitations. I remember taking cold baths because I thought it would toughen me for what lay ahead. How funny that seems now, when cold water is likely to kill me.

There is real mystique to the Vendée Globe. It was founded by Philippe Jeantot, the great French single-handed yachtsman who won the first two BOC Challenge round-the-world races, a phenomenal achievement. His idea was to hold what he called a 'pure race' – an event that circled the world, with no stop-overs or ports of call for repairs or resupplies – the ultimate challenge for single-handed sailors.

Philippe created an event that taxed not only the courage and endurance of man and boat, but also the skills of yacht designers, naval architects, sailmakers and equipment manufacturers. Some of the French competitors had budgets worth millions of pounds.

Ocean racing is like a religion in France, and single-handed yachtsmen are the high priests. I used to find it very flattering to be recognised in the streets of Paris, Brest or Lyon and to have young boys ask for my autograph and people bring gifts to the boat, like home-baked cakes, before the start of the race. I don't think even Lal appreciated this until she saw the reception I received when *Exide Challenger* was towed out of the harbour to the starting line of the race. There must have been 300,000 spectators lining the shores, and they didn't just cheer the French superstars, they cheered every competitor.

Lal stood on the open deck of the fishing boat as it pulled me along, waving occasionally. My last memory is of her waving goodbye as the tow line was released from *Exide Challenger* and I headed for the starting line under my own power.

7

~~~~~~

SOUTHERN OCEAN
11:28 A.M., Monday, 6 January 1997

Flight Lieutenant 'Simmo' Simpson keyed one of his long-range HF radios.

'Air Force Sydney, Air Force Sydney, this is Rescue 251, over.'

The pilot, Flight Lieutenant Ludo Dierickx, listened as static filled the silence. A voice broke through: 'Rescue 251 this is Air Force Sydney, over.'

'This is Rescue 251. Request relay to 92 Wing Operations. Estimated time of arrival on task 0448 Zulu. En route weather poor. North-west winds in excess of six zero knots, cloud cover heavy, ceiling one five zero zero feet, base unknown, sea state unknown, over.'

'Rescue 251 this is Air Force Sydney, roger, out.'

Dierickx took a sip of coffee and scanned the flight instrument panels. It had been nearly four hours since the P-3C Orion took off from Perth airport and ten hours since it left RAAF Edinburgh in Adelaide. Like the rest of the thirteen-man crew, he'd been summoned from bed at three in the morning, interrupting the last few days of his Christmas leave.

Squadron Leader Vic Lewkowski, the current duty executive of 10 Squadron, had briefed them in the bunker at 92 Wing. The crew leaders, already in their flying suits, had sat on chairs and tables listening to the barest bones of detail.

'There is one person on board each yacht and there has been no communication from either. Each has activated two beacons and these are giving different positions. Therefore we have four targets but only two possible survivors.

'The suspicion is that the yachtsmen have taken to life-rafts and may be separated from their parent vessel. But the truth is we simply don't know. They could be with the yachts, in their life-rafts or in the water.'

Lindsay Campbell handed out descriptions of the yachts and the safety equipment on board. 'Apart from the Argos beacons, both yachts are equipped with a 406 MHz EPIRB but no signals have been picked up from these. We're getting updates on the co-ordinates every two and a half hours.'

The transit to Perth and refuelling had gone smoothly for Rescue 251. After take-off it had climbed quickly to 28,000 feet to conserve fuel in the thinner air. The crew knew they were pushing the Orion to the edge of its capabilities. At most they would have three hours 'on task' in the search area before having to turn back.

The normal contingency was to complete a mission with forty-five minutes of reserve fuel in case runways were blocked or the pilots missed an approach. This time they'd been given permission to cut this to fifteen minutes. This put added pressure on the Tacco (Tactical Co-ordinator), Flight Lieutenant Louis Gameau. If he miscalculated fuel use or possible headwinds, the Orion would land with its wheels in the water before it reached the Australian mainland.

Built by the Lockheed Corporation in America, the P-3C Orion is a long-range patrol aircraft, ideal for anti-submarine warfare, maritime reconnaissance and search and rescue. It has a ceiling of 30,000 feet and a cruising speed of 410mph.

'Okay let's go down and have a look,' said Dierickx, letting the P-3C drop into the porridge-like clouds. Flying on instruments, it descended slowly, buffeted by turbulence, until breaking through the cloud at 700 feet.

'Will you look at that?' muttered Gameau.

Beneath them, in the cold grey light, the sea was a foaming cauldron. Waves the size of five-storey buildings driven by 70mph winds rumbled across the surface, turning it almost completely white. Salt spray lashed the windscreen and the wiper blades struggled to cope.

'Heaven help those poor bastards,' said Dierickx.

Simpson peered over his shoulder. 'White hulls, white water, we're never going to find them.'

Dierickx shrugged, 'Maybe not, but since we've come so far, it wouldn't be polite to go home without saying hello.'

As the SEM (Sensor Employment Manager) began scanning to pick up any 121.5 beacon signals, Dierickx took the Orion down to 300 feet above the wave-tops.

'Just look out for icebergs, okay?' he joked.

At every available window and vantage point, members of crew had taken up positions, scanning the sea for some sign of *Pour Amnesty International*, the nearest of the two yachts, according to the latest satellite co-ordinates.

Argos claimed to be able to pinpoint a transmitter to within a few hundred metres, but a drifting yacht, life-raft or body can be carried for miles in the space of three hours. The crew had to take the last known location for a beacon and then set up a search pattern down-wind.

'I'm getting a 121.5 [signal],' called Simpson. 'Cross-fixing now . . . 51 17S 101 48E.' This was sixty nautical miles from the northern-most datum position given by the Argos satellite. The co-ordinates were already punched into the computer and the Orion altered course by thirty degrees, homing in on the signal. Descending even further, the crew began scanning the whitewash and pounding waves.

'What have you got?'

'Nothing.'

'Ditto.'

'I've still got the signal,' said Simpson.

'Mark, mark, mark,' cried Flight Lieutenant Don Hickey in the starboard aft lookout position. 'Right, three o'clock, half a mile.'

Dierickx hit the 'mark on top' button at 0504 Zulu time, registering the plane's exact location. He executed a long sweeping turn and came back down the same track.

'I can't see a thing.'

'It's there, I'm sure of it,' said Hickey. 'It's disappeared in a trough.'

'There it is. There!' exclaimed Gameau.

An upturned hull rose on the crest of a wave. Astonishingly, the keel still seemed in place, which meant the yacht should have righted itself. Flying as low and as slowly as possible, the Orion swept overhead.

'There's something on ... on the rudder ... it's him, it's him!'

Thierry Dubois waved frantically as the aircraft passed overhead. The Frenchman's eyes were so encrusted with salt that he could barely see. For more than half a day he'd been lashed to the rudder of his yacht, battered by huge waves and weakened by the cold. Without a survival suit, the wind chill would have killed him within an hour.

The storm had hit *Pour Amnesty International* on Saturday, with winds of 65 knots and above. Dubois ran with the wind, keeping aloft four square metres of sail to avoid too much speed. Twice the yacht had been knocked down, with the mast in the water. The third time, it somersaulted completely and the mast broke.

Dubois crawled along the deck with a hacksaw and a knife, managing to free the mast as water crashed over the deck, covering him completely. He had already worked out what to do. When the weather improved, he'd rig a makeshift mast and sail and head for Perth.

Suddenly, the boat somersaulted again, pulling the Argos positional beacon from the deck. Dubois switched on a second beacon, but not in distress mode. He still felt he could ride out the storm.

During Sunday night and Monday, he stayed inside the cabin, zipped into his sleeping bag, as the storm raged around him. Hit by two waves, one on top of the other, the yacht rolled again, this time only 180 degrees. The Frenchman waited for the weight of the keel to pull her upright but, inexplicably, it didn't happen.

With water leaking into the hull, Dubois prepared his life-raft and survival container, which had food, water, clothes and an SSB radio. Outside, he pulled the cord but the raft only half-inflated and the force of the waves tore it loose. Meanwhile, the hatch had jammed shut and Dubois couldn't get back inside the yacht. Somehow he managed to scramble on to the upturned hull and hold on to the rudders. He had his two

remaining emergency beacons around his neck and he activated both. Several times in the following hours, he was
washed from the hull by waves and had to swim back to the
rudders.

'Air Force Sydney, this is Rescue 251. We have located a
survivor. Deploying ASRK [Air Sea Rescue Kit].'
Loaded into the bomb-bay of the Orion were two life-rafts
and two survival packages, with each component linked by
175-metre sections of buoyant rope. The idea was to drop the
packages up-wind and up-current, trying to straddle the
stricken yacht, so the rafts would drift towards Dubois and he
could grab the rope and pull the nearest one to him.
This is easier said than done when the Orion's slowest speed
is 160 knots, the surface wind is 70mph and the altimeter is
fluctuating between 80 and 120 feet because of the waves.
Having made several passes over the yacht, weighing up the
possibilities, the crew dropped smoke markers in the water so
Ludo Dierickx could line up the drop. Working on a calcu-
lation of 50 yards plus 10 yards for every knot of wind, he
planned to release the life-rafts 650 yards up-wind.
The plane began its final approach with the bomb-bay doors
open, ready for release.
'Where are the smoke markers?' shouted Dierickx, unable
to see them in the white water. He glimpsed the yacht on his
starboard side, with the dark shape of Dubois clinging to the
twin rudders.
'Okay, this has got to be mark-one eyeball stuff.'
With a finger poised on the release button, he continued on
the run, relying now on his judgement and the practice drills.
He hit the button. The first dinghy fell, then a container,
then nothing. The other packages had jammed in the bomb-
bay station. The Orion did a figure of eight and returned. The
single life-raft might not drift close enough for Dubois to grab
the floating line, so the crew chose to drop the second ASRK. It
was a life-or-death deployment, because they had no more
rafts.
The Orion turned and made the final up-wind approach.
Salt had encrusted on the windshield at the edge of the wiper
blades, cutting visibility even further, but Dierickx could just

make out *Pour Amnesty International* riding the roller-coaster waves.

'Wait ... wait ... wait, just a little further. Now!' he told himself.

This time the rafts and containers deployed correctly. It looked good. They had landed about 300 yards up-wind and appeared to straddle the hull. The wind and waves should carry them right to Dubois.

'How long have we got?' Dierickx asked.

'Forty-five minutes to PLE [prudent limit of endurance],' replied Gameau.

'Let's see if we can find the other yacht. We'll come past here on our way back.'

Turning south, the Orion climbed to 10,000 feet and began to scan for the two beacons belonging to *Exide Challenger*. When this failed, the crew began a visual search using a parallel track system with a spacing of one nautical mile between each track. They based the search on the last recorded satellite positions for the beacons and estimated a drift speed of two knots.

Apart from the two pilots and the engineer, another three members of the crew were crammed into the cockpit, peering over shoulders and out through the windscreen. Every other window in the aircraft had a dedicated observer. With so much white water being kicked up by the storm, the chances of spotting a white hull were remote, while they knew that finding a life-raft would be damn near impossible.

'We've got to go,' said Paul 'Darvo' Darveniza, the flight engineer, monitoring the fuel level.

'Can you give us a few more minutes?' asked Dierickx.

'No. As it is we'll have to shut down an engine on the way home.'

Before climbing to altitude, the crew had one final sighting of Thierry Dubois. What they saw horrified them. The rafts from the second ASRK appeared to be drifting slower then the upturned hull. Instead of getting closer, they were getting further away.

Waves had inverted the rafts and the canopies acted like large sea anchors. At the same time, the keel of *Pour Amnesty International* was acting like a sail and increasing the drift rate of the yacht. Still clinging to a rudder, Dubois could only watch in frustration. If he tried to swim for the life-rafts, he'd probably perish in the huge seas or die of cold before he could reach them.

'We've got to go now,' demanded Gameau.

'But we can't leave him,' pleaded a young crewman.

'We have to,' said Dierickx. 'There's nothing more we can do for him.'

'Look at him! How can we go? There must be something . . .'

'Listen, we're at PLE. We turn back now, or we join him down there – simple as that.'

In despair Thierry Dubois watched the aircraft leave. How much longer could he survive? Would there be another plane? Should he risk it and swim for the rafts?

An hour later, at 1934 AEST (Australian Eastern Standard Time) Rescue 252 dropped through the clouds and began searching for *Pour Amnesty International*. At his station in the main cabin of the plane, Flight Lieutenant Phil Buckley sat before a bank of green screens, flanked by two acoustic operators. The RAAF Orions are packed with high-tech listening equipment and have the ability to identify and track virtually anything in the water, from Russian submarines to whales.

As the Sensor Employment Manager, Buckley's job was to recognise the most important information picked up by the sensors and acoustic operators and to pass this on to the Tactical Co-ordinator of the flight. Buckley, a Royal Air Force officer on exchange duties with the RAAF, had been in Australia for two and a half years and had another six months to go before returning to RAF Kinloss in Scotland.

Using a homing signal from an SAR datum buoy dropped by Rescue 251 to mark the stricken yacht's position, Rescue 252 found *Pour Amnesty International* along with several liferafts drifting in the vicinity. Dubois was no longer on the upturned hull.

'Where the hell is he?' muttered the pilot, Flight Lieutenant Ian Whyte. Had he tried to reach a raft or been washed off the hull? Either way, they had little chance of finding a body in the whitewash.

'What about the rafts?' asked Phil Buckley. 'I reckon the last one we topped might have had someone in it.'

The aircraft back-tracked and found Dubois, waving frantically. Having seen the first Orion fly away, the Frenchman had decided to swim for the nearest life-raft, fifty metres away. Just as he managed to climb on board, a huge wave flipped the raft and threw him out.

Later he recalled: 'I found myself in the water, without a life-raft, with no water, no food and telling myself with calm [sic] that I was going to die. I felt a feeling of regret for all the things I still wanted to do in my life. I'm only twenty-nine years old. But I did not panic, ever.'

He crawled back into the damaged raft and lay there as it slowly deflated around him. The second Orion arrived with only minutes to spare and quickly prepared to launch another ASRK.

'It must seem like an eternity to him,' said Buckley, as they turned and dropped smoke flares before the final approach. The winds had eased slightly, but visibility was still shockingly bad. Ian Whyte hit the button. For Dubois the dinghies seemed to arrive from heaven. This time the connecting rope fell 'right into his hands', according to Buckley, and the crew watched him scramble inside.

It had taken Rescue 252 more than twenty-five minutes to drop the life-rafts, and attention now turned to finding *Exide Challenger*. It would soon be dark, and the next Orion would not arrive until first light the next day.

'God, I wish I knew what we were looking for,' said Whyte as they began a search pattern. 'Is it a life-raft, a beacon or a yacht?'

Every window and available space in the cockpit was again taken up by a member of the crew. Buckley sat on the forward radar cabinet, looking out the forward left quarter of the aeroplane. The cloud base was down to 300 feet and visibility less than a half a mile. Every so often, Whyte deliberately flew into a rain shower to wash the salt spray from the windshield.

Buckley had seen wild conditions in the North Sea, and had also done some sailing in the Baltic in seas he thought were pretty rough stuff, but nothing like this. He estimated the waves to be four storeys high with spray howling off the top of them.

Initially, the crew attempted an electronic search, unsuccessfully trying to pick up signals from the beacons. Then they applied a creeping line-search pattern based on the last known position of the transmitters. This entailed a great deal of 'fudge factor' because of different drift rates for a yacht, life-raft or man in the water.

Sweeping back and forth over the area, each track never tight with the last, the Orion was flying at its slowest possible speed without stalling. For fifty minutes the crew scanned the ocean, thankfully not long enough for the mind to become fixated and begin deceiving the eyes. When this happens, the brain tells you there is something in the water – a body or a mermaid or a boat – when it's just a break in the whitewash or a shadow. Conversely, a person can become so accustomed to looking at the same scene, a fatigue sets in and they fail to see a change. A battleship could steam right in front of them and they'll see only waves.

'Mark, mark, mark!' screamed over the intercom.

The mark-on top button registered in a computer.

'Upturned hull, 200 yards, just going astern.'

The Orion had flown right past the hull and a designated observer at the rear had seen it emerge from the whitewash. The Tactical Co-ordinator used the mark-on screen to plot a position and the Orion came back round.

'I still can't see it,' said Whyte.

'There it is,' declared Buckley, pointing over the pilot's shoulder.

Exide Challenger rose on a wave, the number '33' clearly visible on her side. Her keel had been snapped off and left a black mark like an open wound along the highest point of the hull. Broken masts and rigging were visible beneath the water.

Rescue 252 made several photographic passes and twice saw the yacht buried by a wave and completely submerge.

'He surely can't be inside that,' muttered a crew-member.

'Yes, he can,' said Buckley, trying to raise spirits. 'That's probably the safest place he could be.'

'I hope he's in his life-raft,' said Whyte, shaking his head.

The crew spied what appeared to be an emergency beacon beside the hull, transmitting on 119.25 MHz. They had less than fifteen minutes of fuel, and began a search to the south for any possible life-raft or another beacon.

'Air Force Sydney, Air Force Sydney, this is Rescue 252, over.'

'Rescue 252 this is Air Force Sydney, over.'

'Upturned hull of *Exide Challenger* sighted at position 52 11S, 101 14E, at 1049 Zulu. No sign of any survivor. We are now going off station, over.'

As the Orion turned for home, it made two passes over Thierry Dubois, who should now have been safely zipped into a life-raft with plenty of water and food for the days ahead. Instead, they found him back in the water, with the raft upside down.

With no time to drop another ASRK, they had to watch helplessly as the Frenchman tried to right the raft and crawl inside.

8

BRISTOL, ENGLAND
Sunday evening, 5 January 1997

All day I don't hear from Tony. He's probably trying to call me but can't get through. When the phone rings at 10:00 P.M. I think it's him, but instead it's the coastguard from Portsmouth.

'Mrs Bullimore, there's a reporter wanting your number, but I didn't give it to him.'

'Why does he want me?' I ask, surprised.

'Well, you know what reporters are like. Have you heard from Tony?'

'Yes, yesterday.'

'Was he all right?'

'Yes, as far as I know. Why?'

'Oh, it's nothing – just these reporters.'

After he's gone, I feel myself frown. 'Don't be silly, Lal. He's fine,' I say, and go back to the lounge. I only spoke to him less than a day ago.

When I go to bed, I half-expect Tony to wake me in the middle of the night. That's what he did on Saturday morning at 2:00 A.M. He's always been like that, even when he used to go away on business. If he couldn't sleep he used to call me. It doesn't bother me any more, not when he's sailing. I'm happy to hear from him.

He tends to stay on the phone for a long while, asking about day-to-day things. Who I've been seeing, did I go shopping, how are the nieces and nephews? If he phones during the day and I'm not here, he'll call and call until he gets me.

'Did you go out today?' he'll say, when he finally gets through.

'Yes.'

'How long were you out for?'

'Why?'

'Because I phoned.'

'When?'

'Four times.'

'You checking up on me?' I laugh.

I can tell if something is wrong on the boat or something is bothering him. He won't tell me but I know his voice. On Saturday he sounded happy. The seas were picking up and he'd just reefed the sails.

'I love you. I'll speak to you tomorrow,' he'd told me.

'Okay. You be careful.'

When Tony first goes away on a long voyage, I'm pleased to be rid of him. He's so single-minded and charged up in the weeks beforehand that he's a nightmare to live with. 'Thank God the bugger's gone,' I think. 'Now I can get some peace.'

And then, within a day or so, I start thinking, 'Oh, Tony, where are you? When are you coming back?'

This time has been worse than before – maybe because we're older. I miss him terribly.

Monday morning and the phone rings. That'll be Tony, I think. But no, it's Yvonne, my niece.

'Aunt Lal, put the television on. I think there's something wrong with Uncle.'

I go downstairs in my dressing-gown, my mind blank. The TV takes several seconds to warm up and then a picture emerges of a boat upside-down. I can't hear the newsreader's voice, but I see the number 33 on the hull. It's Tony.

I can't bring myself to turn up the volume – I don't want to hear if they've found a body.

Three steps into the kitchen and I pick up the phone to call Steve Mulvany, Tony's nephew. Numbly I listen to it ring and ring. Finally he answers.

'Turn on your television,' I say.

'Why?'

'Just put it on.'

I hang up and stare at the screen. My head has gone. I can't move. I don't know whether to go upstairs and get dressed, or make myself a cup of tea. I just keep pacing the drawing-room, watching the screen, seeing *Exide Challenger*, thinking about Tony.

The phone rings. It's a reporter from Radio Bristol.

'Mrs Bullimore, I'm sorry to trouble you, I wanted to ask you about your husband.'

'I can't talk,' I say, hanging up.

It rings again. A reporter from the *Evening Post* says, 'Mrs Bullimore, I want to get a few details about your husband's sailing career. Has he ever done any single-handed races before?'

'You should be ashamed of yourself,' I say angrily. 'He's lived in Bristol for more than thirty years, building boats here and sailing them. Look in your library and stop asking me stupid questions.' I hang up.

Next time it rings I simply stare at it. I can't talk to any reporters. But what if it's news about Tony? I pick it up.

'Mrs Bullimore, this is the *Daily Mail*...'

I bash it down again.

Almost simultaneously, the doorbell rings. I have an intercom.

'Who is it?'

'Mrs Bullimore, I'm sorry to trouble you—'

'Please go away. Please leave me alone. I've only just heard.'

'I just wanted to ask you—'

'I'm not talking to you. Please go.'

I'm on my own for four hours before someone I know arrives. Wesley Massam, the builder of *Exide Challenger*, hears the news when he arrives at work and rings his wife Jane. She comes to the house and stays with me. A few minutes before her, Dave Mathieson, a childhood friend of Tony's from Southend-on-Sea, also arrives and immediately begins dealing with the media.

Just before this, an Australian journalist posted in London telephones, and I'm about to put down the receiver when he says, 'Mrs Bullimore, don't hang up. I know you're distressed. I know you don't want to talk to anybody, but don't hang up.' He's really nice and calms me down.

'I'm not going to ask you questions, I just want you to talk to me. Have you heard from the race organisers?'

'No.'

'How did you get the news?'

'From the television.'

'Right, I tell you what I'll do. I'll try to find out what I can and I will ring you back. I promise.'

Later, when he does ring back, Dave takes the call.

'Two yachts have capsized,' he tells me. 'One of the skippers has been sighted and they've dropped him a life-raft. There's a boat on the way down there.'

'Which skipper?' I ask, feeling my voice tremble.

'They haven't said.'

I'm trying hard not to cry. 'They're only going to find one alive, aren't they? They're not going to find both.'

I shuffle towards the door.

'Where are you going?' asks Jane.

'I'd better get dressed. I may have to rush off.'

Upstairs, I turn on the shower and step under the water. Suddenly, the tears are flowing and I just can't stop them. 'Where are you, Tony? Are you all right? Don't do this to me. Talk to me. Please.' I lean against the wall and sob until my chest hurts and I'm exhausted.

Downstairs, Dave and Jane are still fielding media calls. Jane makes me a cup of tea and the tears all come out again. I'm standing in the kitchen by the dishwasher sobbing like a child. I don't know whether I can cope with this.

All day we hear nothing from the race organisers in France. All our information is coming from the television and radio - much of it conflicting. Eventually they announce that the lone yachtsman in the life-raft is a Frenchman, Thierry Dubois, and that the missing skipper is Tony.

'He's in the boat,' I say.

'What do you mean?' scoffs Dave.

'Tony is in the boat.'

'Don't be stupid, Lalel. It's only going to hurt more when you find out that he's gone.'

'He hasn't gone - he's alive,' I say angrily.

'How do you know?'

'Because my stomach tells me so. My head has gone but my

stomach is solid. He's alive, Dave, he's in there.'

Later in the afternoon, a fax arrives from Raphael Dinelli's sister in France. I've never met her, but it's kind of her to think of me.

Dinelli family to the Bullimore family,

Good morning,

we know how it feels when you have to wait for news of somebody you love. We don't really know Tony but he belongs to a kind of sea-man of whom we are so proud. I sure, soon you have good news about Tony. Don't worry, to do what he has done already makes him strong, very strong.

  (Sorry for my horrible english)

        Isabelle Dinelli (Raphael's sister)

Wesley arrives when he finishes work and immediately sits me down in an armchair. He kneels in front of me and talks sternly. 'Lalel, don't listen to the television any more. Don't listen to the radio. Every story is going to be different and they're all going to speculate. You don't want that. You just want the facts. I'm going to find out all the information that I can and I'll let you know.' Then he phones the Portsmouth coastguard and gets a number for the Maritime Rescue Co-ordination Centre in Canberra.

I've known Wesley since he was a teenager. He helped build two of Tony's previous boats, *IT82* and *Spirit of Apricot*, as well as *Exide Challenger*. A part of him, I realise, is crying out to know if something he did, or didn't do, is behind the accident. Was it a design fault, a building fault or a freak event that caused the yacht to lose its keel?

Putting down the receiver, he tells me that an Australian warship is being sent to the search area.

'He's alive, Wesley. He's in there.'

'Yeah, I think so too,' he replies.

'When will they get there?'

I can see Wesley doesn't want to tell me. 'It's going to take three days.'

My hand covers my mouth. Poor, poor Tony.

Midnight comes and I can't sleep. I sit in a chair in the living-room or go upstairs and kneel beside my bed with my Bible, praying. Everywhere I look I see little reminders of Tony. On the sideboard is a card that he sent me when he went to Jamaica on business. It hadn't been my birthday or Christmas or any anniversary, he just wanted to send me a card.

The inscription reads:

This morning I woke up and saw a beautiful tree swaying in the wind, so elegant and free, reminding me of what you and I are so fortunate to share from the depths of our soul whether we are far or near.

Love Tony. xxx

He's always been like that. Impossible to live with one moment and then the next moment buying me a present to say he's sorry. I still remember when I first set eyes on him in 1963. My younger sister and I had arrived from Jamaica only a few months earlier. She'd been keen to work in England in a scheme being run by the British government, and I decided she needed a chaperone. Five years we gave ourselves, and then we'd go home.

My father had a small farm in the hills of Jamaica and had managed to support a wife and eight children. He and my mother have never left the island.

Doreen and I arrived in the summer and went to stay with a family we knew in Swindon. We both got jobs in a local factory making table mats. On a cold, grey summer's day the doorbell rang at our terrace house and a rather cheeky young salesman began trying to sell my sister blankets and sheets. He made us laugh, and eventually I had to close the door on him.

About five minutes later, the doorbell rang again. It was another salesman, this one immaculately dressed in a coat and tie. He looked surprised to see me. Although he only looked to be in his mid-twenties, he was obviously running the show, but I couldn't understand why he decided to try his luck when the other chap had failed.

'My name's Tony,' he said.

'I've told your friend that we don't want anything.'

'Oh, I'm not here to sell. My cousin Syd just came and told me that two of the most beautiful girls he'd ever seen lived in this house and I just had to come and see for myself.'

I have to admit I was flattered. Tony wouldn't go away. He

kept wanting me to invite him inside. Then he wanted my telephone number. I kept saying no, and eventually had to shut the door on his foot.

I underestimated Tony – not for the first time. When he couldn't get my number, he began sending me notes. I'd come home from work to find them slipped through the door. Dozens of them. Although Tony lived in Bristol, he had offices in Plymouth and would deliberately cut across to Swindon to post another note, asking me out for coffee or to the pictures.

This went on for three weeks until a girlfriend of mine told me: 'Oh, just go out with him. Don't go to the pictures because it's dark, go to a pub where it's light and everyone can see you. Then he'll see how everyone stares at the white man with the black woman. He'll see how they behave and he won't pester you any more.'

So I said yes, and Tony picked me up one Saturday lunchtime and took me to a country pub just outside Swindon. I knew people were staring at us and I thought, 'Oh, Lal, you've gone mad. What are you doing?'

Rather than putting Tony off, though, it made things worse. When he dropped me home he asked when he could see me again.

'I don't think it's a good idea,' I said.

'Why?'

'I don't think I can cope with this.'

Tony looked genuinely shocked.

'You saw them. They looked at me as if I were a prostitute.'

'Don't be silly.'

'Yes they did. A black woman with a white man, she must be a prostitute. That's what they thought.'

Tony looked directly into my eyes. 'I don't care what they think. I really don't.'

Over the next two months, Tony redoubled his efforts and put even more notes through the letterbox. Soon I realised that he wasn't going to go away. It wasn't just his perseverance, something else got to me. He was charming and very sweet in an old-fashioned way. Over-protective, I suppose, but I needed that then. Only later did I discover that he'd just come back from three years in South Africa, and had chosen to leave because of his anti-apartheid views.

Tony didn't care about colour. I don't think he even noticed people staring, but I did. They would talk behind their hands and I'd catch occasional snatches of conversation, words like 'disgusting' and 'slut'. Sometimes it upset me, but Tony has such a reassuring presence, he gave me strength. I knew I wasn't a prostitute. I'd been brought up in a decent, humble family who went to church every Sunday. I knew deep down that I was respectable and didn't deserve the insults.

After about six months Tony and I became lovers, and he invited me down to meet his parents in Southend-on-Sea. I have never been so nervous. Tony's sister, Doody, met me at the door and her first words were, 'Oh, you're not as black as he said you were.'

My heart sank.

We spent the weekend there, and Tony's parents were very nice to me. His dad didn't say much, but his mother eventually took me aside and said, 'He's going to marry you.'

'Why?'

'Because you're the first girl he's ever brought home and said, "This is my girlfriend".'

I felt wonderful.

One evening at his flat in Aberdeen Road, Bristol, Tony asked me to marry him. We'd talked about the possibility before but always said that we'd wait. Something obviously made up his mind because he looked across the sofa and said, 'It's time we got married.'

I asked him again, 'Are you really sure?'

'Yes, that's what I want.'

We'd been together long enough to know all the problems we faced, and knew they were unlikely to get any worse. As for any future children, we decided that if we brought them up honestly and let them learn both ways and cultures, they would grow to be strong and tolerant.

'It's a privilege to have two cultures,' declared Tony, believing it passionately. He also used to say, 'Wouldn't it be great if Britain could show the world how wonderful it is when the best of different cultures combine.' Maybe that's naïve, but what a wonderful thought.

Whenever someone upset me with a whispered insult or snide comment, Tony wouldn't let me dwell on it. 'Don't let people upset you,' he'd say. 'Don't let them turn you off. Not every white person is like that.'

He's right, of course, and the bigotry works both ways. Many black people said the marriage wouldn't succeed, and some were openly hostile towards Tony. I took the view that our love would overcome any obstacles. Marriage isn't about struggle and hard work – it has to be strong enough to survive by itself.

With some misgivings, my parents accepted that I wanted to marry Tony. In Jamaica, race isn't an issue and the prejudices involve class rather than skin colour. Sadly, it isn't the same in Southend-on-Sea. Rather than being welcomed into Tony's family, as I'd first thought, they completely disapproved of me. Tony had always been a favourite with his parents. They were enormously proud of him and he didn't like to disappoint them. This is probably why he didn't tell them about the marriage.

'It's just between you and me,' he said. 'Nothing to do with anyone else.'

Although I wanted a church wedding, surrounded by our family and friends, I quickly realised it was never going to happen. It didn't really matter; we loved each other – that's what counts. The deed was done in a register office in Bristol. We couldn't afford a honeymoon.

Tony didn't tell his parents until a few days before his mother died of cancer. He went to visit her in hospital and broke the news to her. She cried and told him, 'You've thrown away your life, you silly boy.'

I've always seen the fact that Tony married me when he knew that his mother disapproved as a testament to how much he loved me. I can say this because I know that she meant the world to him.

Kneeling in the dark beside my bed, I start to cry again. Dave, Jane and Wesley are asleep somewhere in the house. The clock on my bedside table shows it's 3:41 A.M.

'Where are you, Tony?' I whisper.

'Oh, Lal, the boat rolled over.'

'Yes, I know.'

'It was such a big storm. I couldn't save her.'

'But you have to save yourself now, do you hear?'

'I don't know how, Lal.'

'There's a rescue ship coming. It'll be there soon.'

'How soon?'

'Not long. Not long.' I can't bear to tell him the truth.

'I tell you what,' I say. 'We'll use the Third Eye. Do you remember?'

'Yes.'

It's a game we used to play a long time ago. I can't remember the last time. The 'Third Eye' is like an inner strength or a guardian angel.

'I'm sorry, Lal.'

'What are you apologising for?'

'For putting you through this.'

'Don't worry about me, you just stay alive. Are you warm enough?'

'Yes.'

'Don't lie to me.'

'I won't.'

We keep talking and he asks me questions about what I did during the day and if there'd been any mail. I picture him sitting on a box inside the hull, resting his head in his hands. He's not injured.

'You should go to bed,' he tells me.

'No, I couldn't possibly.'

'Do you mind if I get some sleep?'

'No. Just you make sure you wake up.'

9

PERTH, AUSTRALIA
8:00 A.M., Monday, 6 January 1997

Chief Petty Officer Pete Wicker caught the tail-end of the radio news as he drove through the gates of HMAS Stirling, Garden Island, Western Australia. Summarising the main headlines, the announcer said something about a search for missing yachtsmen in the Southern Ocean.

'Poor buggers,' thought Wicker, as he turned along the four-kilometre causeway towards the docks. He was contemplating a short 'day at the office' before getting back home for the final week of his Christmas leave. After twenty-three years in the Royal Australian Navy, spending months at a stretch away from home, he had a great love for homely pleasures like family barbecues, taking his teenage daughters to the beach and relaxing under the pergola with a beer.

Ahead of him he could see the gun-metal grey stern of his ship, HMAS *Adelaide*, a 4,000-tonne guided-missile frigate. She, too, had been given a holiday and a maintenance check. Most of her crew were still on leave, but Wicker and several others were back a few days early to run some tests on the ship and make sure she was ready for an up-coming naval exercise in the Pacific.

His first task was to 'wind the ship', which meant turning her around so that she could be painted on the other side, using pontoons as a platform. He walked up the gangway and saw the grinning face of Quartermaster Jimmy Sharma.

'You know we're sailing, don't you?' he said.

'Yeah, we're going to the wind the ship at 8:30. It's been programmed.'

'No, no. We're sailing.'

'What's happened?'

'Two yachtsmen are missing down south. We're the duty vessel.'

'But we're not ready. There's no crew.'

'They're being recalled – as many as we can find. We sail at 1600 hours.'

Wicker went straight to the Chief Petty Officers' Mess and saw the officer of the day.

'What's going on?' he asked.

'You better decide who you'll need and start recalling them.'

Briefings were being conducted throughout the ship, with the heads of various departments having to organise hundreds of tasks before the *Adelaide* could put to sea. Because of the maintenance period tools, awnings and equipment had to be packed away and stored. The ship had to be fully fuelled and loaded with supplies, including enough fresh food to last fourteen days.

Captain Raydon Gates addressed the crew over the public-address system shortly after 8:00 A.M. He confirmed that there would be nothing routine about the voyage. HMAS *Adelaide* would be sailing further south than any Australian warship had ever ventured on a rescue attempt.

'There has to be someone closer than us,' said Wicker as the broadcast ended.

'Apparently not,' said a colleague. 'There are two French boats – a scientific vessel being loaded at Kerguélen Island and another en route to Heard Island – but neither can muster more than 11 knots. *Adelaide* will beat them down there.'

A young Able Seaman asked: 'Shouldn't we wait until the Air Force actually find something? There might be no one alive to rescue.'

'We're the response vessel. We have to be ready,' replied Wicker.

By early afternoon, two-thirds of the normal crew had been recalled. As the bosun, Pete Wicker handled the maintenance and general seamanship around the upper deck. He also looked after small-arms weapons training and close-range gunnery.

'Anything on the upper deck is my responsibility,' he would tell the young ratings. 'If it breaks, leaks, corrodes, falls off or blows up, then I take the blame. That's why, when I ask you to fix something, you do it.'

As well as the maintenance materials, dismantled machinery had to be reassembled and stores had to be broken down and securely stowed for a rolling sea. At midday, Wicker drove home and picked up his thermal underwear and shaving gear. He had a quick lunch with his wife Dael and then she drove him back to HMAS Stirling.

Meanwhile, on the bridge, Captain Gates juggled phone calls from Fleet Headquarters and had hourly briefings with his senior officers. He'd been awake since a telephone call at 1:00 A.M., when advance warning had been given by Fleet Headquarters of a possible search-and-rescue operation.

After twenty-five years in the navy Gates knew how to wake up quickly, and he immediately began considering the logistics of preparing his ship. He'd been in command of HMAS *Adelaide* for eighteen months, and before that had captained her sister ship HMAS *Canberra* for twenty-one months, including a stint patrolling the Red Sea as part of the UN sanctions against Iraq. As well as being the most senior commanding officer afloat in Western Australia, he had class-co-ordinator responsibilities for the six guided-missile frigates in the Australian navy.

At 3:30 A.M. the phone rang again and the likelihood of the SAR operation had firmed. Gates moved into his study, not wanting to wake his wife Alison, and began discussing the recall of key personnel. In particular, he was concerned about the *Adelaide*'s helicopter crew, who were 2,000 miles away on the east coast of Australia at the naval air station at Nowra doing contingency training and flight trials. Somehow, they had to get back to Perth.

'Okay, they're three hours ahead of us in NSW,' Gates told the officer on duty. 'I want you to call Flight Commander Arthur Heather and tell him to start making bookings for his crew to get back here.'

Gates then began making a list of all the special require-
ments for an SAR operation in the Southern Ocean. How long
would it take? How cold would it be? How much fuel would he
need? As always, he planned for the worst and hoped for the
best.

At 7:00 A.M. he had a call from Captain Rowan Moffitt, the
Chief Staff Officer (Operations) at Fleet Headquarters, to say
that the Admiral was expected to give the order to sail at any
moment.

'What time can you be ready?'

Gates knew the *Adelaide* would officially become the ORV
(Operational Response Vessel) at 8:00 A.M. As such, it was
expected to be sea-ready at eight hours' notice. Without hesi-
tation, he said, 'We'll be ready to sail at 1600 hours.'

Arriving on board at 7:40 A.M., Gates attended the traditional 'colours' ceremony and then held a briefing in his
cabin with all his heads of department to lay out a plan. What
personnel would have to be recalled? Who wasn't available?
Could replacements be found?

Because no one on board had ever been that far south, there
were no SOPs (standard operating procedures) to help with the
planning. They were making their own rules. How to combat
the cold was the major concern. Central Stores had no Arctic
clothing or thermals available, and the local submarine
school could provide only a limited number of heavy-duty
polo-neck white sweaters. Clearly this wasn't enough, and the
crew were told that if they had suitable clothing like beanies,
gloves and ski jackets at home they should quickly go and
collect them.

Gates wanted a doctor on board as well as the usual Petty
Officer medic. He also arranged to have specialist medical
equipment for treating hypothermia, frostbite and salt-water
injuries. On top of this he organised three body-bags, just in
case.

Meanwhile, a military helicopter was ferrying the air crew
from Nowra to Kingsford Smith Airport in Sydney, where
they walked on to a Qantas flight which arrived in Perth at
1450 hours. From there they reached the HMAS Stirling
aviation facility at 1530, only half an hour before the
Adelaide sailed. Gates waited until he knew they were with

the helicopter before giving the order to sail. The S70B Seahawk would be able to ferry them to the frigate.

The recall had gone relatively smoothly, considering so many of the crew were on Christmas leave. However, only two chefs could be found – not enough for such a long voyage – so replacements were seconded from other ships, along with engineers with specialist skills, several aviation maintainers, an extra steward and a couple of Officers of the Watch to work on the bridge.

At 4:00 P.M., as the famous cooling wind known as the 'Fremantle Doctor' arrived from the west, HMAS *Adelaide* slipped her moorings, eased away from the wharf and headed down the narrow channel known as the Success Parmelia Passage into Cockburn Sound. On board were 143 crew – two-thirds of the normal compliment – and eight media representatives, working in a defence pool system. The navigation officer Ken Burleigh took the ship out, leaving at 'slow ahead', while the Executive Officer ('XO'), Jim Manson made sure all the lines and the anchor were securely stowed.

In moderate winds and calm seas, the warship headed west until it passed the northern tip of Rotternest Island and then turned south. Her ETA (estimated time of arrival) in the search area, depending on weather conditions, had been calculated at 0800 hours on 9 January – exactly three days.

Shortly after departure, the news arrived that Thierry Dubois had been found alive and had been dropped a life-raft. Until then the crew had been working towards an unknown goal, but now their purpose was clear – the fate of at least one lone yachtsman depended on the ship reaching him as quickly as possible.

Meanwhile, rescue co-ordinators in Canberra sent an urgent INMARSAT-C message to the master of the oil tanker *Sanko Phoenix*, giving Dubois' position in the life-raft:

REQUEST IF POSSIBLE YOUR VESSEL ALTERS COURSE TO THIS POSITION. REQUEST MAXIMUM POSSIBLE SPEED. ONE SURVIVOR HAS BEEN SIGHTED. PLEASE ADVISE ETA. PLEASE ACKNOWLEDGE THIS MESSAGE URGENTLY.

Ten minutes later, the *Sanko Phoenix* replied:

BEST ETA TO POSITION OF DISTRESS FROM PRESENT POSITION IS 710 NAUTICAL
MILES TO GO, AT AVERAGE SPEED 11 KNOTS, 2 DAYS 14 HOURS.

Almost immediately, the message flashed back:

REQUEST YOU DIVERT TO POSITION TO PICK UP SURVIVOR ... AUSTRALIAN
WARSHIP ADELAIDE DEPARTING PERTH 0800Z BUT WILL TAKE AT LEAST THREE DAYS
TO REACH POSITION.

An hour out, as the *Adelaide* moved around the top of
Rotternest Island, Flight Commander Arthur Heather
informed the bridge that the Seahawk helicopter had been
grounded at Stirling by a leak in the hydraulics. Only one aircraft maintainer had been left behind to start the Seahawk
and fly out with the air crew; the rest were on board. Unless
the chopper could be fixed quickly, the *Adelaide* would sail
out of range.

Captain Gates had to make a decision. If he turned back, a
two- or three-hour delay could be fatal for Thierry Dubois and
Tony Bullimore. At the same time, the Seahawk gave him
vital extra options in any rescue attempt.

'I'm not going back,' he announced to the bridge crew. 'Ask
Stirling if they can send an RIB [rigid-hulled inflatable boat]
to intercept us. If it can come out round Garden Island, we'll
come in from Rotternest as close to the reef as we dare. It can
pick up the maintainers and take them back. If they can fix
the problem, the Seahawk might reach us before we sail out of
range.'

This lateral thinking proved successful. Late that night,
the Seahawk landed in darkness on the frigate 130 nautical
miles south-west of Fremantle. What started out as bad luck
and turned into a good omen.

Meanwhile *Exide Challenger* had been sighted by the
RAAF, with no sign of life. The *Adelaide* was tasked to proceed
'at maximum possible speed' to the search area, firstly to pick
up Thierry Dubois and then to investigate the British yacht.

In the Chief Petty Officers' Mess, Pete Wicker heard the news
about Tony Bullimore as he sat down to a hot meal and a mug
of tea. The main topic of conversation centred on whether the

1. My dad – 'Bert' Bullimore – on stage some time in the 1930s.

2. Me, aged about eleven, with my dad in Blackpool in 1950.

3. My mum in 1952.

4.   Me aged twenty-five, when all I wanted was to become a successful businessman.

5.   With Lalel (and a few trophies) in the Orange Grove restaurant at the Bamboo Club, 1969.

6. Aboard *Toria*, before the start of the 1976 OSTAR (Observer Single-handed Trans-Atlantic Race).

7. With Nigel Irens, whose design for *IT82* marked the start of a long and fruitful partnership.

8. Sitting pretty on *City of Birmingham,* 1983.

9. At the helm of *Spirit of Apricot* during the 1985 Europe Race.

10. *Spirit of Apricot* in full flow, before the 1988 Royal Western Yacht Club single-handed trans-Atlantic race from Plymouth to Newport, Rhode Island.

11. A nice cup of tea: in the galley of *Spirit of Apricot*.

12. The men who built *Exide Challenger*: team photo in 1992.

13. *Exide Challenger* on sea trials, 1994.

14. Lalel crewing on *Exide Challenger* in the Solent.

15. Me at the helm of *Exide Challenger* in the 1995 Europe Race.

16.   The 1996/97 Vendée Globe: at the helm off Les Sables d'Olonne.

17.   At Les Sables d'Olonne just before the start of the Vendée Globe.

18. November 1996: off towards the horizon - and the Southern Ocean.

lone sailor could possibly be alive inside the hull.

'They'll probably find him in a life-raft tomorrow,' said Wicker, keeping an open mind.

The ship's 'jungle telegraph' kept everyone informed of the latest news from Fleet Headquarters and 92 Wing. The general feeling was one of optimism, particularly regarding the Frenchman. As long as nothing untoward happened to him, the ship would reach him in time.

But the fate of Tony Bullimore appeared far less certain. People wanted to believe, but most of them were experienced mariners who knew the odds. When Tuesday dawned, their doubts only increased. Already a chill could be felt in the air, and white-caps stretched from horizon to horizon.

10

SOUTHERN OCEAN
Monday, 6 January 1997

What is that? A knocking sound outside the hull.

'Tap ... tap ... tap ... tap ...'

Is it man-made or just the tangled rigging being washed against the side?

'Tap ... tap ... tap ...'

I want so much for it to be help. My heart wants to believe, but my head tells me not to be stupid. There are two shattered masts outside and hundreds of feet of rope and wire. Every so often, I hear a louder bang and a scraping sound. I imagine the boom or the mast is slowly boring a hole through the side of the hull. Any moment and water will come gushing in.

How long have I slept? Maybe only ten minutes, maybe hours. I look at the water-line in the engine-room and see that it's higher. She shouldn't be sinking. She can't sink. Not until I free the life-raft.

There's nothing I can do in the darkness apart from stay warm and save my strength. I'll try again for the raft at sunrise when green light begins filtering through the submerged windows in the doghouse.

At least the storm has passed - the rocking of the boat isn't so violent. There's also less water leaking through the hole where the keel board snapped. If I stand in the doorway to the engine-room and look up at an angle of about forty-five degrees, I can see through a gap in the doghouse 'ceiling' (formerly the floor) and glimpse a small piece of the night sky. I even convince myself that I see stars when the clouds occasionally separate. At least it means I'm not going to run out of air – unless the boat sinks, of course.

Surprisingly, I'm getting used to the darkness and the strange sounds. Normally when I'm sailing I can read every groan, creak and whisper of a boat. It's like a mechanic who can immediately tell what's wrong with an engine when he hears it ticking over. Now I can hear only waves slapping against the side of the hull and the 'tap ... tap ... tap' of the rigging.

But there's something else. I can only make it out occasionally when there's a lull in the background noise, but I swear I can hear water running into the forward compartment of the boat, beyond the cuddy. I put my ear to the bulkhead and listen. It sounds like someone pouring a bucket of water into a bathtub. What the hell is it?

Exide Challenger is designed with a number of water-tight compartments for buoyancy, including a front compartment used to store sails that can only be reached through a hatch on the deck. This sits behind a 'crash box zone' on the bow which is designed to crumple if the boat is involved in a collision and protect it from major structural damage.

If the forepeak compartment which I use as a sail locker is filling, I'm in serious trouble. It probably only needs two or three tons of water. That might sound like a lot, but 250 gallons weighs as much a ton and that is a drip compared to how much water is around me.

Think about it rationally, Tony, don't jump to conclusions. *Exide Challenger* is lower in the water at the stern, which means the forepeak compartment must be holding.

For a long while I keep my ear pressed to the bulkhead, listening. I'm still not sure. Think positively. If the forward compartment is filling, the stern may rise. If it lifts high enough, I might get a chance to free the life-raft. It's a long shot. Most likely the whole boat will settle lower in the water, making it even more difficult to survive.

*

I have no idea of time, but the tapping on the hull can sound like a clock ticking. At first light I climb down from my shelf and rip open the top of the Mars bar, taking two bites. The paper is sodden and the chocolate tastes salty.

The water level in the cuddy is halfway up my thighs and littered with floating rubbish. If I'd been a little bit smarter, maybe I could have saved some more food from the engine-room and cuddy and got it above the water-line in air-tight containers. Now the biscuits and cereals are sodden or have been sucked out. I'd been wrong about the water level and hadn't factored the vacuum effect of the broken window. Even so, a lot of the stuff that's disappeared was either useless, damaged beyond repair, or had no bearing on my survival or rescue.

Odd bits I wish I'd saved. A few pieces of clothing, for instance, which I might have been able to dry out in the life-raft, if I had two or three sunny days. My binoculars and a torch might also have been useful. It's too late now.

Using my knife, I open an emergency sachet of water. I only have two left now. Dehydration will become a problem unless I start using the Survivor water-maker. It's odd how you get more dehydrated in cold weather than you do in the heat – doesn't seem right, does it?

Out into the doghouse, feeling the cold wrap its finger around my chest, I plunge under twice, feeling my head ache, and then push open the companionway entrance. On the first swim I manage to locate the rope which is the toggle to inflate the raft. On the second swim I cut the others and wrap my hands around the plastic container, trying to pull it back towards the doghouse.

My lungs are bursting and I can feel the bruising in my ribs caused by crawling on to the shelf. Come on you bastard, why won't you move?

Then it dawns on me. The life-raft package is being held against the cockpit sole by its own buoyancy. For me to get it to the open sea, I would have to be strong enough to pull against its buoyancy and drag it below the the raised flush decking around the cockpit sole and the stanchions. Two men might be able to do it, but not one.

Exploding up through the water, into the stale air of the doghouse, I slap the side of the hull in frustration. I really am going to die. No one's coming. Even if they did send a plane, they'll take one look at the hull and fly home. They'll think there's no one alive inside here. Face it, Tony, you're history.

I crawl up on the shelf in my black hole and try to get warm. Slowly my heart rate returns to normal and my breathing grows less ragged. I think about the little bird that I found in the cupboard of the doghouse. Too weak to fly away, the poor thing had chosen somewhere dark and quiet to die. Is that what I'm doing? Is the cuddy going to be my final resting-place?

Morbid thoughts turn madly in on themselves until my mind begins to settle. No, not yet. Think about the other bird that managed to fly away. The strong survive and the weak perish. I have to be strong. Forget about any self-pity. It's vital just to be here, alive and conscious, and able to change things. I know my reaction times and brain are beginning to slow because of the cold - everything seems to take a little longer than before - but I still have some control over my own destiny.

I make a silent agreement with myself that I'm not to think about dying at least for another day. It sounds coldly rational, but when the truth is staring you in the face, it's hard to defend a lie. I curl and uncurl my toes, bunch my fingers and squeeze my hands.

When I finally begin to warm a little, I decide to take the remaining distress beacons and lash them close to the companionway entrance. That way I can grab them quickly if the boat starts to sink and I have to dive out. Perhaps I can put in one supreme effort and pull the life-raft into the open sea. I take the beacons into the doghouse and find some rope for the job. The water is up to my chin, and occasionally I have to hold my breath as a mini-wave rolls inside the hull and covers my face.

With a rope in each hand and another between my teeth, I have trouble using the knife and tying the knots. Each time the boat rocks, I have to drop a rope and use one hand to stop myself falling.

Suddenly the boat pitches and the rope wrenches through my teeth. The pain jars and seems to bounce around my jaw and through my neck. I've lost a filling, and when I gingerly move my tongue around my teeth, I can feel several of them are loose. More bills.

I retrieve the rope and start again, but as I try to untangle a section, my Wishard knife makes a neat opening in the palm of my hand. Instinctively, I drop the knife and hear it splash into the water. I plunge my good hand down after it, frantically feeling for the handle. There's all sorts of shit down there - a mini-tape recorder, a pen, hundreds of feet of rope - it's like spaghetti junction.

'Please don't lose the knife,' I tell myself. 'Remember what happened last time.'

My fingers close around the blade. Be careful, you've already lost one finger. I slide them along the handle and lift it to the surface.

My mind goes back to Portishead Docks in 1989. *Spirit of Apricot*, my sixty-foot trimaran, had just had a refit and looked immaculate. I set sail with four crew on board - Patrick and Ben, both in their early twenties, Mervyn, an old mate of mine, and David, a hydraulics engineer from Cornwall.

Patrick and Mervyn were going to be two of my crew in the next Europe Race, while Ben and David were helping me to deliver *Spirit of Apricot* to Plymouth for the Round Britain and Ireland Race, due to begin in a fortnight.

We left on a beautiful summer's day and spent all morning sailing down the Bristol Channel heading for Lands End. By late afternoon we were off the coast of Devon, and I gave the helm to Patrick and went below with Mervyn to brew a cup of tea. As I broke out the biscuits, Mervyn asked me if he could borrow my knife for something he wanted to do.

I always carried a Wishard knife in my pocket, honed as sharp as a razor.

'Where's your knife?' I asked him.

'I didn't bring it with me.'

'You know better than that.'

'Yeah, I know.'

I think Mervyn thought I was over-reacting, but I gave him

my knife as we chatted and dunked biscuits. Outside, the wind began to pick up.

Spirit of Apricot was one of the fastest boats in the world, capable of doing a steady 30 knots if the conditions were right. The slightest strengthening of the wind and she would power up. It's like dropping down a gear in a sports car and then hitting the accelerator.

'The helm's getting heavy,' Patrick told Ben.

I heard them call me as a strong gust of wind came through which suddenly accelerated the yacht. On deck like a shot, I arrived in time to see the bow begin to dig into the water as the trimaran tried to pitch-pole.

'Have you let go of the sheets?' I shouted.

'Yes,' cried Ben.

I took the helm, but it was too late. The rudders were in the air and the starboard outrigger was deep in the water. 'We're going over,' I yelled.

The mast hit the water and buckled and I was thrown forward out of the cockpit like a rock from a slingshot. I broke my nose on the bottom of the mast but didn't pass out. Instead I became trapped beneath the safety nets slung between the hulls. Pushing my face into the netting, I fought to get air but only took mouthfuls of water. Then I reached straight for my knife. Damn! It was still inside the main hull, along with Mervyn, who was trying to open a safety hatch. Sadly, David was already lost.

I lost consciousness and was saved from death by Ben and Patrick, who began digging their hands through the safety nets and pulling me along to the crossbeam, where they could get me out of the water. Ben gave me mouth-to-mouth resuscitation and I was airlifted by RAF helicopter to the intensive care ward of North Devon Hospital. The doctors told Lal that my heart had stopped and I'd technically drowned before being revived.

The first thing I remember is seeing two big RSM-type nurses peering over me, one of them looked like Hattie Jacques. Lal sat next to the bed, and she smiled when I opened my eyes. I'd been unconscious for two days.

'How's the boat?' I asked.

She didn't answer.

'What's wrong?'

'They haven't found David.'

Helicopters and life-boats searched for five days but could find no trace of the 43-year-old. I followed the search on TV, heavy-hearted and desperately sorry for his family.

I still don't know what went wrong that day. Local fishermen and yachtsmen say that that area of the coast is renowned for sudden squalls if the conditions are right. It's feasible that one of these could have overpowered *Spirit of Apricot* and caused her to pitch-pole. In truth, I can't be sure of what happened because I wasn't on the helm at the time.

Tragically, a very good man died, and I learned a very painful lesson about never letting go of my knife.

My hand stops bleeding after about an hour. For a while I think I might have to stitch the wound. That's a thought! I've got a proper first-aid kit bolted to the bulkhead in the engine-room. It's a marvellous thing, beautifully laid out with shelves and tiny drawers, each of them labelled. I've got everything in there from sticking plasters to morphine. Antibiotics for infection, Valium for insomnia, and sterilised bandages, scalpels, needles and sutures.

I go to the box and find the key is missing. It's floated away and been sucked into the abyss. Careful not to break the tip, I try prying the lock with my knife. I'm rocking all over the place and my hands feel like lumps of wood hanging from my wrists. I could thump them with a hammer and not feel any pain.

After twenty minutes I give up on the first-aid kit. I know that I can open the box if it becomes vital, but right now I don't need antibiotics and, even if I could tie a bandage with these hands, it would soon be sodden and falling off. The morphine is not an option. Even if I was suffering great pain, I'd think twice about using the drug because I need to keep my wits about me. The cold is my best painkiller.

I'm still angry about the life-raft. I like to be competent. By my nature I spend a lot of time thinking before I put a plan into action. A difficult task might take only five minutes to complete, but I'll make sure I know exactly what I have to do and how I'm going to do it before I make a start. A lot of people consider themselves to be careful planners, but in reality they're good at outline but not the meticulous detail. They don't have the ability to think things through the whole way and to look at every possibility and contingency.

I've saved the Survivor water-maker, that's vital, but I should have scooped up some food and other useful equipment before the window broke. The ironic thing is, less than twenty feet away, I've got two months' supply of provisions in the water-tight compartments beneath the cockpit sole, yet I can't touch them. There are eight big containers in there, full of pasta, corned beef, spam, beef and dumpling stews, boil-in-the-bag meals, baked beans. One container is full of milk that I've been saving for the second 15,000 miles of the race. There's also some orange juice and two cases of soft drink.

It would be different if I could free the life-raft and set it up. Then I might consider opening the hatches and getting out some food. But the way things are, I can't risk it. What's the use of having a corned-beef sandwich if it makes the boat sink?

God, I'm hungry! What I wouldn't give for one of Lal's soups, or chicken done her special way with steamed vegetables, rice and peas. Although she's proudly Jamaican, Lal cooks the best roast beef and Yorkshire pudding I've ever tasted, as well as fabulous fish dishes and big dumplings.

I grab the can of baked beans I've been saving. Saving for what? I punch the knife through the top and carefully jag it around until I can peel half the lid back. Then I use the knife to scoop out the beans, which have solidified in the cold. I remember a friend of mine who sailed round the world saying that he didn't eat or drink anything hot, not even coffee or tea. It had something to do with hot food causing the body to cool down in response. I don't know if it's true.

There isn't enough room to eat my 'feast' on the shelf, so I stand in the water. I start thinking about how fast the boat is drifting. Perhaps half a mile an hour now that the wind has dropped. Occasionally, a bigger wave will make it heel over quite a long way. I wonder if it's possible that it might yawl over completely - just for a minute or two. Then I might run out, get the life-raft, open it up and tie it to the boat. I might even have time to open the cockpit hatches and get some more food.

Yes, I have to be ready. It's a long shot, but I'm not going to get many chances down here.

For a while, up on the shelf, I try to will *Exide Challenger* to heel right over and right herself. Occasionally, I feel her move and think it might actually happen, but instead I roll against the netting and hope it doesn't break. Each time I climb up here, I think I'll never feel my toes again. I'm glad I can't see them.

What day is it today? How long have I been here? Three days? No, two days and three nights? I honestly can't remember. Heard Island seems like a lifetime ago. If I close my eyes and imagine hard enough, I can smell land - a sweet breeze full of wet earth, wood smoke and leaves. It's funny how after a few weeks at sea the memory pattern is lost and you forget what lands smells like. That's why it's so sharp and exciting when it strikes you again. Heard Island had been like that.

I remember reading that of all the senses, smell is the most potent and immediate because the signals go straight to the brain rather than being channelled through an array of different nerves and optic fibres. Apparently that's why an aroma can conjure up such a vivid image of childhood or a particular place. My mind keeps going back to Lal at home in the kitchen. I imagine it's Sunday in Bristol, around midday and she's cutting up vegetables for lunch. I take the car and drive down Ashley Road in St Paul's to meet Ronald, a friend of mine, at the Cambridge for a few drinks. The sky is clear and the sun is shining.

There must be about forty people inside the bar, enjoying a drink before their Sunday lunch. The owner Bertie is pulling pints and tending the cash register. Music is playing - golden oldies from Jamaica and hits from the sixties.

'Nice tune,' I say.

Ronald nods. 'Yes, man - a nice tune.'

We catch up on old times and a few hours slip by. I just start to think about going home and can picture Lal saying, 'Come back, Tony, you've been out long enough.' Then all of a sudden the bar door opens and a bunch of friends come in.

'Hey, Tony! Where you going? Stay for one more. We haven't seen you in ages.'

The music gets turned up, the place starts to swing and the drinks keep coming. Lal's a little mad when I get home so late but when the wine is poured and food is on the table, everyone is happy.

The image fades, replaced by a disconnected series of thoughts and emotions. I drift into a fitful sleep, dreaming of home, a place without darkness and cold.

11

Six months after we married, we moved into the luxury of a tiny one-bedroom flat above a pet shop on the Cheltenham Road in Bristol. Roger, the owner of the pet shop, took us under his wing like a couple of strays who'd wandered into his life. Correspondingly, I arrived home one afternoon with an Alsatian puppy. We called him 'Rain'. He chewed every shoe, slipper, pillow, towel and plastic bowl in the flat, but most of all he just grew bigger and bigger.

It didn't take long to realise that there wasn't room for all three of us, and I had no choice but to find Rain a new home. Luckily, I discovered an elderly couple who had just lost their Alsatian and had a big house and garden. They took an instant shine to Rain. Saying goodbye to him was desperately sad, and I went back to see him a week later to make sure he was settling in to his new home. He remembered me all right - bouncing around and wagging his bushy tail. He then went back to eating his freshly cooked meat and potato dinner. That's when I knew that he wasn't going to miss me too much.

It still surprised me at times to find this beautiful woman waiting at home for me. How could she have married me, I wondered. She had such grace, dignity and humility, and an almost childlike sense of wonder at the world that I wanted to wrap my arms around her and keep her safe.

The small fortune that I'd made as a teenage entrepreneur had disappeared during a three-year stay in Africa. When I left England at the age of eighteen, I imagined coming home weighed down by diamonds and gold, but in reality I had to call my parents from Durban and ask them to send me £40 for an airline ticket.

I can't remember what inspired me to go to Africa. Perhaps it was a book I read as a teenager called *A Jew Went Roaming,* which is about a Jewish guy from the East End who went to South Africa, got into diamond mining and made lots of money. He came back to England, rich beyond his dreams, and bought a house in Park Lane, but he still wasn't accepted in the 'right' circles.

The story captivated me because I loved the idea of being the bold adventurer who sets out to make his fortune in a far-off land. I closed my businesses, bought a ticket on the SS *Cape Town Castle* and sailed, despite my mother's many tears. In the pocket of my waistcoat, folded in two halves, were twenty-five special Bank of England notes – each worth £1,000. I could have bought four houses in London with that sort of money, but I took it all with me.

On the boat I met a retired Jewish bookmaker who spent every winter with his brother in Port Elizabeth.

'Have you travelled before?' he asked me.

'No.'

'Well, there is a way to travel and a way not to. I'm going to teach you how. Now put your clothes in there and your suitcase here. Then you're going to give £5 to the bathroom steward, £5 to the cabin steward and £5 to the waiter upstairs. That way, you'll be looked after.'

I also met a Methodist missionary on board, who must have been eighty years old. He was on his last visit to Africa before he retired in England, and he showed me around Cape Town when I first arrived. I can still remember my sense of wonder at first seeing Table Mountain and feeling the hot, vibrant atmosphere of the streets.

I took a train across the Great Karroo, through Kimberley and Bloemfontein up to Johannesburg. Unsure of what to do next, I booked a reasonably priced room at the Victoria Hotel near the centre of the city and then set out to explore.

A few weeks later I bought an old Ford Squire station wagon and started taking long jaunts to different parts of South Africa, as well as visiting Zimbabwe, Malawi, Mozambique, Tanzania and Zaire. There were no regrets about living it up and spending my money – I looked on it as the equivalent of a university education. I spent three years learning, seeing things and meeting people who had a tremendous effect on my later life.

One important lesson concerned the issue of race. For much of my time I mixed with the sons and daughters of very wealthy white families who couldn't understand my hostility towards apartheid. To them it was simply the natural order, and I was an outsider who they believed, in time, would come to think as they did. It didn't happen.

I took up the sport of judo, and spent hours training each day at a gymnasium in Johannesburg run by Professor Jack Robinson and his son Norman, who both became great friends. Through hard work and dedication I became a Black Belt, First Dan, and in 1960 was selected to represent South Africa in the Springbok judo squad.

This was a great honour, but also ironic. That year South Africa was banned from competing in the Rome Olympics because of the apartheid regime. I had a good chance of being selected to compete at the Olympics in the judo squad, but had already made up my mind to leave because I couldn't tolerate the racial injustice. I firmly supported the sports boycott and believed it was the duty of the free world to use all means possible to pressure the then government into abolishing apartheid, allowing freedom of speech and equal opportunity to flourish.

How sad it was that I could not take Lal to South Africa, to show her the beauty of the country. I have often wondered if my travels through Africa have strengthened my belief in justice for all. The spiritual richness of Africa certainly touched me: I remember sitting by a fire on the shores of Lake Nyasa in Malawi, having just canoed across it from Tanzania on my own. I was eating food with an old African friend who had taken me night hunting – we talked for hours, and it was one of the great moments of my life, one I would never forget. So many beautiful memories...

Another regret was that I never spent much time with my younger sister, Bunny. My parents had adopted her when I was a boy. She was just born, and so lovely, but being young and keen to get on with my life I didn't see that much of her – I was always travelling on some mission or other. Many years later, Bunny came to live in Bristol and we would meet up every now and then, but somehow we still went our own ways. I hope she realises that I love her, that she will always be part of my life and that I'll always be there for her.

By the time Lal and I married, I'd managed to restore my finances. Beginning the old 'knocker business' (selling door-to-door) I started with a single van and eventually employed more than eighty people. I had a main office in King's Square, Bristol, and others in Plymouth, Gloucester and South-ampton.

I sold a wide range of products in the St Paul's area of Bristol, which had a large West Indian community. Some of them became good friends and I would listen to them talking about having nowhere to go at night to play their music and express their culture. There were only a few pubs in St Paul's and a tiny club called the Speed Bird in Grosvenor Road.

The seeds of an idea were planted. In 1964 the knocker business was still going strong but I felt I needed a new challenge. The ideas growing in my mind, made bolder by what I was seeing around me and what I was learning from other people, were shaping my future plans. I was beginning to feel I had a mission. Could I build a club? What would it take? Would it be financially viable? Lal would say it's typical of my nature that I charge right at a problem. I had no experience of building a club, let alone running one, but it didn't stop me looking for a property. A real-estate agent gave me the keys of a warehouse in St Paul's Road, just off Portland Square. The basement had three feet of water in it which I waded through on my own. Emerging blinking into the sunlight, I told him, 'I'll take it.'

The following morning I wandered into the Salvation Army hostel in Portland Square. The place was full of guys who were either unemployed, destitute or too friendly with the bottle.

'Anyone done any plumbing?' I yelled out.

'Yeah, a little,' said one.

'What about any brickwork?' I asked. Two hands went up.

'Okay, I'm offering a pound an hour, cash in hand, no questions asked. It's hard work, good money and I'm a fair man. If you want the work, come with me.'

With a team together, I marched around the corner to the basement and we waded into the water. The first task was to drain the building and stop the leaks. It took eighteen months to transform the place – along with every bit of our savings and £6,000 borrowed from the bank. From six in the morning I'd be out selling blankets and sheets door-to-door, and then I'd work late into the night at the warehouse. The money I made each day had to pay the wages.

The transformation was quite incredible. Joe Gibbs, my carpet man, went to the end of the world to get me a carpet covered in great big banana leaves. Another firm made leather banquette seats and local artists painted murals. We had a proper stage, restaurant, dance floor and a mahogany bar.

At night, I worked on the facts and figures, wondering if the club could be financially viable. Unlike the big nightclubs in London that attract high rollers, I was creating a social club and entertainment centre for West Indians, many of whom did not have a great deal of money.

On 28 October 1966, the Bamboo Club had a big opening night with a band, local dignitaries and the Chief Superintendent of Police. It had cost £15,000 to build, and I knew the first six months would be make or break.

Lal ran the restaurant, the Orange Grove, while I looked after the entertainment and the bar. The hours were horrendous and we often didn't finish until four in the morning, particularly if I'd signed a big band. News of the Bamboo Club spread far and wide. Like the famous Cotton Club in Harlem, it became a magnet for black entertainers and had a clientele of all colours.

Within three months I was booking acts like Derrick Morgan, Laurel Aitken, Owen Gray, Desmond Dekker, Millie Small and the great Bob Marley from Jamaica. Similarly, whenever a big American star came to London, like Joe Tex, Solomon Burke, Ben E. King or Jimmy McGriff, I'd convince them to visit Bristol for a warm-up gig, or to add an extra date to their tour. The Bamboo also supported local bands like the

Atlantic Rollers, and I became their manager.

Initially the club could hold up to 500 people, but later we took over the floor above and turned it into a huge dance floor, doubling the capacity. Then we leased the basement premises next door and extended the restaurant.

Athletes and celebrities, particularly on the black scene, were regular visitors, and at various times we hosted Prime Ministers and foreign diplomats. The Bamboo Club became a showcase for what a West Indian cultural centre could provide. Apart from the bands and nightly disco, there were darts teams, domino tournaments, a drama group and regular coach trips to different parts of the country. We also helped found the Bristol West Indian Cricket Club and a similar soccer club. But most of all it was about music, and it became one of the most famous outer-London venues.

Lal and I worked side by side. The club never proved to be a big profit-maker, but it rewarded hard work and I was determined not to price out the people who were our core clientele. For this reason, a lot of the activities were subsidised and were cheaper than elsewhere.

Although I became quite a well-known figure in Bristol, the raised eyebrows and muttered comments were still evident when Lal and I held hands in public or leaned close over a restaurant table. It could be something as simple as a shop assistant leaving Lal's change on the counter rather than handing it to her and saying, 'thank you, Madam'.

One summer I took her on a ten-day cruise of the Mediterranean, leaving from Venice, and on the first night we walked into the dining-room and the conversation simply stopped dead. In silence, we were escorted to our table. Seated around it were a group of middle-aged, quite matronly women. The look on their faces said it all.

Trying to break the ice, I made the introductions and chatted about the lovely weather and how nice they all looked. They were all far too polite to say anything to our faces, but I knew what some of them were thinking. At one point, when I left the table for a few minutes, a woman came across and said to Lal, 'I'm sorry, you are obviously at the wrong table, you'll have to move.'

*

By 1970 the Bamboo Club had reached its maximum size, and some nights we had to organise three sittings at the restaurant to satisfy the demand. I never tired of the business, whether it was negotiating for bands or doing secret deals with recording studios to get first use of the latest recordings.

There were surprisingly few problems, apart from the occasional argument, fist fight or bomb scare. Someone rang up one night when Bob Marley and Jimmy Cliff were on the bill and claimed there was a bomb in the club. We evacuated and the police sent in sniffer dogs.

Marley got back on stage, shook his head about the pointlessness of it all and launched into 'One Love':

One love, one heart
Let's get together and feel all right
Hear the children crying (one love)
Hear the children crying (one heart)
Sayin' give thanks and praise to the Lord and I will feel all right
Sayin' let's get together and feel all right . . .

Early one Sunday morning in December 1977, I was woken by a telephone call from the catering company upstairs from the club. Someone had seen smoke and summoned the fire brigade. By the time I arrived, smoke billowed out of windows and two or three units were pumping water. The officer in charge yelled over the noise, 'Don't worry, sir, we'll soon have it under control.'

Unfortunately, he wasn't a fireman. Fire crews throughout Britain were on strike and emergency calls were being handled by local army units. All of a sudden there was an implosion. Heat had built up inside and suddenly roared upwards, causing the roof to collapse. I could see my office burning, along with 15,000 records – a great collection of West Indian music, mainly Jamaican, but also with soul and jazz from the USA, West African music and lots more. It broke my heart, and the tears rolled down my cheeks.

Although the Bamboo Club adhered to all the fire and building regulations, it was an old wooden building with no sprinklers. Once the flames had taken hold, not much could have saved her. Dreadfully sad, I stood on the footpath watching it disappear, and wondering how I would tell Lal. The club had been seriously under-insured in a bid to keep the costs down, so it wasn't simply a matter of rebuilding.

By the time I arrived home, Lal had already heard the news on the radio. Forensic experts believed the fire had started in the wiring - not an unreasonable likelihood, given the hundreds of wires and complex lighting in the club.

'What are we going do?' I asked Lal, when she'd dried her tears. 'Do you want to build again?'

'No.' She shook her head. 'It's too much hard work and it will never be the same.'

'What shall we do?'

'What about the Bingley Hall?' she asked.

A few months earlier I had promoted a concert at the Bingley Hall, a very historic but run-down exhibition centre in Birmingham. Since then I'd been talking about trying for a longer lease on the building and doing some renovations. Perhaps I could restore it to its former glory and run it as an exhibition centre?

The Bamboo Club had been one of the highlights of my life. A lot of people have tried and failed to re-create the magic, perhaps because everything has a time and a place and we were lucky enough to have both. At odd times afterwards I used to say to Lal, 'Maybe it's time to build another club,' but she would never agree. By then I was forever running off on boats and she knew my heart had been lost to another mistress - the sea.

12

CANBERRA, AUSTRALIA
10:50 P.M., Monday, 6 January 1997

At the Maritime Rescue Co-ordination Centre, Mike Jackson-Calway heard about the discovery of *Exide Challenger* as he arrived for his second night-shift. All his instincts and actions had been right, although he took little comfort from the fact. The life of one lone yachtsman and possibly that of a second now depended on a large number of factors that he couldn't control.

Looking at the six-hourly forecasts, it was obvious to Jackson-Calway that weather conditions had improved only slightly in the search area. There were scattered showers, surface winds of 45 knots from the south-west and heavy swells of four to five metres. Visibility in the showers was down to 4,000 metres and the sea surface temperature was 4°C.

These conditions would directly affect the speed at which the *Sanko Phoenix* and HMAS *Adelaide* could close on the search area. Neither could plough through rough weather without risking damage. Modern warships aren't designed with the fourteen-inch steel hulls of World War II battleships like the *Missouri*, which had to counter enemy torpedoes and mines. Nowadays, warships are comparatively light and are built for speed, manoeuvrability and early detection. HMAS *Adelaide* had a hull thickness of only three-eighths of an inch.

As Jackson-Calway scanned the dupe file, Mahesh sat down opposite him.

'All right, Mike, what do you think? Is he alive in there?'

The older man didn't raise his eyes from the file. 'It's possible, I suppose. I don't know how much air he'd have. He'd be out of the wind.'

Mahesh shivered. 'I couldn't stay in there ... not if I had a choice. I'd prefer to take my chances in a life-raft.'

Jackson-Calway closed the file and began thinking out loud. 'Yes, but if he is inside, why hasn't he operated his 406 EPIRB? Then we'd know for sure.'

'Maybe he's trapped in there,' said Mahesh. 'He might have triggered his other beacon before the boat rolled.'

'Or he could be injured.'

They sat and contemplated this for several minutes, until a phone call interrupted their thoughts.

'Hello, I'm Wesley Massam, calling from Bristol.'

'Yes,' said Jackson-Calway.

'I'm the builder of *Exide Challenger* and a friend of Tony Bullimore. What's the latest news?'

'The yacht is upside-down and missing a keel.'

'Christ!'

'There appears to be no sign of life, but we'll have another plane over the hull at first light.'

'Does it seem to be floating high out of the water?'

'I'm afraid I can't answer that. From what I know, it's lower at the stern.'

'Yes, yes, that makes sense,' said Wesley. 'It's a windward boat with the weight centred towards the stern.'

'Have you any idea how long it will stay afloat?'

'Indefinitely. Even upside-down the boat will be very stable and a man could be inside, warm and dry.'

'But how will we know that?'

'He might come out if he hears a plane or when the rescue boat gets there.'

'The rescue boats are a warship and a merchant vessel; neither can get too close to the hull.'

'Believe me. I know Tony. I know what he's like. He's a survivor. He'll be inside.'

'I wish I had your faith.'

'Well, take some of it. He's alive. I promise you.'

Jackson-Calway had heard promises like this dozens of times over the previous fifteen years. Grieving mothers, fathers, wives and girlfriends would call and plead with him not to abandon the search for their loved ones. He'd even had someone tell him: 'I know Harry's still out there, he's too fucking mean to die because I owe him five bucks.'

Yet something in Wesley Massam's voice buoyed him, and he felt more confident that there was someone alive in *Exide Challenger*. This positive outlook had a galvanising effect, particularly when men's lives were being put at risk to fly so far south. If a P-3C Orion got into serious trouble in the Southern Ocean, the nearest airfield for an emergency landing was in Antarctica. Even if it could land on the ice it would never take off again. At the same time, if it ditched in the ocean, the survivors would be in the same predicament as the men they had set out to rescue.

The telephone calls continued throughout the night, mainly from journalists in France and Britain wanting the latest news, but also from members of the public. A lady in Oxfordshire called to say that she'd been sleeping and suddenly woken with a jolt. 'I believe the English yachtsman is alive, but is very cold and terrified. I've never had this happen to me before and I feel quite silly. Normally, I don't believe in premonitions.'

Tuesday morning's newspapers were already being printed and the front pages were dominated by stories of the rescue attempt. There were editorials about the cost of the operation. This issue had blown up a week earlier when Raphael Dinelli arrived in Hobart after being picked up by Pete Goss. A French magazine which had bought the yachtsman's story whisked him away and denied the Australian media a press conference. Not surprisingly, the Australian journalists hit back savagely. They argued that the RAAF had found Dinelli and Australian taxpayers had footed the bill: at the very least they deserved a thank-you.

With two more Vendée Globe yachts dismasted and capsized, there were demands for restrictions on how far south competitors could sail in round-the-world races. Some yachting experts argued that such regulations would diminish the spirit of adventure in the sport. Others wanted to stop competitors 'cutting the corner'.

Jackson-Calway had mixed feelings. Lone yachtsmen in races such as the Vendée Globe go to enormous lengths to make their boats safe and to carry all the proper emergency equipment. It's rare for them to get into trouble, and normally they get themselves out again without signalling mayday. He had far less time for the weekend sailors or holiday skippers who pack their family off on a boat and have little idea about navigation, safety procedures, emergency beacons or even life-vests.

At one stage, the MRCC had to rescue the same yacht three times off the coast of Western Australia before it finally ran aground and broke up. A chap had bought the boat in Carnarvon, sailed it once around the harbour with the previous owner and then said, 'Great, I'm off to Perth,' 500 miles away. He had never sailed before in his life.

Shortly before 7:00 A.M., Jackson-Calway sent an urgent message to 'the bunker' at 92 Air Wing.

YACHTS IN DISTRESS – SOUTHERN OCEAN

1. FRENCH AUTHORITIES ADVISE ARGOS BEACON POSITION FOR EXIDE CHALLENGER AT 061136Z (1136 ZULU TIME, 6 JANUARY) IS 52 10.2S 101 14.3E.

2. THIS LAST DETECTION HAS BEEN MADE ON 'ALARM' MODE (AS OPPOSED TO ALL PREVIOUS DETECTIONS WHICH WERE ON 'NORMAL' MODE). ARGOS SOCIETY CONFIRMS THAT THE CREWMEMBER MUST HAVE ACTED ON HIS BEACON TO CHANGE ITS MODE OF EMISSION.

3. THIS OBVIOUSLY SUGGESTS THAT THE CREWMEMBER OF EXIDE CHALLENGER IS ALIVE AND IN THE VICINITY OF THE LATEST BEACON POSITION, POSSIBLY IN A LIFE-RAFT.

If proven to be correct, then Tony Bullimore had survived the capsize. But where was he? And why had such an experienced sailor initially triggered the beacon in 'normal mode' instead of 'distress' mode? Had he only just realised his mistake, or had the first signal been misinterpreted?

Although buoyed by the news, Jackson-Calway felt uneasy.

He looked at his watch. In another three hours the next Orion would be over the search area. Hopefully, it would find the *Exide Challenger* and then begin a downwind search for a possible life-raft. Perhaps then they would know the true position.

13

BRISTOL, ENGLAND
Tuesday morning, 7 January 1997

For the second night I can't sleep. Someone says to me, 'Lal, you have to rest, you'll make yourself ill.' But how can I?

'Do you want me to call the doctor?' asks Jane. She thinks I'm going to have a nervous breakdown.

'No, no. He'll give me tranquillisers and they mess you up. They make it worse because you can't think properly.'

Instead, I cook. The house is full and somebody has to feed them. Apart from Jane, Wesley, Dave and Steve, there's also Yvonne, Lois, Alan, Anthony, Jasmine and Joyce. I stay in the kitchen, moving between the stove and the dining table.

'There you are,' I say. 'Help yourselves.'

I force myself to eat a little and drink a few glasses of wine during the evening. Then someone will say something - they might use a word that Tony uses, or mention a place that we've been. That's all it takes and I'm crying again.

The reporters are still phoning. They're camped outside and we've had to shut the curtains on the back windows because someone spied a photographer in a neighbouring garden. Steve handles most of the calls and has given some interviews. I don't want to speak to any of them, I've got nothing to say.

'After they find him, alive or dead, then I'll talk to them,' I say.

We hear about the change of beacon signal on the radio. I keep looking from face to face, saying, 'Does that mean he's alive?'

'Yes,' says Wesley.

'Don't be stupid,' Dave barks. 'It's rubbish. You're just getting her hopes up.'

I can hear them arguing as Wesley makes a telephone call to the race organisers in Paris. He asks them to fax us the details of the beacon change. It means unplugging the telephone for a few minutes so we can hook up the fax machine.

'Here you are, this is what they sent me,' says Wesley.

I read it three times. Each competitor has three Argos beacons and one of them is permanently fixed outside, transmitting position reports. The other two are inside. One of these had changed from 'normal mode' to 'distress mode'.

The last paragraph reads: 'The beacon number one must have been pulled away and is now drifting fifteen miles from the sailing boat. All this information allows us to conclude that Tony Bullimore was aboard the vessel when it capsized and after the accident. He was clear-headed and could have switched on the beacon number two.'

Dave still doesn't believe it. I wish he'd let me hope.

Upstairs in my room, I lie on the bed and close my eyes. Tony is there.

'Oh Lal, I'm in a mess,' he says with a little boy's voice.

'I know, I know.'

'Oh Lal, it's wet. The boat won't stop rolling.'

'Yes, but you wedge yourself in a corner. Don't break anything.'

'And I'm cold, Lal.'

'Yes, but you can hang on. A boat's coming. Just be good. Just do everything you can.'

'I don't know if I can, Lal. I don't know if I can hold on.'

'Yes, you can. You're a tough little man, Tony Bullimore. You're Captain Bulldog. Don't you dare go away and leave me behind. Don't you dare.'

I keep thinking about the start of the race. That bloody will! When Tony gave it to me on the morning of the race, I got angry at him. How could he? Why then?

I know he thinks that I can't take care of myself because I'm so quiet. That's why he pays all the bills and organises all the household chores before he goes away on a race. He's been protective of me since the first day we met, and sometimes I hate him for it. He thinks I'm a bloody idiot and can't do things for myself. It drives me mad.

But I know he does it out of love and perhaps because he feels guilty for going away so often. The truth is I've never been afraid of prejudice when Tony is with me; he's wrapped me up in a protective shield.

When he gave me the will I got scared. We were hugging in the bedroom and I could hear voices outside saying, 'Tony, we have to go. The cars are waiting. We have to leave now.'

I didn't want to let him go. I felt sure he wasn't telling me something about the race and what he thought might happen. After he'd gone I sat there for a long time, waiting for the tears to stop. 'It will be all right,' whispered Yvonne. 'Don't you upset yourself.'

Jim Doxey came to take us to the docks.

'C'mon Aunt Lal, we have to go or we'll miss the start,' said Yvonne.

A few minutes before *Exide Challenger* left the dock, I went on board and kissed Tony goodbye. 'Take care, be good,' I said.

'Don't worry, I'll be back. I'll phone you later.'

There was a problem over the boat that was to tow Tony to the starting line. The race organisers had arranged a boat that was too small to let us go on board and see the start of the race. Tony was having none of it. He told the organisers that if they didn't provide a proper boat for his family to see the start then he'd withdraw from the race.

Quickly, they found a fishing boat with a rather surly skipper who didn't appreciate his vessel being commandeered. He looked at us sour-faced as we jumped on board, myself, Yvonne, Jim, Dave and Jane.

I'll never forget travelling down the channel. There were 300,000 people lining the banks and they started to chant, 'To-nee! To-nee! To-nee!' and clap their hands in rhythm. I couldn't believe it. Every so often, Tony gave them a little wave and they cheered even louder. 'To-nee! To-nee! To-nee!'

Even the French fisherman was moved; he began smiling

triumphantly and sharing our sandwiches. Of course, I couldn't stop crying, but these were different tears. I'd never felt so proud.

Laying here now, in the dark of my room, I tell myself that if I never see Tony again, at least I can remember that day. I can think of him being towed down the channel with all those people chanting his name. To them he was 'the old wolf of the sea'.

More than any other race, the Vendée Globe frightened me. Even though I'd waved Tony off dozens of times before, none of the previous races were this difficult or, potentially, this dangerous. I remember Tony bringing home a video of sailing in the Southern Ocean and it had a story about a yachtsman who went mad sailing around Cape Horn. It terrified me, and I kept imagining that this is where Tony would most likely have trouble.

When he first started sailing, twenty-five years ago, the sea meant nothing to me and I found it hard to understand his passion. Now I know it can be an evil, vicious place and it makes it even harder to comprehend how Tony can play with it, like a little boy with a toy. I suppose it's like a drug to him. He gets a high even when he's just talking about the boat ripping through the water.

I've never tried to stop him and I never will, because it isn't fair. This is what he wants to do. If I try to stop him he won't be happy, and we're at the stage in our lives where we need to be happy. Once he gets a whim, Tony just charges into it. I remember when he first came home and said he wanted to buy a boat. Up until then, he had not had a lot of time to go sailing, and would go out occasionally with his old friend, Arthur Ellis, who was a member of the Bamboo Club. Arthur had a boat called *Nimble Fortune* and it was the first proper sailing boat that Tony had ever been aboard. Later Arthur bought a 38-foot trimaran, *Cornish Clipper*, and Tony helped sail it from Canvey Island near Southend-on-Sea back to Bristol in mid-winter. On the first weekend they got as far as Plymouth and then completed the voyage a week later. Tony was hooked.

'I'm thinking of buying a boat,' he said one day. The statement had an ominous sound. Tony does nothing by half-measures, and I knew he wouldn't be happy pottering around in a little trailer-sailer. He'd want a big yacht.

It was 1972, and he'd seen an advertisement for a boat in a magazine and phoned the owner, who lived a few miles from Plymouth. He was selling a 42-foot trimaran, which had been built about six years previously and won line honours in the Round Britain and Ireland Race in 1966, with Derek Kelsall and Martin Minter-Kemp on board. The owner had loaned the boat to the Drakes Island Outward Bound School, a centre to give young people, mainly from the inner cities, an opportunity for an adventure holiday that could teach them about teamwork, leadership and accepting responsibilities. The yacht was moored at Mevagissey, a small fishing port in Cornwall, about thirty miles along the coast from Plymouth. The owner had told Tony he could go and have a look over the boat, as long as the school didn't object, because it would be late in the evening.

Without telling me, Tony drove down there with Arthur. They arrived after dark, when all the youngsters were in their bunks in sleeping bags. The organisers of the school said Tony could either wait till morning or look around carefully without waking the boys.

Later that night, he arrived home at the flat and rather cagily said: 'I'm thinking of buying a boat, Lal. I'm getting the itch for it.'

'Oh yes?' I answered.

'I've seen a boat that I'd like. It's fantastic. Very flash. A beauty. I want you to have a look at it.'

'When did you see this boat?'

'Tonight, with Arthur. You should have seen her, Lal, gleaming in the moonlight. She looked beautiful.'

'No, we're buying a house,' I told him. 'We've been saving for a proper house with a garden.'

'Just come and have a look at the boat, Lal.'

'I don't want to come and see it, I want my house.'

Tony started to sulk a little, but then he spied a big jar of sixpences on the sideboard. 'Listen,' he said, 'I'll make a deal with you. We'll share out the sixpences from the jar. Whoever gets the last sixpence gets to choose what we do with the money.'

I don't know why I agreed with him. We sat there and he put the jar on the coffee table and began counting it out. 'One for you ... one for me ... one for you ... one for me ...'

I should have known that the last sixpence would be Tony's. I wouldn't put it past him to have secretly counted them out beforehand so he knew exactly how many were inside.

'You promised to come and see her,' he said, as he left to buy the yacht.

I felt like saying 'To hell with your stupid boat,' but I went with him. The sheer joy on his face as he pointed things out to me and stood with his hands on the helm made me realise how much it meant to him. I had to wait another three years for my house and garden.

In those days I had no idea about the dangers of ocean racing. Sailing seemed to be a leisurely, almost sedentary hobby for the wealthy and the well-to-do. Sometimes Tony took me weekend sailing along the coast of Cornwall and we spent one holiday cruising to the Scilly Islands.

We were working such long hours at the Bamboo Club that I quite liked the idea of Tony having a hobby. He used to read all the magazines and every book he could find about sailing - fiction or non-fiction, historical or present-day. When Arthur couldn't teach him any more, Tony took private lessons from a Master Mariner, a teacher from Brunell Technical College in Bristol. He learned about coastal navigation, off-shore navigation and general seamanship. I should have seen this leading somewhere, of course. Tony had bought a thorough-bred yacht, albeit an ageing one, and he wanted to race.

14

SOUTHERN OCEAN
Tuesday, 7 January 1997

My tongue is swollen, making it difficult to swallow. Don't
worry, Tony, you've got nothing left to eat now. One less
problem to worry about. In a peculiar way it's refreshing to be
faced with no choices. I can't free the life-raft, I'm out of food,
the boat is lower in the water, my fingers and toes are starting
to blacken with frostbite ... all unavoidable facts.

Cold is such a creeping, insidious enemy. It's going to take
me piece by piece. That's what happens with hypothermia. The
body takes warm blood away from the extremities and the skin
to protect the heart and brain. This maintains the core body
temperature but you begin to freeze from the outside, first the
fingers, then the toes, then your nose and your ears ... bit by
bit.

It's started already. My hands and feet feel like lumps of
petrified wood and are about as useless. There's a swelling and
hardening of my index finger and second finger on my right
hand. No amount of movement seems to get the circulation
flowing, but I have to keep trying. I bang my feet against the
bulkhead, counting to a hundred, '... seventy-five, seventy-six,
seventy-seven ...' Then I tap my fingers, careful not to knock
the severed pinkie.

I try to think about my diaphragm. How cold am I? I unzip
the front of the survival suit and put my hand in. My hand is

freezing compared to my chest, but I can still sense the temperature inside me is dropping. I try to make my teeth chatter. If that happens it's a definite sign of coldness or fear.

Normal core body temperature is about 37°C. If it drops to 35°C then there's a significant degree of hypothermia. Once it gets to anything like 32°C degrees then I'm gone. I won't be able to get warm again without assistance. I'll start imagining things and want to lie down and sleep. At 28°C, the rhythm of my heart will begin fluttering rather than beating. I wonder if I'll dream before I die.

How much longer will that be? Twelve hours? Twenty-four? If rescue doesn't come by then, I may as well slip off the shelf into the water and let the cold take me quickly. But I'm not going to die in this prison. I'll swim outside and see the stars or the sky one last time. Yes, then I'll swim around until I get tired or overcome by the cold.

I'm not a particularly strong swimmer, which isn't a bad thing. I can cover a few miles if I have to, but not ten or twenty. And I can't tread water for hours and hours, even if it weren't so cold.

I've always been fond of the story that John Mortimer tells in his autobiography, *Clinging to the Wreckage*, about the time he asked a grizzled old mariner whether yachting was a dangerous sport.

'Not dangerous at all, provided you don't learn to swim,' the skipper replied. 'When you're in a spot of trouble, if you can swim you try to strike out for the shore. You invariably drown. As I can't swim, I cling to the wreckage and they send a helicopter out for me. That's my tip, if you ever find yourself in trouble, cling to the wreckage!'

I think I'm smiling, but I can't tell because my face is so cold. I trace a fingertip over my lips, but it's gone.

Keep warm, just keep warm. I huddle on my shelf and work out the time factors. If they pick up the beacon signal, how many days will it take to get a ship down here? Three, possibly four. First they'll send a plane - so why haven't I heard it? They're not coming, that's why. They've given up on me, or they don't know I'm here, or the plane has flown home, thinking it's all over for the Pom.

I have to believe they're coming. Two years ago the Australians rescued Isabelle Autissier, a French yachtswoman and a good friend of mine, who had run into problems during the previous Vendée Globe. Mercifully, Isabelle was still able to use her radio and managed to tell her rescuers what had gone wrong and direct them to her yacht. In my case, they don't know I'm alive, all they can hear is the beacon, an electronic cry for help.

I doze in the pitch-black cuddy, listening to the water rolling from side to side smashing against the underside of the shelf. Every twenty seconds or so, it hits me right in the eyes, making it impossible to sleep. I get an old towel and drape it over my face. I can feel the water hitting the towel. My nose and forehead are becoming frostbitten.

God, I'm thirsty! My mouth is full of salt. I try to lash the water-maker to the netting, so I can pump with one hand and stay on my shelf, but it takes me an age to get even a dribble of water in my mouth. I need both hands and more space, which means getting back in the water. Some choice! Do I freeze to death or die of thirst?

I slip back into the water and unlash the pump. Leaning against the bulkhead, I put one plastic pipe in the water at my feet, the other in my mouth and the third trails away. The filter unit is tucked against my chest and I pump a dozen times with each hand, resting and alternating between each.

I pump five hundred times and drink about half a cup. It's gone in a gulp but I feel terrible because now the craving is worse. I tell myself, 'Tony, you've had enough to survive. You're not going to die of thirst. Get back on the shelf and get warm.'

Growing up, I had a friend called Tony James, whose mum Lil ran a nice little dress shop in Southend-on-Sea. His father, Harry, was the manager of a factory, a real steady man. Tony and I were about the same age, although he went to private school while I went to the local Fairfax School. We used to talk about sailing around the world together, even though the only boats we'd ever been aboard were fishing boats or the passenger boats that used to take day-trippers around the pier for two and sixpence. Sailing was an elitist sport and neither of us would ever get the opportunity to learn when we were young.

Another memory I have is of Jimmy O'Connell, a merchant

seaman who used to stay at our B & B. Jimmy reminded me of
Matthew Lawe in Nicholas Monsarrat's 'Master Mariner'
series, a man who is cursed to sail the seven seas until the seas
run dry. He would tell me stories about the exotic places he'd
visited; islands with palm trees, snow-white beaches and
water that ran backwards. Jimmy would stay with us for a few
weeks and then I'd come home from school one day to find out
that he'd gone. He was off to sea again to get some money
together and then he'd be back to gamble it away before
getting on the next ship.

One weekend, when I was about seventeen years old, I went
down to a boatyard at Burnham-on-Crouch on the River
Blackwater, about twenty miles from Southend. The yard had
boats of all shapes, sizes and types, but one in particular
caught my eye. It was a Land-to-Sea Air Rescue launch, built
to go into the channel and pick up pilots during the war. It was
twenty-two feet long, with a doghouse and two large engines.

'So what do you want the boat for?' asked the salesman.

'I want to sail around the world,' I said.

His head almost fell off, he laughed so hard. Then he showed
me a real sailing boat. 'This is what you need.'

She was magnificent; forty feet of polished wood and var-
nish, with gleaming fittings and arrow-straight masts. He
wanted £3,750 for her – far more than I could afford. 'One day,'
I told myself. 'One day.'

Over the years, little things happened which kept the
embers alive. On the *Cape Town Castle*, on my way to South
Africa, we crossed the Bay of Biscay in rough weather and I
remember going up on deck and seeing a tiny Portuguese
fishing boat battling the seas. It kept disappearing completely
into the troughs, but the fisherman, holding on to the rigging,
didn't look worried or frightened, he had everything under
control. It seemed so romantic and adventurous that I said to
myself, 'That's what I want to do.'

In South Africa I did some dinghy sailing and enjoyed the
cold beers and boat talk afterwards, but the real passion came
much later in Bristol when Arthur Ellis took me out in his
trimaran *Nimble Fortune*. The first time we sailed out of
sight of land I felt exhilarated. There were no roads or one-way
signs or traffic lights. We were pushing across a massive,

moveable canvas; a natural wonder without which there could be no life on earth.

When I bought *Toria* in 1972, I still hadn't done a lot of sailing. I negotiated the owner down to £1,800 and Arthur helped me sail her back to Bristol. There were two big outboard engines and brackets, which weren't needed, so I sold them and used the money to buy a smaller engine and new ropes.

Toria had been designed by Derek Kelsall – he had a daughter called Victoria and named the trimaran after her. The boat won the first Round Britain and Ireland Race and was still quick, although sailing technology had moved forward since then.

I always intended to race her, and Arthur agreed to partner me in the 1974 Round Britain and Ireland Race, a two-handed event which began in Plymouth in July. Beforehand, we took the boat out of the water, sanded the hull and got her ready. We spent hours poring over the charts at night, discussing the route.

Although Arthur had more experience, he'd never done a race of this length. It was totally new to me: I turned up at Plymouth having only just finished learning off-shore navigation. There was an enormous buzz around the docks and a great feeling of camaraderie. Initially, the boat crews seemed to stick together, staying with their boat, checking the deck gear and loading provisions on board. The only social interaction was a nod of the head in the yacht-club bar when we picked up a pint and a sandwich for lunch.

'Hey, Arthur, have you noticed how some of the others have got corporate gear?' I said one morning.

He looked up. 'How do you mean?'

'Tracksuits and windcheaters. We should have some of those.'

'But we don't have a corporate sponsor.'

'Ah, that's only a technicality, Arthur.'

I dashed down to Woolworths and picked us up a couple of matching T-shirts with stripes on them. We looked like two escapees from Dartmoor.

Looking across the marina, it was clear that the winner would come from one of perhaps half a dozen boats. They had the latest designs and equipment, as well as the most experienced crews. *Toria* had a high profile, having won the race before, but she'd been well and truly bastardised since then, with a new cabin added. Although I knew we couldn't win, our ambition was simply to finish and get a good position.

In the morning, before the race, they towed us out of Millbay Docks into Plymouth Sound. I went on the helm and Arthur sorted out the sails and worked the winches. The ten-minute gun was fired and the flag went up. I checked my watch. We weren't interested in being first across the starting line; unless you time the run perfectly there is a risk of being pushed over the line early and having to go back around the buoy, losing valuable time. I just wanted a nice clean start.

'Five minutes, Arthur, I want to get closer up to the line.'

'Watch your port side, two boats.'

'I see them.'

We crept closer, making our last tack forty seconds before the gun fired on a Royal Navy ship.

'Okay, Arthur, wind her up. Let's put some zip into the old girl.'

We were about twentieth across, and I had a grin from ear to ear.

Once outside Plymouth Sound we were in the open sea. In those days we didn't have sophisticated navigation equipment like Global Positioning Systems, which can give you an instant fix via satellite on your exact location. Instead we relied on our charts, clocks and sextant.

The first leg of the race was to Crosshaven in southern Ireland. We arrived at about three in the morning, and Lalel was standing waiting on the dockside. She'd taken the car-ferry across to Cork and then driven to Crosshaven. Another yachtsman, Mike McMullen, sat next to her on the steps, serenading her with his guitar and inventing songs about wives who get left behind. A lovely ex-Army man, Mike was among the favourites in the race with his trimaran, *Three Cheers*, which had arrived hours before us. I first met Mike and his wife Liz at a boatyard in Upton, outside Bristol, when we both had our boats out of the water, sanding the hulls.

Each leg had a 48-hour stop-over, which gave us a chance to relax and make running repairs, as well as enjoy a drink at the Royal Cork Yacht Club, the oldest in the world. The initial coolness between the crews had begun to disappear, and now we swapped stories and bought each other beers. They were a good bunch of guys, although one or two were a bit snooty. They came from all walks of life, but really it didn't matter if you were a dustman or a duke – the sea had drawn us closer together.

For many it was the first and perhaps only big ocean race they would ever compete in, and afterwards they would go back to their respective yacht clubs, prop up the bar and tell stories about their big adventure.

After Crosshaven, we sailed up the west coast of Ireland to Barra in the Hebrides. We were halfway across when suddenly the boat accelerated and the wheel spun aimlessly. I looked back to find there was no rudder. It had jumped off the gudgeons and pintles (hinges) and was floating about twenty feet away. Thankfully, before we left Plymouth, I had drilled a half-inch hole through the top of the transom-hung rudder and tied a rope through it, which I fastened to a padeye on the deck. I knew the pintles had worn badly.

We spent four hours trying to lift the rudder back on and then changed course for Islay, a sparsely populated island, closer than Barra, where hopefully we could get the gudgeons and pintles replaced. As it turned out, the main industry on the island and the biggest local employers were several malt whisky distilleries.

I dropped anchor in the bay and a local schoolteacher came out in a rowing boat and took us ashore. I didn't have any money with me, but the landlord of the local pub said, 'Have what you like and you can pay me tomorrow.' Then he laughed. 'Because if you don't pay, you won't be getting out of here.'

After a few large whiskies, I was taken to see the local blacksmith, a man-mountain with shoulders as wide as a tractor and a black bushy beard. Overnight, he made us some new parts and the next day helped us fit them to the boat. Afterwards, I bought him a whisky and asked him how much we owed him for the repairs.

'Four shilling,' he said.

'Ah, that can't be right. Surely it's more.'

He glared at me and muttered darkly, 'That's what I want and that's what I'll get.'

He did us a tremendous favour because he knew we didn't have much money. Within two hours we were sailing again.

By now the leading boats were days ahead of us, and we were simply trying to keep up with yachts of a similar speed and size. From the Hebrides, we went out around St Kilda in the Atlantic, then north to Lerwick in the Shetlands. Then down through the North Sea to Lowestoft and back to the finishing line in Plymouth. It took us about twenty days of sea time, and we finished about nineteenth out of about sixty boats. The placing had far more to do with having a good boat than our racing skills.

I knew straight away that I wasn't the sort of person who could be happy pleasure-sailing around the coast and competing in local regattas; I needed the challenge and incentive of major off-shore races. Nothing could compare with the sense of freedom and sheer excitement of being at sea and pushing a yacht to its limits.

John Steinbeck once wrote that the sight of a boat riding in the water clenches a fist of emotion in a man's chest. A thoroughbred horse or a beautiful dog sometimes arouse the same emotion, he argued, but no inanimate object other than a boat can do the same. That's why you see people - even if they've never sailed - run their fingers over the smooth surfaces of a yacht and knock on the hull to hear the sound.

Not long after I bought *Toria*, I became a member of the Royal Western Yacht Club of England (RWYC) in Plymouth. I hadn't grown up around yacht clubs and for years I regarded them as being out of my reach. As a kid I used to look through the fence surrounding the yacht club at Thorpe Bay, wishing I could have a go on one of the sailing boats, but knowing it was impossible.

When I became a member of the RWYC, I didn't feel comfortable at the club. So many people were so full of what they knew and I felt that some of the members looked down at me. I felt a bit lost, and found it hard to join in, particularly because I lived in Bristol and the club was in Plymouth. I didn't have much opportunity to take part in social activities and get to know other members.

However, there were a lot of people I did like at the club, such as Captain Terrence Shaw, Commander Lloyd Foster and dear old Alec Blagdon, who ran a local boatyard and who would always help me if I had a problem before the start of a race. They were tough days and it was hard to win acceptance, but I've always taken the view that unless I do things for myself I will never get anywhere.

When I entered the Observer Single-handed Trans-Atlantic Race (OSTAR) in 1976 – a race organised by the RWYC – I still had relatively little experience of ocean racing. Apart from the 500-mile qualifying passage and a few miles in the Bristol Channel, I had never sailed alone, yet here I was attempting to sail single-handed from Plymouth to Newport, Rhode Island. I think a part of me felt as if I'd discovered my great passion ten years too late, and I wanted to make up for lost time.

Lone sailing had become quite fashionable thanks to the exploits of Sir Francis Chichester, and the OSTAR had become a very high-profile race, attracting competitors from around the world. Although I enjoy good company and good conversation, I've always regarded myself as a bit of a loner. Perhaps it's a state of mind rather than something obvious to others. I can happily fit into a team and race with a crew, but I like the individual challenge of single-handed racing, where success or failure rests squarely on my shoulders.

At the same time, it's impossible to prepare for a major event like the OSTAR without a dedicated team of helpers who can assist in finding sponsors, organising the boat and checking hundreds of last minute details. I've never been very good at delegating responsibility, but in ocean racing I had to learn because it simply isn't possible for one person to do it all.

In the months beforehand, I collected all the charts and read up on the race, studying weather maps and the routes taken by past winners. There were three basic options. The shortest route, the 'Rhum Line', is not necessarily the quickest because it means pushing against the Gulf Stream and working constantly on boat speed. Alternatively, I could go south into warmer waters and then swing north, making the journey longer but with fewer storms and lighter winds. This route had never produced the winner. Lastly, I could go north and gamble on the winds and currents. It would mean spending long hours in freezing temperatures, negotiating icebergs and the dense fog off the Newfoundland Banks.

I chose the more direct route and set about preparing *Toria*. She had sailed in the OSTAR once before, in 1968, when Martin Minter-Kemp brought in her seventh, covering the 2,810 miles in twenty-seven days. She had handled well in a good breeze, making as much as 14 knots, although he had a problem with the outriggers filling with water.

Now eight years older and beginning to show her age, I hoped that *Toria* could at least match Minter-Kemp's time. After completing the qualifier, I arrived in Plymouth a week before the race started and based *Toria* in Millbay Dock. A few days earlier, the BBC had approached me with the idea of doing a documentary called 'The Lone Sailor', and asked if I would take cameras on board to film the voyage.

They equipped me with two cameras – a hand-held Super-8 and a larger camera that could be clipped anywhere on the safety rails of *Toria*. Someone from the BBC's engineering department had made the brackets and said to me, 'These things will never break.' During the voyage I was supposed to set up the camera, point it in the right direction, press the button and film a race diary of how the boat was performing and how I was feeling.

Of course, it was quite ridiculous to be tackling a crash course in camera techniques only days before departure, with the boat in chaos and so many chores to be done. I hadn't even bought any food for the voyage. With two days to go, Lal and I went to the local supermarket, pushing a trolley along the aisles picking up a few tins of this and a few packets of that. It was so amateurish compared to later races, when I had diet sheets that guaranteed I consumed a certain number of calories a day, as well as all the proper vitamins and minerals.

Eventually, I had cardboard boxes full of cornflakes and corned beef all over the yacht, with no proper containers and not enough time to store them properly. Every extra pound is critical to a multihull, yet I had 280lb of food and drink – far too much. Arthur helped me check the sails and fittings, while Lal sorted out my clothes.

On the morning of the race, Millbay Dock became a sea of colour with balloons, bands, holiday crowds, hot-dog vans and ice-cream sellers. There was a carnival atmosphere, and I hooked up the camera to film some of the celebrations as they towed me out to the starting line.

Lal waved me goodbye from a spectator boat as I took my place among the 125 competitors, waiting for the gun. I don't think she realised the implications of a trans-Atlantic voyage. When I first told her about sailing in the OSTAR, she looked at me and said, 'Is it dangerous?'

'Of course not, people do it all the time,' I said.

I didn't mention the storms or being run down by freighters in the fog. To be honest, I didn't regard the voyage as dangerous. My only concern was navigation, because I'd only just completed my private lessons. Other yachts had the latest weather equipment and SSB radios, while I had simple wind instruments, a plastic sextant that cost me £8 10 shillings and a VHF radio that was good for about twenty-five miles, line of sight.

When I got out of Plymouth Sound into the open sea it was quite an experience. Here I am, all by myself, I thought.

About five days out, the first of the storms arrived. I'd never been in anything so rough and soon the main cabin was littered with sodden boxes and spilled food. *Toria* seemed to be handling things, but I made slow progress with reefed sails.

Another storm arrived almost on top of the first, without any respite. The seas were enormous and I ran under bare poles in a 50-knot wind. Inside the boat, water began dripping over the chart table and there were more drips over the bunk. I tried to seal the leaks and shivered in damp clothes.

Each new storm seemed to run into the previous one. I edged slightly north, trying not to beat straight into the wind and waves. The main camera had disappeared during the first storm and all I found was a wire dangling from the safety rail. 'Shit, they're going to be pleased,' I muttered.

Trying to fight off the cold, I cooked blindingly hot curries and shovelled them down. I also had a big German sausage hanging from the roof and I'd carve off chunks and eat it with bread and some pickles and mustard. At no stage did I contemplate retiring from the race; it would simply take me longer than I expected. Nor did I feel frightened, because I'd made the decision before the start of the race that I'd just go for it, whatever the weather conditions.

On 12 June I discovered that the starboard outrigger had taken a lot of water and, being the lee float, because of the direction I was sailing, I needed to bale it out quickly. Ironically, Martin Minter-Kemp had suffered the same problem when he sailed *Toria* in the OSTAR.

The wind had dropped a little so I decided to bale out the water and tidy things up. The whole living area was a mess, littered with great boxes of BBC film, sodden food, spilled oil, sails and ropes. Putting the kettle on for a hot drink, I lit the Tilly lamp in the main cabin to help dry things out and provide some warmth. Then I unhooked the safety harness from its usual place in the cockpit and re-hooked it to a sturdy ring-bolt by the starboard winch.

Kneeling on the outrigger, I tied a canvas bucket to the safety net, lifted the hatch cover and climbed inside the float. There was about eighteen inches of water inside, which I think had leaked through the daggerboard case because of the tremendous strain on the daggerboards during the previous few days. I'd spent about 90 per cent of the race on a starboard tack.

I began baling out water with the bucket, and eventually removed most of it. The rest I would sponge out later, I thought.

Looking up, I noticed black smoke billowing out of the cabin.

'What the hell is that?'

I scrambled over the nets and looked into the doorway. There were flames between the bunks on the cabin sole. The Tilly lamp had fallen over, setting fire to a sail under the forward crossbeam. Flames quickly spread to the film and I dashed inside, using both fire extinguishers and trying to drag out the burning sail. Suddenly there was a flash and I shut my eyes tight. Turning quickly, I scrambled outside with singed hair and a burnt left arm. The big German sausage swung above the flames and began to sizzle.

The blaze had taken hold, and I thought of the gas canisters, petrol and other flammable products on board. *Toria* was doomed and survival was all that counted now. I took the life-raft, threw it over the side and pulled the rip-cord. Reaching into the flames, I managed to pick up a lump of cheese from the chart table, a bottle of water, a knife, matches, a torch and an old-fashioned distress beacon kept by the door.

The yacht had started to crackle and pop. Time to leave, Tony. I tied the raft to a long rope and gradually let out the thin nylon line as I drifted away. The rope went taut at about forty feet. There were flames coming from the top and sides of the main cabin and I picked up the little hand-held camera and began filming.

Suddenly, a gas bottle exploded and lumps of burning boat poured down into the water. 'Blow this for a bunch of grapes,' I thought. 'If one of those lands on the life-raft, I'm in big trouble.' Cutting the rope felt like severing an umbilical cord. The boat jerked and drifted free. I wanted to cry.

Continuing to film, I watched the mast bend and then crumple. The main hull collapsed and the outriggers caved inwards, so the daggerboards that usually dug into the water were floating flat. I was alone, 500 miles into the Atlantic, with the seas building again before an approaching storm.

After triggering the beacon – which could only be picked up by an aircraft flying overhead, or perhaps a passing ship – I lit a cigarette, ate a bit of cheese and began wondering how long it would take to be rescued. The fire had started mid-morning and destroyed *Toria* in less than half an hour. It was amazing to think that she could burn that quickly.

I lay down in the raft, feeling sorry for myself and contemplating the days ahead. Less than three hours later, the blast of a ship's whistle nearly split my eardrums. Poking my head out of the canopy, I looked up ... and up ... and up. A bloody great tanker towered over me.

The *Ocean Chemist* had been steaming towards America when one of the crew spotted the remains of *Toria* broken up in the water. He alerted the German captain and a powerful telescope scanned the horizon. They saw an orange object several miles away and initially thought it was a tender that had broken away from the boat. The captain didn't want to change course, but eventually decided to investigate.

The tanker lowered a boat into the water, with two crew, and they pulled me on board and towed my life-raft back to the ship. The tender was hoisted on deck and the captain looked over the side and grinned.

'Are you okay?' he asked, with a heavy German accent.

'Yes, thank you for saving me.'

'Where is the rest of your crew?'

'There isn't anyone else – I'm on my own.'

'What do you mean?' he frowned in disbelief. I guess he thought I'd mutinied and drowned my crew.

'Single-handed. I had a fire.'

'Ah, I see. Do you want your life-raft?'

'Yes, thank you.'

They took me down below to the owner's cabin where my burns were bathed and bandaged. The captain donated a T-shirt, some underwear, a pair of old slippers and a shaving kit. Then his wife turned up with a huge pot of tea and a plate of sandwiches.

'Shower in there,' she barked. It sounded like an order. I didn't argue because she looked like an East German shot-putter.

Afterwards, someone came and escorted me to the captain's cabin.

'Is there anyone you want me to contact?' he asked.

'Yes, my wife.'

He took me to the radio room where the radio officer had already sent a message to the coast guard in England: TONY BULLIMORE SAFE. ABANDONED YACHT DUE TO FIRE. PICKED UP BY TANKER 'OCEAN CHEMIST' TODAY PM. PLEASE NOTIFY OSTAR RACE OFFICE, PLYMOUTH.

I couldn't get a ship-to-shore call through to Lal until the following day, but I knew the race organisers would pass on the news. With any luck, she'd know I was safe before she even knew I was missing.

Toria wasn't the only casualty of the roughest OSTAR on record. About a third of the fleet had pulled out of the race and several yachts were missing or in trouble. *Gauloises* and *Saint Milcent* had both gone down, the latter after a collision. Saddest of all, Mike McMullen's boat *Three Cheers* was missing. Tragically, Mike's wife Liz had died only three days before the start of the race. She'd been sanding under the yacht at a boatyard near Plymouth when she dropped an electric polisher into the mud and electrocuted herself.

Although absolutely heartbroken, Mike had decided to sail in the OSTAR. I don't know what happened. Maybe he didn't fight as hard as he could have done, or the sea hadn't exacted enough pain from him. Whatever the case, nothing was found of *Three Cheers* until four years later, when a piece of wreckage was picked up off the coast of Iceland.

For the next few days, I could do nothing but enjoy the hospitality of the ship and spend my time playing chess with the captain's wife. At one point, we diverted to the aid of another competitor, *Kriter III*, and found the big catamaran climbing over mountainous seas. Did I really sail in that, I wondered, as I watched the yacht being tossed around like a child's toy in a bathtub. The skipper, Jean Yves Terlain, thought he could manage and declined our help, but a day later the boat broke up and he had to be rescued by another merchant ship.

The *Ocean Chemist* was on its way to the Gulf of Mexico, via New York, and the BBC were waiting for me as I made my rather ignominious arrival in America. They filmed me carrying the life-raft down the gangway.

Although I'd lost the main camera, the producer John Humphries was actually quite excited that I'd filmed *Toria* as she sank. He took me to the Ramada Hotel, ran the BBC credit card through the desk and told me I could get anything I wanted. Then he put his hand in his pocket and gave me $40. 'Take this, it's all I've got on me,' he said. 'I'll see you tomorrow.'

I had a wash and a shave before going out and buying a bottle of Kentucky whiskey. On the way back to the hotel, I managed to get lost and had to ask for directions from a guy in a pin-striped suit.

'Excuse me, which way—'

'I've got no change,' he muttered, walking straight past me. I suppose I did look like a tramp in my canvas trousers, the Captain's T-shirt and an old pair of slippers.

Back in my room, I drank about half the whiskey while sitting on the edge of the bed. Then I toppled backwards and slept for twelve hours.

Lal flew to New York and brought £500 for an airfare home. The race organisers asked if we wanted to visit Newport, Rhode Island, to watch the remainder of the fleet arrive, but we were desperately short of money. Instead we stayed in New

York for two or three days, courtesy of the BBC, seeing Times Square and some of the other sights. I didn't feel much like sightseeing really, and spent most of my time sitting in a café on Eighth Avenue, drinking coffee and planning my next campaign. Losing *Toria* meant the end of sailing for a while, but there was no question of me giving up. I had a dream to build my own boat, a multihull that could take on and beat the fastest boats on the high seas.

15

PERTH AIRPORT
9:30 A.M., Tuesday, 7 January 1997

The temperature on the tarmac at Perth Airport had scorched to 42°C, and the only shade for the maintenance crews was beneath the fifty-foot wings of the Orions. They worked twelve-hour shifts, without a break, at times turning an aircraft around within an hour and forty minutes without even turning off the power during refuelling.

Vic Lewkowski emerged from the shimmering heat haze and found the shift boss, Sgt 'Rocky' Johnstone, beneath the wing. Around him teams of men were checking the engine, airframe, radios and avionics.

'What have you got?'

'Problems with the comms.'

'When will she be ready?'

'Another hour.'

Lewkowski looked at his watch. What had started as a small detachment of two aircraft with a couple of maintainers on both, had become the largest RAAF search-and-rescue operation in peacetime. By Wednesday morning, there were five aircraft, six crews (from 10 and 11 Squadrons), seventeen maintainers and a Hercules ferrying personnel between Adelaide and Perth.

With eighteen hours of daylight in the search area, up to six Orion sorties a day were needed to provide coverage, with each aircraft 'on task' for three hours over the scene. At the end of each eleven-hour mission, the crews needed a minimum of sixteen hours' rest.

Lewkowski would have preferred to give 24-hour coverage, but the enormous distance and logistics made it too difficult. At least the Argos beacons were still transmitting, so the break for darkness wouldn't cause the Orions to lose touch. Unfortunately, some of the positional reports were seven hours out of date by the time they reached the aircrews.

Putting someone over the top of Thierry Dubois had become the first priority. Apart from checking his welfare and giving him confidence, it was also an insurance policy against his life-raft being destroyed by a wave or the yachtsman being thrown into the water.

'How long do you think Bullimore's got in there?' asked Rocky. The beacon change had convinced many that he might still be inside *Exide Challenger.*

Lewkowski shrugged. 'The designers estimate he has about 148 hours of air. They've studied the photographs.'

'Which means he could hang in there for another few days.'

'If the cold doesn't kill him first.'

With a maximum fuel load, Rescue 253 used most of the 3,500-metre runway to get airborne in the oppressive heat. At the controls, Lieutenant Larry Smith took her to 21,000 feet, unable to go higher in the hot air. He'd push her up another 8,000 feet on the journey south.

Although the Orion had 2,000lb of extra fuel, the crew had to work on the principle of having an emergency down there and, if possible, shut down one and sometimes two engines to extend their endurance. With moisture in the air and extreme cold, there was a risk of ice forming on turbine blades and causing damage when the engine was restarted. Similarly, if the cabin pressurisation failed they would have to descend to 10,000 feet, using more fuel in the process.

Each Orion had immersion suits, locater beacons and life-rafts in case it had to ditch in the ocean. In theory, the plane would float for long enough for the life-rafts to be thrown out of the emergency exits and the wings would provide a relatively stable platform for the crew to scramble on board the rafts. The big unknown in such a scenario is whether a plane could survive impact. Hitting a wave at high speed would be like colliding with a brick wall.

'You're the ugliest hostie I've ever seen,' joked Smith, as a sensor operator handed him a coffee. RAAF catering staff had provided a bunch of 'frozoes' – TV dinners that could be reheated in the galley – as well as fresh rations to make sandwiches. The curries and breakfast trays seemed to be favourite.

Rescue 253 had been briefed to find the *Exide Challenger* and then search downwind for a life-raft. If time permitted, the crew would attempt a radio drop to Thierry Dubois. MRCC was keen to discover if the Frenchman had any idea what had happened to Tony Bullimore. Perhaps the two yachtsmen had been in radio contact before their boats capsized.

The crew arrived over the search area shortly after first light, and found that the weather conditions had improved slightly, with the wind at 30 knots and a cloud base of 300 feet. Descending further, the Orion seemed to be almost skimming across the surface.

'Any lower and we'll be surfing,' said Smith, as he watched the radio-altimeter fluctuate with each wave. To everyone's relief, Dubois was still in his life-raft and managed to wave his arms as they swept overhead.

Diverting to the last known position of *Exide Challenger*, they located the yacht 70 nautical miles to the south and set up a downtrack search configuration based on a life-raft or a man drifting at two to three knots for possibly the past seventy-two hours.

Eight nautical miles from the upturned hull, they spotted what appeared to be a pink buoy in the water. This was thought to be the first Argos beacon that had broken away from the yacht when it capsized. The accuracy of the location was later down-graded to being nearer to twenty nautical miles.

After nearly two hours of searching, the crew back-tracked to Dubois' life-raft and prepared to drop a radio using a helibox – a simple cardboard carton with flaps cut and tied to create a rotor effect as it fell from the aircraft. The spinning slowed the rate of descent, protecting the contents from impact, but the accuracy of the drop depended entirely on pilot judgement. During training the crews had done as many as twenty or thirty passes, but the most accurate of the drops had been five metres from the target. This might be fine when dropping supplies to people stranded by flood waters, but this time they had to be much closer. No one wanted Dubois to leave his life-raft and risk not being able to get back again.

After an initial run to drop a smoke flare, Smith flew down-range and then set up a procedural turn. With a wing span of only 100 feet and four powerful engines, the Orion isn't noted for its smooth ride and the crew could feel every bump.

'Standby for helibox drop,' ordered Smith. 'Open main cabin door.'

Behind him, a sensor operator had taken the aircraft ladder out of the tracks at the port door and was sitting on the floor, anchoring himself to the aircraft before the door opened. An observer sat strapped in a seat beside him. The rush of wind and spray seemed to explode into the airframe.

'Standby, thirty seconds to drop,' said Smith.

The roaring engines and rushing air made legible speech almost impossible, so the dropmeister acknowledged by keying his mike once.

'Standby, ten seconds to drop.'

Bracing himself to kick the helibox, the operator watched the ocean flash beneath him. Meanwhile, Larry Smith had lined up the Orion straight into the wind, flying directly over the life-raft at 100 feet.

'Standby to drop . . . on my mark . . .'

Dubois seemed to race towards them and then disappear beneath the nose.

'. . . drop now!'

Kicked into the slipstream the helibox spun in the aircraft's wake.

'Store gone. Main door closed.'

'Roger.'

A sensor operator picked up the descent using an IRDS (Infra-Red Detection System), tracking the helibox using a camera beneath the fuselage.

'Looking good . . . looking good. God damn, you put it right by his door!'

'He's got it. He's got it.'

The crew were cheering. 'He didn't even get wet!'

'We should have put some chocolate in there.'

Miraculously, Smith had managed to land the helibox within three feet of the target. Dubois could simply lean over and pull it inside the life-raft. The simple radio had only one button and one frequency, along with a picture of an ear and a mouth as a kind of 'idiot's guide'.

One crewmember joked, 'You wait, he won't speak English.'

Smith gave Dubois several minutes and then tried to establish contact. 'Life-raft survivor, life-raft survivor, this is the Royal Australian Air Force P-3C Orion. Port side, overhead now. Do you read me?'

He waited thirty seconds and tried again.

'*Amnesty International* survivor this is Royal Australian Air Force Orion, are you okay?'

Dubois' voice burst into the cockpit. 'Yes, everything is okay, a little bit cold but everything okay, I have food, water, and no problem.'

'Survivor of *Amnesty International*, expect rescue in forty-eight hours, repeat forty-eight hours, ship coming to pick you up.'

'Good, good.'

'We will maintain airborne contact with you until a ship arrives and a helicopter picks you up. There should be another aircraft on top of this position in three hours.'

'Okay, another aircraft in three hours, is this correct?'

'Affirmative. *Amnesty International* survivor there is another vessel in your vicinity, *Exide Challenger*, which is also in distress. Do you have any information?'

'I have no information.'

'That's affirmative.'

Dubois then asked about the weather outlook, and clearly sounded concerned. Smith had no forecasts, but wanted to keep his hopes up.

'Outlook for the next two days, weather will be good.'

'Weather will be good? It's okay?'

'Yes, weather will be okay.'

A relieved Dubois said, 'Okay, okay. Thanks a lot, thanks a lot, guys.'

Smith instructed him to keep his radio turned off until he

saw an aircraft overhead because the batteries had to last another two days.

'*Amnesty*, this is Orion. Request you confirm you have enough food and water to last two days, over.'

'Yes, okay, okay. I think I will be good for two days of food and water, no problem.'

Rescue 254, piloted by Ludo Dierickx, arrived in the search area shortly after midday, as the weather began to deteriorate. As with the earlier flight, the crew managed to spot the drifting Argos beacon, amid coils of rope, but could find no trace of any life-raft from *Exide Challenger*.

Thankfully, the submerged hull did not appear to be any lower in the water, but further photographs were taken to confirm this analysis. These images became more important when the next Orion on task, Rescue 255, failed to find any trace of the British yacht. With darkness having fallen in the Southern Ocean, searchers knew it would be another six hours before they could attempt to relocate the partly submerged hull.

At the next crew briefing in Perth, Flight Lieutenant 'Ajax' Jackson was told that if Rescue 256 managed to find the yacht, they would attempt to get a response from a survivor by dropping an MK84 electronic Signal Underwater Sound (SUS) beacon adjacent to the hull, along with a sonobuoy that would possibly pick up the sound of someone inside.

A SUS beacon puts an electronic 'ping' into the water that is normally used to transmit basic messages to a submerged submarine using one of five signal patterns. In this instance, 92 Wing hoped that a survivor within the yacht would hear the sound and respond by making a noise.

When he heard the plan, Phil Buckley was sceptical. As a sensor expert, he knew the capabilities of the devices being used and argued, 'Unless he's washing his hair in there, he's not going to hear a SUS. He'd have to be underwater.'

However, the idea of dropping a sonobuoy was a good one, he thought. Rather than merely radiating a signal like a SUS beacon, a sonobuoy can transmit and receive energy 'bounced' off a target. Consisting of a hydrophone (an underwater microphone), with a radio transmitter attached, it can pick up sounds from within several miles depending on the intensity of the source and the level of background noise.

Ajax had the co-pilot's seat, with Squadron Leader Richard Moth beside him, as Rescue 256 dropped through the clouds at first light on Wednesday morning. It took them an hour to find Dubois' life-raft and they had to buzz him three times to get a response. It had been a bad night for the Frenchman.

'When is the helicopter coming? When is the helicopter coming?' he asked desperately.

'HMAS *Adelaide* has told us they are trying to get to you before sunset, but you may have to wait until tomorrow morning,' answered Moth.

'I do not understand. I do not understand.'

'Maybe tonight, maybe tomorrow morning.'

'Okay, you tell them as soon as possible. Very bad night. Very cold.'

Having been promised better weather, the stricken yachtsman had been beaten up all night by a huge front that almost flipped the raft half a dozen times. Ajax could hear the desperation in Dubois' voice. 'Poor bugger, I hope they reach him today.'

'What is the weather?' the survivor asked.

Moth took the Orion up to 10,000 feet and looked at the radar, 'Well, it seems to have calmed down.'

'You're sure? No more bad weather?'

'There doesn't appear to be anything worse coming through. I have no proper forecast.'

The radar provided a reading for weather in excess of 100 nautical miles from the aircraft, but fronts in the Southern Ocean travel very quickly and were passing through the search area every twelve hours.

Concentrating on the *Exide Challenger*, the crew flew south-east in worsening conditions. Everyone on board was fully aware that it had been more than ten hours since the yacht had been sighted. Another failure would raise the spectre that it had disappeared completely beneath the waves.

Rain showers, fierce winds and squalls cut visibility to half a mile as they began a search based on the last DATUM buoy dropped near the yacht. Using radio directional equipment, they also scanned for the Argos beacon signal, but the alarm message was designed to be picked up by satellite rather than an aircraft. It transmitted in very short bursts of information every minute.

The TACCO (Tactical Co-ordinator), Flight Lieutenant Ian Forsyth, used the last known position of the Dubois raft compared to where the crew had found him to help calculate how far *Exide Challenger* might have drifted since last seen. He programmed into the equation a 'fudge factor' because a boat well down in the water wouldn't drift as fast as a life-raft.

'Mark! Mark! Mark!' came the cry. Flying Officer Sean Corkhill had sighted the hull just as it flashed past the tail of the Orion on the port side. The crew felt a tremendous sense of relief. The yacht had drifted further than anyone expected but, mercifully, had remained afloat.

'I'm happy, we're visual. Let's make another run,' said Moth at the controls. 'How long have we got, Nav?'

'Eighteen minutes.'

The Orion crossed low overhead, allowing a photographer and infra-red camera operator to take close-ups of the hull which would assist the crew of HMAS *Adelaide*. Side-on to the swell, waves were crashing over the yacht, burying it beneath the wash.

'It doesn't look good,' said Ajax. 'It's too low in the water.'

'There's no bastard alive in that,' muttered a TV news cameraman who had accompanied the flight.

Although no one voiced agreement, many of those watching felt the same way. The hull had a morbid, ghost-like feel, like a broken child's toy that had been washed down a storm drain and found its way to the ocean. Beneath the water, Ajax could make out dark shapes and silhouetting from the twisted masts and rigging. He half expected to see a body.

A cable draped out of the gashed section of the hull, where the keel had broken off. On one pass a crew-member thought he saw the cable wiggling. Richard Moth did a procedural turn and came in again.

'C'mon, wake up, God damn it,' he muttered.

'If he's alive, he must be able to hear us,' said Corkhill. 'We're almost knocking on his door.'

They decided to launch the SUS beacon and sonobuoy. In the belly of the Orion, behind the bomb bay, a series of chutes with metal lids allow the ordinance operator to drop the high-tech listening equipment. The TACCO gave the order and the torpedo-shaped sonobuoy, three feet long and five inches in diameter, was slid into place.

On the next run, it was jettisoned by a small explosive charge and hit the water only a few yards from the hull. The base of the sonobuoy then opened and released a sensitive underwater microphone on a length of cable.

On board, the acoustic operators held headphones tight to their ears, staring at green screens that portrayed, in linear form, every sound recorded. They knew the frequency of everything in the water.

Rescue 256 managed to make six passes above the *Exide Challenger*, picking up no audible response from anyone inside.

16

SOUTHERN OCEAN
Tuesday, 7 January 1997

What's that?

It's sort of a low humming noise like a child makes when he pretends to be an aeroplane swooping down to drop imaginary bombs. Maybe it's the wind blowing through some rigging thrown up on to the hull.

I strain to hear it again, but it seems to have gone. I know that I should get off my perch, but I'm so cold, bruised and exhausted that it becomes a mental struggle. I don't want to get back in the water, I just want to curl up and cling to life.

But what if it's a plane? What if they see the yacht and then fly away, thinking I'm already dead? What should I do?

No, no, it's just the wind in the rigging. My mind is playing tricks on me.

There it is again! I'm sure of it. That same low hum, getting louder and louder. Maybe this is my one chance. I roll off the shelf, stumbling as my legs hit the water and falling face down. The shock of the cold sharpens the senses, blowing away the fog in my brain.

I have to swim out; they don't know I'm here. 'You're only going to get one chance, Tony. Don't blow it.'

The sound has gone again. What if it doesn't come back a third time? Maybe I'll get outside just as the plane is flying away, or it could be too high to see me, or hidden by cloud or mist. Has it even seen the yacht? How can I be sure?

I shiver in the doghouse, trying to decide whether I should swim for the surface. What if I can't get back inside and I'm trapped out there? I'll surely die. I need some way to signal them ... the flares!

I rip open the hold-all and pull out a rocket flare. If I stand at the entrance to the engine-room, looking up at an angle, I can see the hole where the keel snapped. It's almost as if it broke from the inside. Water pours through the gash each time a wave washes over the hull.

I can see the grey clouds but the hole is only about a foot wide. Raising the rocket flare, I stretch my arm towards the gap, testing my aim. Could I do it? How accurate is a rocket flare in the first six feet of its flight? If I don't get it outside, it will explode in the hull. There are diesel tanks beneath the doghouse floor.

Bracing myself against the doorway, I stretch my arm out again and close one eye. I take aim using the end of the flare and the hole but each time the boat pitches and rolls I lose the target. At best I can hold it steady for a fraction of a second. Not long enough. The cold has dulled my reflexes and I take an age to react. My brain might say 'Now!' but my finger won't squeeze the trigger until it's too late. Shit! Shit! Shit!

What about the transducer holes - round holes maybe an inch across where the depth sounder and a boat speed paddle run through the hull. I could take out the instruments and clear the holes. But are they wide enough to fire a flare through? No. And I don't have the tools to ram a hole through the hull.

Oh dear God, Tony, you've blown it, haven't you? They're not coming back for you. I'm sorry, Lal. I'm so sorry. I've been here too long and it's taken everything I have to give.

I listen for a long while and hear nothing but the slap of waves, dripping water and the tapping of rigging. I wonder if I imagined it all. Maybe it *was* just the wind. Crawling on to my shelf, I tilt my legs higher, letting the water run out of my rubber seaboots. I begin tapping my feet against the bulkhead.

From now on, I can't afford to miss any opportunity. When I'm sure of something, I have to act quickly. Forget the cold and the hurt - just go for it!

I doze for a while, feeling the cold slap of water against the towel on my face. The movement of the boat has become almost comforting. After a while, almost unconsciously, I find myself humming a song that is all around me. The rhythm is being tapped out by the rigging. It's from a far-off place that is quietly beckoning me to come:

In Dublin's fair city
Where girls are so pretty
'Twas there that I first met
Sweet Molly Malone
As she wheeled her wheelbarrow
Through streets broad and narrow
Crying, 'Cockles and mussels, alive, alive-oh . . .'

My mind wanders to the backstreets of my youth, when as a little boy I used to sometimes stay with my Aunt Gladys at Golders Green. Because of the war, families seemed to be all mixed up and trying to find stability. I had to share a bed with my Grandad Fred, a real old boozer who used to come home having had a few, flop down on the bed and squash me up against the wall. I didn't say anything, I just tried to sleep.

Every Friday, my uncle Len would bring home some fresh fish from his job at Billingsgate and on Sunday morning Grandad Fred would hitch up a horse and cart and head off down the road with a little set of hand scales, a bunch of old newspapers and a bucket full of cockles, mussels and whelks.

Often I'd go with him, helping brush down the horse and hold her steady while Fred slipped on the bridle. Then he hooked up the two-wheeled cart, clicked his tongue and we ambled slowly down a long, very steep hill. All the while, Grandad would give a kind of war cry which sounded like gibberish but the local housewives knew what it meant, 'Fresh cockles. Get your fresh cockles and whelks,' or something approximating this. Everyone knew old Fred and I sat up next to him in my short trousers and old shoes, feeling very important.

At the bottom of the hill, Grandad would park outside the pub, tell me to mind the cart and then disappear inside. Periodically, he emerged to give me cold lemonade and packets of crisps and then disappeared inside again. Eventually, at closing time, he waddled outside.

'Come on Tone, show us how to handle the reins,' he'd say, handing me the leather straps. We'd head back up the hill, but the poor old horse could only get about halfway before his hooves would start slipping on the cobblestones, creating sparks. I had to jump down quickly and throw chock-blocks behind the wheels so the cart didn't run backwards. The blocks were on ropes and each time the cart moved a few feet forward, I would throw them under again.

Once we got to the top, we'd just plod along to the stable where the horse got a nose-bag of oats, fresh straw and a good rub down.

I haven't thought about that in ... in ... God knows how long.

What else can I hear? I listen hard, letting the rhythm of the tapping fill my head with countless tunes from the past.

For auld lang syne, my dear,
For auld lang syne,
We'll take a cup o' kindness yet,
For auld lang syne.

The beat is so slow it's almost like a funeral dirge. My funeral?

The melody continues to play in my head but I don't sing. Instead I let time pass and listen to an endless chorus.

Cold is creeping further into me and I'm quite fascinated by the sensations I feel. How will it take me, I wonder. It's as though there's something living within me, eating its way through my veins and arteries, turning muscle to stone. When I try to pick up the water-maker it wants to slide through my fingers before they can close. I grab it with my left hand before it can fall, then shake my head, trying to clear the fog.

I didn't think I'd be so unemotional about death. I thought I'd scream and shake and hiss at the unfairness of it all. Maybe if it frightened me more, I'd fight even harder. Maybe it's the cold. I slip down into the grey water of the cuddy and begin pumping. The first few drops from the Survivor are salty, but I don't have the energy to spit them out. I keep pumping with jerky motions, trying to quench my craving for liquid.

Every so often, I discover that I've stopped pumping and drifted off into a dark limbo of twisted thoughts. Then I shake my head and realise that I've been out of touch for a few minutes.

I try to question everything I've done. What have I forgotten? Is there something more I can do? What about the other beacons? I've been saving them for a reason. If I do manage to get the life-raft free, I'll need a beacon to take with me or they'll never find me. Or if the boat sinks and I have to swim outside, I'll strap a beacon around my waist. Who knows, maybe they'll get to me before I drown. Every minute I can stay alive gives them a little longer to reach me.

The 406 EPIRB will transmit for about forty-eight hours before the batteries start to run down, so I'll save that one till last. Giving my arms a break from pumping, I wade into the doghouse and untie the last Argos beacon. Scared of letting it fall, I cradle it like a baby and let my whole body roll with the boat. Twice I fall sideways, once into the water and the second time I hit my head against what's left of the galley. Another bruise for the collection.

Sitting in the doorway of the engine-room, with water lapping around my waist, I turn on the beacon's test switch. A red light glows brightly in the semi-darkness. I doubt if the signal can penetrate the hull of a yacht, but I decide to turn the distress mode on and off every so often. Maybe, if they can pick it up, they'll realise that I'm alive.

After half an hour the red light starts flickering. There's something wrong with the beacon. I turn it off and turn it on again. The light is definitely not as strong. I lash the beacon to the shelf using five-millimetre cord and go back to pumping with the Survivor. Most of the water is pouring down the waste pipe, but just a dribble is clean and every so often, I tilt my head back and let it trickle down my throat.

After *Toria* had burned during the OSTAR, I spent the next few years chartering yachts and competing in cross-Channel races. In the meantime, I saved every penny and held on to my dream of building a competitive boat.

By 1981 I had the money together, so I approached Walter

Green, an American designer who had a great track record with multihulls. Walter was busy on another project and suggested I talk to Nigel Irens, a Bristol designer who had some good ideas. I knew Nigel and met him at a café down in the docks. We talked through Nigel's ideas and soon I was really excited; I couldn't wait to get the project off the ground.

'When can you start?' I asked.

'As soon as I get the deposit.'

'I want her to be ready for the next Round Britain and Ireland, as well as the Quebec to St Malo race.'

Nigel scribbled a few calculations on a sheet of paper. 'I think we can do that.'

On the strength of a handshake and a deposit, he set about building a forty-foot trimaran to be called *IT82*. It cost £50,000 and took nine months to complete. Several days a week I went down to the docks, watching the sleek hull and out-riggers take shape. Some boats you just know are going to be fast, and this one looked unstoppable.

Although she almost broke the bank, it all seemed worth-while as a crane lifted the bright red trimaran into the water in the spring of 1982. We fitted the mast and cracked a bottle of champagne over the bow, cheered on by family and friends. For Nigel, a 'hands-on' designer, it had become a labour of love.

On a Tuesday morning we took her out into the Bristol Channel, myself, Nigel and a mate of his called Mark Priddy, who had the nickname 'Yeti'. Mark was a huge guy, as strong as a bloody ox, and we let him crank everything up to see if he could break her. Eventually he looked round at us and said, 'She's okay, she's a winner.'

Taking things slowly, I took *IT82* through a series of manoeuvres and started to wind her up. She surged forwards up to 12 knots, to 14, then 16. 'Bloody hell, this thing is like lightning,' I yelled. She felt like a wonderful sea boat, hugging the water without any sense of instability. When I finally steered her off wind, I had a grin from ear to ear. There was no telling how fast she could go. I finally had the boat I'd been searching for.

Nigel had already agreed to partner me in the two-handed Round Britain and Ireland Race. We had three months to get ready, working hard to shake out any of the problems and fine-

1. The search: RAAF flight Rescue 251 scans the seas for signs of life from me and Thierry Dubois. Flight Lieutenant Ludo Dierickx (left) and sonar operator Liam Craig keep their eyes and ears peeled.

2. An early sighting of the capsized *Exide Challenger*, taken from one of the P-3C Orions of 92 Wing at RAAF Edinburgh in Adelaide.

3. A closer view: Tuesday, 7 January 1997. Note the ragged remains of the keel.

4. Wednesday, 8 January: Thierry Dubois waves to an RAAF plane from one of the life-rafts they dropped for him. He was rescued later that day.

5, 6 & 7.   Thursday, 9 January, and it's my turn - up and out and ready to be picked up by the Zodiac dinghy from HMAS *Adelaide*.

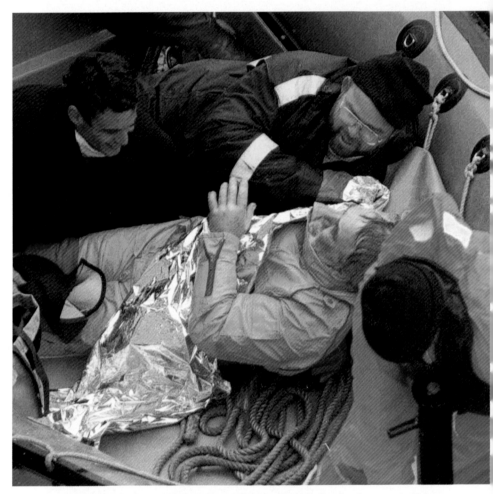

8. Saved: Chief Petty Officer Peter Wicker (top) helps load me on to the frigate *Adelaide* having pulled me out of the water.

9. Thierry and I celebrate on board HMAS *Adelaide* with some of the many men responsible for our rescue.

10. Dry land: a congratulatory pat for Thierry as we arrive at Fremantle on 13 January.

11. Lalel, with proof at last that I've made it.

12. Facing the media at a press conference on my return to the UK in February.

13. Lalel with her niece Yvonne Murray, who was a tower of strength during Lalel's own ordeal.

14. Together again: a kiss for Lalel.

tune the yacht. Arriving in Plymouth a week before the start, it was nice to know that this time other sailors at Millbay Dock were looking enviously at *IT82*, knowing that we were among the favourites in our class.

The race itself became almost a procession. Although we couldn't expect to beat the 'class one' yachts without a little luck, we did finish fifth overall, beating many of the bigger boats and winning our class. Line honours were taken by *Colt Cars GB*, sailed by the late Rob James and his wife Naomi.

Nigel and I worked well together, although we had our little disagreements because he sometimes thought I pushed the boat too hard. He is the sort of sailor who will ease off to protect equipment while I'm more interested in going to the edge, because if you don't push, you don't win.

When we crossed the line in Plymouth Nigel and I were over the moon, and I bounded up the steps to the RWYC and gave Lal a big hug and a kiss. I needed a shave and looked pretty rough, but I'd never been so happy. In the bar of the Royal Western Yacht Club people were slapping our backs and talking about *IT82*. Hours later, full of excitement, still drinking and enjoying the company at the club, the anti-climax started to show through and only Lal recognised the signs. She knew me too well to think that I'd be satisfied with just winning my class.

'What's wrong?' she asked.

'Nothing. I'm happy as a clam.'

'No, something's wrong. I always know when that mind of yours is ticking over. What are you thinking, Tony Bullimore?'

I shrugged and feigned ignorance.

'Let me guess. You want to build another boat, don't you? You want to build one that can win outright.'

'Yes.'

'Oh Tony!' she sighed.

'Not now, love. But one day I want a yacht that can leave the rest of the fleet standing.'

The following year, *IT82* won her class superbly in the Trophée des Multicoques at La Trinité in France and achieved a similar result in the Plymouth-Villamoura-Plymouth Race.

Then in 1984 I sailed her in the OSTAR, making it to Rhode Island in under twenty days and finishing third in my class. Halfway across the Atlantic I hit terrible weather and for two days battled high winds and rough seas. *IT82* handled the storm without a problem.

Yet already taking shape in a barn outside Bristol, sur-rounded by cow pens and chicken runs, was a new sixty-foot trimaran with a revolutionary wing mast and a budget of £280,000. A hole had to be cut into the barn to accommodate the size and a ceiling-to-ground tarpaulin hung the length of the workshop.

I sold *IT82* to Richard Tolkien, a good friend and great yachtsman. The incoming funds went towards the new boat, but again it was a terrible financial struggle to finish the yacht and an equally difficult search to find sponsorship to fund a racing programme. Eventually, I secured the backing of Apricot Computers and the new multihull was launched under the name *Apricot*.

I knew that 1985 was going to be my year. *Apricot* won the Round Island Race (the Isle of White) and broke the record. Then she won the Round Britain and Ireland Race, taking line honours and failing by a few hours to take that record as well. In the Europe Race, a few weeks later, she won all eight legs, crossing the line hours ahead of high-powered maxi-yachts that were a third longer.

In the leg to Toulon, we came around the headland, with an eight-mile run-in, almost eight hours ahead of the fleet. As we entered the marina, there were carnations strewn over the water, TV cameras on the shore and a band playing in those funny uniforms that always look six sizes too small. Thous-ands of French spectators were stunned into silence. They had come to cheer on their home-grown champions and discovered an English boat crossing the line first. Then they started to cheer, because they appreciate their sailing in France and recognised that *Apricot* had pulled off a stunning win.

At dinner that night, I sat next to a French Admiral who turned to me and said, 'You know, Mr Bullimore, the British have won many great battles against the French in years gone by and the French have beaten the British on many occasions.' Everyone around us leaned closer.

'Yes, I have great respect for French yachtsmen.'

'Yes,' he went on, 'but I can't understand how you in your little boat beat the others.'

I laughed and thought about all the things I could possibly say.

'I guess we were lucky with the weather, sir.'

Other yachtsmen and designers were intrigued by the 78-foot wing mast, made from carbon, Kevlar and titanium. Others had dabbled with such a revolutionary concept but had not got it right. However, Barry Noble and Martin Smith, who designed and built the wing mast, had gone to the cutting edge of the new technology and we seemed to be going in the right direction.

Apricot dominated almost every major event in 1985, and in the wake of her success, Nigel Irens and I were jointly voted 'Yachtsmen of the Year' by British sailing journalists. At the age of forty-seven, I had finally reached the top of the tree.

It was great to win and collect the trophies, particularly after all the hard work and expense. Although there were still a few sailing people who found it hard to say something nice about me, most of them were tremendously supportive and encouraging.

At the end of 1986 I set off on the single-handed Route du Rhum, from St Malo in France to Guadeloupe in the Caribbean, 4,000 miles away. This is one of the top single-handed races in the world and certainly one of the most prestigious in France. About eighteen hours into the race, as I was rounding Ushant, the wind began to blow and I battened down in a Force Nine gale. So early in a long race, I decided to take it easy until the weather had gone through, rather than risk breaking equipment for a couple of extra knots of boat speed.

At 0700 the next morning, I went on deck and slowly walked to the bow checking for damage. Being on a port tack, the left outrigger was out of the water, but the damage was clear. The outrigger had snapped off on the port side forward of the front crossbeam. This may have been caused by an unusually powerful wave, but later I discovered that a container ship had shed a load of wooden telegraph poles in the storm and I possibly hit one of these. My race was over.

Looking at the charts, I considered whether I could sail to Plymouth, but it was simply too far. Instead I looked for somewhere closer, where the prevailing wind would take me without the damaged port outrigger being in the water. Brest appeared to be the logical choice.

'St Lys Radio, St Lys Radio, this is *Apricot*, racing yacht *Apricot*.'

'Hello *Apricot*. What do you require?'

'A telephone call to Paris. It's urgent.'

The operator patched me through to the race office and a member of the morning staff answered. 'Hello Tony, how are you?'

'I've got problems. I'm out of the race. My port outrigger has broken off at the forward section.'

'Are you in trouble?'

'No, I'm okay. I'm making for Brest. I'll be there in about eight hours. Can you arrange a tow vessel? I'm worried about the outrigger. I won't be able to get into the harbour with the damage. I'll need extra crew on board the tow vessel to help me with the tow lines.'

'Of course, of course. I'll arrange it now. Is there anyone else you want me to contact?'

'No. Just make sure the tow vessel is standing by, the weather looks like it may be deteriorating.'

I limped onwards to Brest and arrived by early evening, but still had a few miles to cover before I reached the safety of the marina. I checked on the radio to find out when the tow vessel would be with me and gave my position. I was told to stand by because it was on its way. In the meantime, Cross Corsen, the French rescue service, contacted me because they heard me on the radio. They had called the race officials and asked if any assistance was required, but were told, 'No, everything is under control.'

Meanwhile, I waited and waited. Where was my tow? Surely they can't have forgotten me. On the headland above, the military lighthouse-keeper had kept watch through his binoculars, having recognised the famous *Apricot*.

He radioed on the VHF: 'Don't worry. Stay where you are. The tow vessel is coming.'

The seas were now coming with a vengeance from the south-west, wanting to carry *Apricot* towards the rocks. I kept radioing the harbour authorities every fifteen minutes, growing angry as well as concerned. 'Try to calm down,' I told myself, as I cut a big chunk of fruit cake and washed it down with a mug of tea.

Apricot was taking a real buffeting from the wind and the seas had started to build. When the anchor chains began to drag, I radioed the shore to find out what had happened.

'The tow vessel has not come, another hour has passed, I am now drifting towards the rocks and I have no more time. I must put out a "Mayday".'

Growing distraught, I sent out a distress call, giving my position. 'Mayday, mayday, this is *Apricot*, racing yacht *Apricot*, urgent assistance required.'

I tried to take her further offshore, but with a busted outrigger and no time to get sails aloft, *Apricot* drifted closer and closer to disaster. I could hear the waves smashing and spilling over rocks that jutted from the foam like rotting teeth.

Suddenly, a small launch turned up, powered by an outboard engine. It couldn't have towed a fly off a rice pudding. Standing on the bow, holding the tow lines aloft, I screamed into the wind, 'Tow! Tow!'

The speedboat owner took one look at the rocks and wouldn't come near me. If anything he backed away. All of a sudden I felt a shudder and heard the crunch as *Apricot* rolled over the rocks. I stripped off my oilies down to my thermal long-johns and went down below. Already the main cabin was half full of water. Desperately, I looked around, wondering what I should take. First I grabbed my camera case and then thought, this is nonsense, it's too heavy to swim with.

A wave smashed into *Apricot*, spearing her further across the rocks that ripped out the bottom. Time to go – I'm getting out of here. Standing on the deck, I peered into the darkness. *Apricot* had been sucked back into a trough and I waited for the next wave. As it came over the boat, I leapt towards a big smooth rock, letting the water pick me up and throw me forwards. I threw my arms around the slickness of the stone and clung on for dear life as the water ran back down. Then I tried to crawl forwards, lying down and clinging tightly each time a wave crashed over me.

Finally I struggled out of the wash. In the starlight I could see a seventy-foot cliff above me. My feet and hands were bleeding but I had nowhere to go except up. Feeling my way, I started climbing, slipping twice when loose rocks gave way beneath my toes.

Exhausted, I reached the top and lay on my back, trying to get oxygen into my lungs. There was a wire perimeter fence flanking the cliff face, with coils of razor wire at the top and signs saying 'Keep Out!'. As I peered through the link, two enormous Alsatians appeared out of the darkness and threw themselves at the fence, all teeth and fury. I stumbled backwards and took a few seconds to realise that they were inside the fence, chained to a wire that ran around the perimeter.

Following the fence, I tried to calm the dogs and by the time I reached a gate they seemed to have disappeared. Peering inwards, I noticed several Nissen-style huts used by the military, and there was a light burning at one window. I climbed on to the ten-foot gate and sat there, searching for the dogs.

All clear. I jumped down and started running. Reaching the hut, I pressed my face to the dirty windowpane and saw two soldiers sitting in front a television, with their feet up and shirts unbuttoned.

When one of them answered my knock at the door, he looked as if he'd seen a ghost. I looked a mess in my sodden, filthy long-johns, with bleeding hands and feet.

'Tony Bullimore. I am Tony Bullimore. My yacht *Apricot* is on the rocks . . .'

'Ah, *Apricot*, oui, oui,' he said, bustling me inside and pouring me a brandy. After he'd phoned the local police, he showed me to a shower and gave me a uniform to wear. After about my third brandy, I began to warm up but felt an enormous sense of outrage at having lost my yacht because of someone else's incompetence.

Two gendarmes arrived, looking like Little and Large. One of them was so tall he had to virtually double himself over to fit into the little Citroën police car. The other needed a cushion to see over the steering wheel. The latter, who seemed to imagine that I had done something wrong, took one look at me in a military shirt, came face to face and ripped the insignia off my shoulders, as if court-martialling me.

Feeling so devastated, I barely noticed. At the police station, I filled out several forms that were designed for motor accidents, not yachts, and had to bite my lip hard to stop exploding. Didn't they understand what had happened? I'd almost died out there.

The following morning, I went back to the scene and felt like crying as I looked at the seagulls wheeling overhead, picking up scraps of floating food. *Apricot* was no more. She'd broken up and been forced beneath a submerged rock shelf. The yacht had not been insured because it would have cost another £50,000 on top of the £280,000 to build her. I simply couldn't afford it.

'At least you're alive,' said Lal, giving me a hug. 'Maybe it's time to call it a day.'

I shook my head. 'Not yet. Not yet.'

17

〰〰〰

HMAS *ADELAIDE*
Tuesday, 7 January 1997

Taking advantage of a moderate northerly flow, Captain Raydon Gates pushed HMAS *Adelaide* southwards at 24 knots – a critical speed for the frigate. To go any faster would require the second turbine, and every extra knot increased fuel consumption by 3 per cent.

Fuel use had become a crucial issue because the warship did not have enough to steam into the Southern Ocean at maximum speed, effect a search and then get back to the Australian mainland. At the same time, the Captain knew that every extra hour of the voyage could threaten the safety of survivors in the freezing temperatures. Somehow, he had to strike a balance between speed, safety and conserving fuel.

Throughout Tuesday he discussed with Rear-Admiral Chris Oxenbould the possibility of HMAS *Westralia,* the largest vessel in the Australian fleet, rendezvousing with the frigate in mid-ocean to refuel her on the return journey to Perth. That afternoon he was given direct command of the tanker, which sailed the following day from Fremantle. Immediately, Gates brought on the second turbine and increased the Adelaide's speed to 27 knots. Although still 880 nautical miles from the search area, he hoped to arrive by first light on Thursday morning.

The heaters on board were operating at full blast and many

of the crew wore a ragbag of assorted ski-jackets, beanies and windproof pullovers to keep warm on watch. There were a few cases of seasickness but nothing to affect the tasking.

The bridge crew were monitoring the HF transmissions of the Orions, updating the latest positions for the stricken yachts. This allowed the navigator to fine-tune the ship's course so as not to waste any fuel.

Planning the rescues now dominated the captain's thinking. Twice each day he held meetings with his heads of department and specialist personnel such as senior engineers and shipwrights. Discussions centred on how they could cut through the hull of *Exide Challenger* if it proved necessary.

'If he's sheltering inside, how much air would he have?' asked Commander Allen Lo, the chief engineer.

'About seven to eight days, according to Fleet,' said Gates. 'Cold is the biggest worry. If he's wearing an immersion suit and can stay out of the water there's a chance he'll survive.'

'And what if he's immersed?'

'The experts give him twelve to forty-eight hours, which means he could already be dead.'

Captain Gates had left Fremantle with what he referred to as 'my two baskets'. One had been full of confidence that the missing yachtsman was alive and the other full of hope. As time passed, his confidence 'basket' had slowly emptied and the hope 'basket' had filled.

With two turbines now operating, at least he had the extra option of launching the Seahawk before last light on Wednesday to pick up Thierry Dubois in a winch operation. To do so, the Adelaide would have to get within 180 nautical miles of the life-raft, with enough daylight remaining for the air crew to perform the recovery. It could be done in darkness but the risks were far greater. Gates regarded this as a long shot and much depended on the weather, which was expected to worsen as the frigate neared the search area. The latest Orion had reported a new front passing through with winds of up to 45 knots, rough seas and a large swell. The temperature at sea level was 2°C.

Gates had heard many stories about the Southern Ocean, some of them almost half-mythical. Ironically, the name appears on few maps. The Indian Ocean, Pacific Ocean and

Atlantic Ocean extend all the way to Antarctica according to the charts, but sailors have invented the Southern Ocean to separate the seas at the bottom of the globe.

More than anything else, the cold worried Gates. With the wind-chill pushing temperatures to below zero, anyone on deck risked exposure and hypothermia. Shifts would have to be changed frequently and any injuries reported.

His second major concern were the squalls that seemed to arrive out of nowhere in the Southern Ocean and blow with a ferocity unparalleled anywhere on the planet. Gates knew from experience that even a warship the size of the *Adelaide* could be damaged by a fierce storm. Earlier in his naval career, he had been on board the aircraft-carrier *Melbourne*, sailing across the Great Australian Bight, when the seas were so rough that waves were breaking across the flight deck. On another RAN ship in the Bay of Hauraki, off Auckland, waves had split one of the main bulkheads in the centre of the vessel at the height of a storm.

The long swells that build up in the Southern Ocean were another problem. If the *Adelaide* began surfing down a swell, she would become difficult to steer and control. Added to this, the Australian Antarctic Division had issued a warning of icebergs in the area below 52 degrees south. These could not be detected by radar and were a danger to any ship travelling at high speed with a hull only three-eighths of an inch thick.

'We can have lookouts during the day, but at night we won't see an iceberg,' said Ops Officer Michael Rothwell.

Ken Burleigh spoke up. 'None of the P-3Cs have reported seeing any in the search area.'

'That's significant,' said Gates. 'They've covered a lot of miles searching for life-rafts. I'd be more worried if they'd sighted ice.'

'How do you want to respond?' asked Burleigh.

'I don't want to slow down. Let's continue as we are. Ask the P-3Cs to keep an eye out and to report any sightings immediately.'

As predicted, the weather began to deteriorate on Wednesday morning and the superstructure took a pounding as it drove into the waves. Although the *Adelaide* reduced speed to avoid damage, the ride became uncomfortable and a large number of the crew came down with seasickness, along with half the media contingent.

In the CPOs' Mess, Pete Wicker had just sat down for a cup of tea when he was joined by the 'XO', Jim Manson, second in command of the warship.

'How are we going to get him out if he's inside?'

'I've been thinking about that,' said Wicker, who from the outset had assumed that any sea-borne rescue would involve his skills in seamanship.

'The helo should be able to pick up Dubois,' said Manson, 'but we'll have to find another answer for the British yacht. The biggest problem is how to get close enough. If we use an RIB, we have to find a way of securing it to the hull – a smooth surface in rough seas ...'

'Couldn't the helo drop someone on top of it?' suggested someone nearby.

'How are they going to hold on?' said Wicker. 'We don't want anyone in the water – not in those temperatures. Unless ...' Wicker looked at Manson. 'What about a diver?'

The 'XO' shook his head. 'Fleet have said that under no circumstances are we to put anyone under the hull without the Admiral's express permission. It's just too dangerous with all that broken rigging.'

'That rules out towing it or winching it on board,' said Wicker.

Manson nodded. 'Which leaves the RIB.'

'Maybe we could drive spikes into the side of the yacht to secure ourselves? Then we could put some sort of deck treading over the hull to give us some grip,' said the Chief Chippy (chief shipwright) 'Syd' Smith.

Wicker: 'Then we still have to cut through. He might be alive inside an air pocket, and we don't want to sink the bloody yacht.'

Manson: 'Fleet is in touch with the designers and the boat builder.'

Smith: 'I don't fancy running oxy equipment and gas hoses from a bouncing RIB on to a moving hull.'

'That's what I want you to decide,' said Manson. 'Come up

SAVED

with some suggestions and we'll talk later.'

Wicker and Smith stayed in the Mess and spent several hours discussing the logistics of a sea-borne rescue and the various cutting tools available. Soon afterwards, the following message was sent to Fleet Headquarters and relayed to MRCC:

OPER/ANTARCTIC ONE.
1.   IN ANTICIPATION OF HAVING TO ENTER THE HULL TO RESCUE OCCUPANT, THE FOLLOWING QUESTIONS ARE RAISED:
    A.   LOCATION OF EPIRB BEACON
    B.   LOCATION OF ANY COMBUSTIBLES, EG. LPG GAS CYLINDERS, PYROS ETC
    C.   LOCATION OF ANY WATERTIGHT BULKHEADS/DIVISIONS
    D.   WEIGHT OF VESSEL
    E.   MATERIAL OF VESSEL
    F.   SIZE OF BALLAST TANKS WITH OPTION OF FILLING WITH COMPRESSED AIR FOR BUOYANCY
    G.   DIMENSIONS OF YACHT
2.   INTEND SEEKING FOLLOWING INFORMATION FROM ON TASK P-3C:
    A.   LAY OF SUBMERGED VESSEL, INCLUDING LIST AND PERCENTAGE SUBMERGED

Meanwhile, Pete Wicker set about choosing his team, approaching them individually. He wanted three crew to handle the RIB and selected three leading seamen: Paul Ellul as the coxswain; Alan Rub, a navy diver; and Chris Smart. He also wanted 'Syd' Smith on board because of his engineering expertise. Counting himself and Jim Manson, that made a crew of six.

The operation would have three phases and two more crews were chosen. The first RIB would attach lines to the hull and hammer on the outside. If there was no response, they would attach some form of template to the hull, showing the best place to cut. The next crew would begin the cutting and be replaced after half an hour because of the bitter cold. No crew would work for any longer than this before having a break.

At Fleet Headquarters, details and diagrams of *Exide Challenger* were received from Wesley Massam and Jim Doxey, along with an inventory of everything on board. These were faxed directly to HMAS *Adelaide*. Syd Smith now had an accurate layout of the yacht and could begin working a template to cut through. In particular he had to be careful of combustibles. There were six plastic drums of diesel, as well as two full and two empty LP gas cylinders that were normally stored beneath the cockpit sole, aft of the mizzen bulkhead. The gas cylinder in use is just inside the companionway entrance, port side. Near this was a yellow plastic flare box containing 12 Para flares. The main fuel tanks were under the doghouse deck.

The position of the various beacons was also vital in determining where a survivor might be sheltering. According to the plans, the EPIRB was attached to a bulkhead in the lower living area. Two Argos beacons were stowed nearby, but a third (positional beacon) had been kept outside on the stern.

The faxed sketches made it clear that there was no access between the living area and the aft stowage compartments of the yacht, which could only be reached through hatches on the deck. The same was true of the sail locker in the forward section, and the bulkheads appeared to be solid and watertight. There were, however, small breaches in some of these bulkheads for wiring.

In the main living compartments there were nonwatertight bulkheads with doorways. This meant that a survivor could possibly move between cabins, but he couldn't go all the way forward into the sail lockers.

Exide Challenger weighed approximately eight tonnes without her keel, with ballast tanks capable of holding two tonnes of water on each side. These could be reached through vents on the deck and could be cleared by using high-pressure air.

The hull material consisted of a core of aertex foam, 40mm thick in the hull and 35mm in the deck. This foam had been laminated with two millimetre thick carbon/Kevlar, inside and out, with heavier concentrations around the keel area and other points of loading.

The report stated: 'The designer believes that the Kevlar would make it very difficult to penetrate the hull with an axe. The foam has a tremendous ability to absorb energy and the inner Kevlar layer will tend to flex when struck. If an axe is not effective, the only tools likely to cut effectively may be a disc cutter with a diamond wheel or a Broco cutter [thermal lance].

'Tests using a Broco are being conducted on a representative sample of material and results will be advised when known. Once skin has been penetrated, it should be possible to cut with hacksaw blades, but Kevlar will rapidly blunt the blades. Caution should be taken to avoid laceration by sharp edges of cut composite material, especially the remnants of the keel.'

That afternoon, Wicker gathered his boat crew together in the empty starboard hangar and began discussing how they could secure the RIB to the upturned hull. With the help of Chris Smart, Paul Ellul and Alan Rub, he began to organise coils of rope, shackles and winches that might be needed. They fashioned a rope ladder with two grappling hooks on one end and a single grappling hook on the other. The idea was to throw the device over the hull and then attach the single grappling hook on an adjustable line that could be pulled tight. This might allow someone to cling to the hull without being washed off by the first wave.

In addition, they prepared a safety harness that could be hooked to the 'ladder'. If someone got into trouble, they could be pulled straight back into the RIB before a wave could smash them against the hull.

'What about the rudders as an anchoring point?' suggested Smart.

'I don't know if they could take the strain of a two and a half tonne RIB,' said Wicker. 'It's the same with the busted keel – we won't know until we get out there.'

This is what concerned him most about the operation. Despite all the preparation, 90 per cent of the decisions would have to be made on the spot.

Down below, 'Syd' Smith had another team in his workshop investigating how they could pierce the carbon/Kevlar hull. Using the design plans and recommendations from Fleet, he created a series of cards showing the best location to cut. This was on the centre-line between two and three metres from the leading edge of the keel, directly above the engine-room.

Importantly, the latest photographs showed that *Exide*

Challenger continued to ride down at the stern, which meant penetrating the hull forward of the keel position was unlikely to cause her to sink.

Tools such as pick-axes and chipping hammers were being sharpened because they might prove useful in providing a grip on the smooth surface. Meanwhile, a decision still had to be made on how they would cut through the hull.

At Fleet Headquarters in Sydney, the operational hierarchy gathered to discuss this question. Among those present were Rear-Admiral Chris Oxenbould, Commodore Tim Cox, the chief engineer Captain Peter Hatcher and two experienced local yachtsmen who had been asked for their input.

Damage control expert Commander Trevor Jones was tasked to locate a sample of the Kevlar GRP composite hull so it could be tested with a range of tools. Thumbing through the yellow pages, he rang various local boat-builders until he found McConachie Yachts in Mona Vale, on Sydney's northern beaches. They had some very similar material and were willing to provide a sample.

On Wednesday afternoon, Warrant Officer Lionel Harris took a Broco cutter to the boat yard and tested it on a three-foot-square section of Kevlar. The thermal lance sliced neatly through the material but generated enormous heat and fumes. Further tests were conducted back at Fleet, using a portable power tool, an axe and a 'damage control hand-saw'.

The recommendations sent to HMAS *Adelaide* suggested that the Broco cutter should be discounted because choking smoke would fill an air pocket within seconds and possibly suffocate any survivor. The portable power cutter, although successful, was regarded as being too dangerous to use on the rolling hull.

'So that leaves the axe and the saw,' said Wicker, glancing at the report. 'We pierce the outer layer of the hull, scoop out the foam and then start cutting with the hand-saw. The Kevlar fibres are going to clog up the teeth, but we'll just have to keep cleaning them.

'We could always use the Broco as a last resort. If he's in a bad way, we could punch a hole to give him some fresh air, tell him to hold his breath and then use the lance. It wouldn't take more than a minute.'

Syd Smith agreed. 'You never know, we might have more time than we think.'

The two men's eyes met. Wicker knew immediately what the 'chief chippy' had implied. If they found Tony Bullimore's body in the hull, it wouldn't matter how long they took to retrieve it.

Although the change of signal on the Argos beacon had raised hopes that the yachtsman might be alive, the lack of any additional evidence since Tuesday morning had seen this optimism begin to fade. The growing consensus seemed to be that 'two out of three isn't bad'. The rescue of Raphael Dinelli had been remarkable and Thierry Dubois was almost within reach, but it was too much to ask of any God, guardian angel or patron saint of sailors to spare a third life.

At the rescue co-ordination centre, Mike Jackson-Calway took over on the day shift at 6:50 A.M. on Wednesday. He read the dupe files and then prepared a situation report for Fleet Headquarters, MRCC ETEL in France, 92 Wing Ops and the British and French Embassies.

1.   FURTHER SORTIES BY RAAF P-3C ORIONS LAST NIGHT CONFIRMED THAT MR DUBOIS WAS SAFE AND WELL IN THE LIFE-RAFT IN IMPROVED WEATHER CONDITIONS WINDS WESTERLY AT 20 KNOTS.

2.   THE EXIDE CHALLENGER WAS LAST LOCATED VISUALLY AT 11.42 AT POSITION 5221S 10159E UPTURNED WITH KEEL MISSING AND MAST AND RIGGING STILL ATTACHED. THERE HAS BEEN NO SIGN OF MR BULLIMORE. ARGOS BEACON POSITION REPORTS FROM EXIDE CHALLENGER CONTINUE TO BE UPDATED BY MRCC ETEL.

3.   MRCC ETEL CONFIRM THAT THE ARGOS BEACON ON ALERT MODE CONTINUES TO TRANSMIT FROM THE STRICKEN VESSEL, HOWEVER A 2ND BEACON APPEARS TO HAVE DRIFTED FROM THE VESSEL, THIS BEING THE 'POSITION INDICATING' BEACON USUALLY LOCATED ON THE STERN OF THE VESSEL.

4.   SONAR DEVICES LISTENED OUT FOR ANY SIGN OF MR BULLIMORE ON THE EXIDE CHALLENGER HOWEVER CONDITIONS WERE NOT SUITABLE TO DETERMINE ANY SIGNS OF LIFE.

5.   FURTHER RAAF P-3C ORION SORTIES TODAY WILL ATTEMPT TO GAIN A RESPONSE FROM EXIDE CHALLENGER AS TO WHETHER MR BULLIMORE IS TRAPPED WITHIN THE HULL.

With each successive Orion mission, the tasking had been almost identical. Firstly, the crew had to confirm Dubois' safety in his life-raft, then it had to establish if the *Exide Challenger* was still afloat, before beginning a search using the co-ordinates supplied by MRCC, based on the drift rate of a life-raft. After covering as wide a track as possible, the crew had to check on Dubois before departing the area.

Meanwhile, the *Sanko Phoenix* continued to steam south at 11 knots in moderate seas. The *Adelaide* had managed to make such good time that by Wednesday morning she was five degrees further south, and would arrive in the search area three hours earlier than the tanker. MRCC suggested the two ships make contact and establish a joint rescue plan. Captain Raydon Gates would be the On-Scene Commander.

By lunchtime in Canberra, as Jackson-Calway ate a sandwich from the canteen, the first Orion had reached the search area. As feared, the weather had deteriorated and Rescue 256 reported 40-knot winds, a four-metre swell, a cloud base of 200 feet and an air temperature of minus 2°C at 300 feet. In a steady drizzle, visibility ranged from zero to 500 metres. The hull of the *Exide Challenger* remained intact, but there was no sign of any survivor.

Upon hearing of the low cloud and air temperature, Captain Gates ruled out any possibility of launching the Seahawk on Wednesday afternoon. The helicopter had no de-icing equipment and he couldn't risk having the main rotors ice up.

Changing the timetable, he planned to launch the helo at 4.30 A.M. (local time) on Thursday morning and arranged with 92 Wing to have an Orion in the area at first light.

OPER/ANTARCTIC ONE.

380NM FROM AMNESTY INTERNATIONAL LIFE-RAFT.

DUE TO PREVAILING WEATHER, SET AGAINST ADELAIDE AND DRIFT OF LIFE-RAFT, RESCUE ATTEMPT RESCHEDULED FOR FIRST LIGHT 9 JANUARY (WEATHER DEPENDENT) . . . FRENCH YACHTSMAN DUBOIS RELOCATED BY RAAF P-3C REPORTED

IN LOW SPIRITS DUE TO WORSENING WEATHER. ADVISED OF ADELAIDE'S PROPOSED
RESCUE TIME. NO JOY WITH SURVIVOR FROM EXIDE CHALLENGER . . .

That afternoon, Jackson-Calway sat down with the manager of SAR operations, Rick Burleigh, to discuss the grounds for calling off the search. Ultimately, the decision would rest with the Australian Federal Minister for Transport, although he might seek Cabinet approval. Normally, Cabinet would accept the recommendations of SAR operations, but the agenda can sometimes be set by the media, particularly in high-profile searches such as this one. If tearful relatives plead for 'just a few more days', it becomes difficult for any politician to say no.

Jackson-Calway and Burleigh knew all about political expedience and image-management. Yet the reality of their world was far more hard-nosed. Neither of them wanted to lose anyone in the Southern Ocean, not Tony Bullimore and certainly not any of the searchers.

'I'm going to recommend the search is suspended if they don't find him on board,' said Burleigh, a grizzled veteran of twenty-one years with the Australian Maritime Safety Authority (AMSA).

Jackson-Calway nodded. 'What grounds are you going to give?'

'If they find his life-raft on board, we'll know he's in the water. No one could survive in those temperatures for this length of time. There's also the fact that he hasn't activated his 406MHz EPIRB.' Burleigh spoke and scribbled notes at the same time. 'Finally, I think we can argue that the effort expended is already enormous and any extension would simply prolong the risk to SAR crews.'

18

PERTH, AUSTRALIA
Wednesday, 8 January 1997

'I don't think we should be trying to coax him out of the boat,' said Phil Buckley, as he sat in the restaurant of the Regency Motor Lodge in Perth. 'If he's in there, it's the best place for him.'

Vic Lewkowski shook his head. 'But if we get him into a life-raft like Dubois, then we can keep an eye on him. He'll have food and water. We could even drop him a radio.'

Buckley sighed. 'Yeah, but think about it. What if he's not strong enough to swim for an ASRK? The poor bastard could drown. And look what happened to Dubois - one of his life-rafts gets shredded by a wave and he spends an hour in the water.'

One of the ground crew joined in the discussion. 'At the very least we should let him know we're looking. It might keep his spirits up.'

Buckley: 'And how do we do that? He's not going to hear the SUS.'

'Why not drop something on the boat, like a helibox?'

'I'll tell you why,' argued Buckley. 'Because when it hits the hull, he's going to think, good they've arrived and he'll swim outside and won't be able to get back in.'

'We don't know that for sure,' said Lewkowski.

'You're right, so why take the risk?'

Someone else suggested dropping an explosive charge in the water, far enough away from the hull for the survivor to hear.

'Hey, great idea, let's bomb the Pom,' said Mick Whitley, the shift boss on the maintenance team.

When the laughter died down, Buckley raised his mug and motioned to the waitress for another coffee. 'I still say we do nothing that might coax him out. We all want to know if he's in there, but not if it means putting him in danger. He probably already knows we're searching. He must have heard us and he's sitting tight.'

'Gee, that'd take some balls, wouldn't it?' said Mort, one of the sensor operators. 'If I heard a plane, I'd be out of there in a flash.'

Buckley: 'Yeah, but this guy's an experienced sailor. He knows to stay with the boat and to stay out of the wind. He's waiting for someone to knock on the hull.'

'So you really think he's alive in there?' asked Mort.

'I'm saying it's possible. We don't know what it's like inside there, he might be dry and warm. If he's not, then he might be better off in a dinghy. Shit, I don't know. All we know for sure is that the boat doesn't seem to be sinking any more.'

This same debate had been taxing the operations staff at 92 Wing. Don Hickey, one of the acoustics operators, had also suggested using an explosive, but this had been discounted as being too dangerous. Wing Commander Ian Pearson could sense the frustration of the Orion crews. If only Tony Bullimore would turn on another beacon or change the mode of signal, then they'd be sure he was alive and inside the vessel. Even if he banged regularly on the hull, a sonobuoy would pick up the sound.

In rapidly deteriorating weather, Rescue 257 had been unable to locate the *Exide Challenger* mid-morning on Wednesday because of the appalling visibility. That afternoon Larry Smith and his crew on Rescue 258 managed to find the yacht (0733 Zulu time) and immediately deployed more sonobuoys and an SUS beacon.

Suddenly, the co-pilot picked up what seemed to be a very

faint 121.5 MHz transmission - the same frequency as an EPIRB distress beacon. 'I got something - just for a few seconds, right overhead, very, very low in the noise.'

'Okay, I'm gonna do a reversal procedure,' said Smith. 'I'll come downwind and I'm gonna mark on top again.'

Maybe a mile past the overflight, as the Orion began to turn, the flight crew picked up something that sounded like muffled speech.

'What's that?'

'Quiet, quiet,' said Smith. 'We might have a 121.5. Nav, were you transmitting?'

'Yeah, but that was a few minutes ago,' said Roger McCutcheon.

'When did you transmit?'

He looked at his screen and gave the time.

'Okay, let's go over it again and see what we can pick up.'

They made three more passes, but couldn't find the signal.

'It could have been a break through from our radio or the ICS system,' suggested McCutcheon. 'Our HF radio can break through and you can hardly hear it. We had the 121.5 pulled up full blast and could barely pick up the signal.'

Smith wasn't convinced. The 406 SARSAT beacon carried by Tony Bullimore normally transmits a side signal at the frequency 121.5 for local homing. While this might explain what the crew had heard, they should also have been able to pick up the main, much stronger, 406 signal.

'How do we want to call it?' asked McCutcheon.

Smith pondered the question. 'I think we should let Ops know we've picked up a possible transmission, but it's more likely to be break through from the aircraft.'

With their remaining time on task, the crew conducted a visual search downwind and then checked on Thierry Dubois before departing for Perth. There would be time for one more flight before dusk, and they relayed details of their mission to Rescue 259 which passed them less than an hour from the search area.

Meanwhile, MRCC in Canberra had been advised that HMAS *Adelaide* would now arrive in the search area at 2300 hours Zulu time on Wednesday 8 January (Thursday morning local time), three hours before the *Sanko Phoenix*. Captain

Raydon Gates would immediately take over co-ordination of the rescue attempt.

After speaking briefly to Thierry Dubois on the radio, Rescue 259 banked sharply and headed south to search for *Exide Challenger,* homing in on the signal from a DATUM buoy dropped by the previous flight.

Pilot Ludo Dierickx kept the 60-tonne Orion at 300 feet, and seven sets of eyes crowded on to the flight deck, scanning the seas. Behind them, sensor operators were trying to pick up the same 121.5 signal that had been heard by Rescue 258.

'There she is,' shouted someone.

On the port side, three-quarters of a mile in front, the hull wallowed in the heavy swell. As they made the first overflight, two sonobuoys were slipped into the launch chutes, ready to be dispatched.

As the TACCO, Louis Gameau took responsibility for the drop. 'Standby for buoy drop.'

'Roger. Search power is on.'

'Standby, thirty seconds to drop ... twenty seconds ... ten seconds ...'

He hit a button on his console and the sonobuoys fired into the ocean, landing within yards of the yacht.

'Two buoys heard.'

'Roger that.'

Two minutes later audio became available to acoustic operators, and within five minutes the screens in front of them began printing useable information. Making another pass, fourteen minutes later at 1242 Zulu time, Rescue 259 deployed a SUS beacon, hoping the loud electronic 'ping' would generate a response from inside the hull.

Instead the crew picked up a very faint 121.5 beacon transmission but only when directly overhead. With a slowest speed of 300km an hour, an Orion can't loiter above a fixed point, so the signal lasted just a few seconds. Using a battery of sensitive radio equipment, they tried to fix its location, but were thwarted by the very short bursts and limited transmission time.

Meanwhile, acoustic operator Don Hickey sat at his sensor station listening to the almost soporific sounds of the ocean.

Waves slapped against the side of the *Exide Challenger,* and deep within the sloshing water they could hear rigging tapping against the broken masts and hull, as well as the creaks and groans of the crippled yacht. It had been fifty minutes since the sonobuoys were deployed, and there appeared to be no sign of life.

'Can you hear that?' said Hickey, motioning to Liam Craig, the SEM.

'What have you got?'

'Listen. Can you hear it? It's a rhythmic banging or tapping sound.'

'You still got it?'

'Yeah.'

Dierickx leapt from the pilot's seat and ran the short distance down the aircraft. He grabbed a set of headphones. 'Put it on the Aux box.'

With a flick of a switch, the sound of sloshing water filled the aircraft. In total silence the crew listened, concentrating hard on picking out a differentiating noise in the background. Ninety seconds after it began, the sound suddenly stopped.

Dierickx had put the aircraft into an orbit at 1,000 feet and the crew analysed the tape, playing it half a dozen times.

'It sounds like rigging,' said one of the cockpit crew.

'I'm not even sure what I'm supposed to be listening for,' said another.

'It's a definite tapping sound,' said Hickey. 'I don't think it can be the rigging. Why would it suddenly start and then stop?'

'Any number of reasons,' said Dierickx. 'It's like a blind blowing in the wind, it won't have a constant rhythm.'

'But this thing did. It was constant. I think he's inside and he's hitting the hull with something.'

Almost an hour later, the acoustic operators picked up the sound again, this time for fifty seconds. It still wasn't enough to be convincing. With the light beginning to fade, the Orion turned back and made one last pass over Dubois. It couldn't get a visual fix on the life-raft and the radio signal was weak, so they turned on their landing lights and Dubois shouted that he could see them. He directed them to turn left and suddenly his orange raft emerged from the gloom 100 metres below. A dim roof light illuminated the canopy.

'*Amnesty International* survivor this is Royal Australian Air Force Orion, do you read me?'

'Yes, yes, I read you guys. Where is the helicopter?'

'The Seahawk can't make it until tomorrow morning. The air temperature is too low and the rotors will ice up. It can't reach you tonight.'

'Okay. Okay.' Dubois couldn't hide his disappointment. He faced yet another cold and uncomfortable night. Dierickx felt desperately sorry for him. 'The *Adelaide* is only 200 nautical miles from you. The chopper should be with you in six hours.'

'Fine. Thanks, guys. I'm okay.'

Climbing to 28,000 feet, the Orion began the long haul back to Perth. The cockpit crew took turns to grab a meal in the galley, eating reheated frozoes of roast chicken and vegetables.

In the 92 Wing bunker at RAAF Edinburgh, Wing Commander Ian Pearson received the latest sit-rep from Rescue 259, with news of the tapping sound. He had to make a decision whether to make it public or keep it under wraps. The fate of Tony Bullimore and Thierry Dubois had become a huge international story and the media's appetite seemed insatiable. Calls were coming in from around the world and each Orion sortie landing in Perth was being met by dozens of journalists.

A tapping sound from inside the hull strongly suggested Tony Bullimore was alive, but what if they were wrong? What if it was just rigging being washed against the yacht? Not only would it prove to be enormously embarrassing to the Air Force, it would unfairly raise the hopes of the yachtsman's family in Britain. Pearson had to be sure.

A copy of the tape was flown to RAAF Edinburgh and handed to Flight Lieutenant John Postle, the 92 Wing Analysis Officer. Every Orion sortie is recorded on audio tape, from the cockpit conversations of the crew to the hours of sonobuoy transmissions. By listening to these various tapes, it is possible for an entire mission to be reconstructed.

The acoustic operators on board each Orion are experts at interpreting signals and have to make a primary analysis on the spot. Postle, however, can do it in slow time from the comfort of his office, running the whole mission through a computer and playing the tapes again and again.

In this case, he didn't have the luxury of time. As he threaded the audio reel into his Honeywell 96 recorder, he knew the bunker needed an answer immediately. Spinning the spool until the tape tightened, he clipped it in place.

The sound of water and all its many subtle movements began to fill the office. Postle wrapped the sound around him and sank within it, feeling almost like a baby returning to his mother's womb. The water and waves seemed to wash over him, swirling through his mind and clearing away all other thoughts.

He had started his RAAF career as an airborne electronics analyst and then changed direction to become a navigator. Since then his remarkable ability to recognise various sounds in the sea had made him a logical choice as the analysis officer for 92 Wing. He was also the squadron's survival training officer.

After fifty minutes he rewound the tape and listened again. He had to be careful because the mind can so easily become lulled by repetitive noise and miss the subtle changes. On top of this, sound travels further and nearly five times faster in water than in air, so the hydrophones had picked up enormous amounts of background noise, some of it possibly generated from several miles away.

Because the Orion is an anti-submarine aircraft, Postle normally listened for anything that made a mechanical noise, like an engine. By measuring the beats of a propeller on a submarine in conjunction with noise made by other parts of the structure, he could tell the size, the make and the speed. People often imagine that this is quite easy because they assume the ocean is a huge pool of silence. In reality, it's quite the opposite. The background noise picked up by sonobuoys is enormous, a symphony of sound that includes an evening and morning marine chorus – a biological phenomenon that explains why it's often better to go fishing early or late in the day.

On top of this there are squealing dolphins, mating whales, seismic activity, surface shipping, under-sea erosion, snapping shrimp and crabs scratching themselves on the ocean floor. Postle's ear had been trained to differentiate and recognise them all.

Having heard the tape three times, Postle called Ian Pearson.

'The boys did a brilliant job picking up the sound,' he said as he began playing the relevant section of the tape.

'Now listen very carefully. That long wavelength sound is the swell washing up against the hull, but about every three seconds you'll hear a slight change in pitch. That's caused by secondary waves being pushed against the boat by the wind. The frequency is slightly different. I want you to listen between those wind waves.'

Pearson leaned closer, straining to pull any sound from what seemed like a constant stream of water running over a weir.

'I hear a tapping sound,' he declared. 'Is that it?'

'No. What you're hearing is the rigging being pushed by the wind wave against the hull. That's what your ear will naturally pick up. I want you to listen behind that sound – forget everything else. You're looking for a very faint, sharper noise about the frequency of someone clicking their fingers together.'

Pearson tried again, staring hard at the tape machine as if somehow looking at it would reveal its secret.

'I hear it! I hear it! It's not a tapping sound at all.'

'No.' Postle shook his head and turned off the tape.

'So what is it?'

'You want my best guess? I'd swear it's someone using a reverse osmosis water pump.'

'He's alive!'

19

SOUTHERN OCEAN
Wednesday, 8 January 1997

Christ, I'm cold. My chest is so badly bruised from sliding on to the shelf that it hurts when I breathe. My jaw aches and my shoulders cramp up because I can't turn over or shift position. One arm is above my head and the other jammed against my side. At least I can still feel a dull ache in my hands. When I squeeze my fingers into a fist, pain shoots up my arms – that's a good sign.

Freezing water splashes on to my forehead and runs down my nose. It's like some form of Chinese water torture, but instead of a persistent drip, it's like half a bucket hurled at my head from across the darkness.

It's night again. I can tell by pushing my head forward and looking through the hatch door of the cuddy into the engine-room. The green filtered light has faded, like someone drawing the curtains.

How long have I been here? Three nights, four nights, I can't remember. My stomach is empty and the cold has found ways to trickle inside me, filling every crack and hollow. There's no calories left to stoke the furnace. Won't be long now, Tony.

If I stare really hard at the black carbon interior, I can almost imagine that I see stars. That's one of the things I love about single-handed sailing, being miles from land and looking up at that huge black canvas and the jewels within it. Years ago, when I lived in South Africa, I visited a major diamond dealer and he lay a piece of black velvet on the table and then took out a small leather pouch. As he emptied the contents, the diamonds spilled outwards across the cloth, catching and fragmenting every piece of light. The night sky is a thousand times more beautiful.

Exide Challenger rolls more violently, throwing me against the nets. For a split second I think she's coming round and I half fall off the shelf, trying to scramble down. My legs buckle and I land face first in the grey polluted water. The shock of the cold makes me inhale and water shoots up my nose and into my lungs. I rear up, spluttering and hacking. It feels like I've swallowed a gallon of diesel and it burns at the back of my throat. A wave of nausea and pain sweeps over me and I wretch. I can hear my coughing, echoing off the cuddy walls, but it doesn't sound like me. It's more like demonic laughter.

Crawling back on to the shelf, I curl up into one big ball of hurt and sink into dazed confusion. My mind refuses to sleep and memories flash through it like disjointed clips from an old silent movie. I see my mother in the kitchen, telling me to hurry up or I'll be late for school. A mug of tea, a piece of toast and jam, sausages sizzling in the frying pan, I wish I could be back there to see her again. She had a tough life, my mum, and she instilled a lot of strength in me. She always said that I'd make something of myself. I hope she's not disappointed.

My dad is talking to me. 'Tone, we all may want to be great poets or great writers, but with good slapstick, you make someone laugh, you make someone cry. Nothing else counts. Remember that.'

He used to tell me that when I was just a kid, and that's how he saw life. When he walked on stage with his walking stick and hat, he could have them rolling in the aisles one minute and crying the next. Then he'd say, 'Let's all be happy, let's sing a song,' and he'd break into a soft-shoe shuffle.

The image changes again and I see my darling Lal, at home with her head in her hands, unable to stop crying. Will she ever forgive me?

She didn't want me to do the Vendée. She thought I was too old. In truth, I think she hoped I might retire eleven years ago, when I became Yachtsman of the Year. But even after losing *Apricot*, she never said to me, 'Tony, if you build another boat I'm leaving you.' Maybe if she had, I might have reconsidered, but I doubt it.

Spirit of Apricot was on the drawing-board, and I was keen to get everything moving forward. What a glutton for punishment I am. Lal looked a little sad but gave me a lot of support once the project got under way. We have an Apache marriage – once joined, never parted – and one of its strengths is that we've never tried to change each other.

More high tech than *Apricot* and using the very latest materials, the new sixty-footer was designed by Barry Noble, a real sailing boffin, and Martyn Smith, a former senior structural engineer with British Aerospace who had worked on the Concorde. However, the real revolution was an enormous 100-foot wing mast, with a girth of about five feet halfway up its length, a straight leading edge and a concave trailing edge.

In the race to get it finished by May 1988, I arrived late for the starting week of the OSTAR and the organisers gave *Spirit of Apricot* a 10 per cent penalty. Many of the other competitors signed a petition asking that my penalty be waived, but the committee stuck to the red tape rule, which meant I couldn't possibly win the race.

I accepted it, although felt it was a little unfair. Ultimately, I finished sixth overall and ninth on paper after the penalty. It wasn't a bad result considering I had so little time to get ready and become accustomed to the idiosyncrasies of a new boat.

Yet as soon as she began to win races, *Spirit of Apricot* quickly established herself as perhaps the greatest light weather boat in the world. I was even approached by an American design team who wanted the plans to the wing mast because they were building a multihull to defend the America's Cup in 1991 off San Diego, against a huge mono-hull being built by New Zealand. I asked for $250,000, because I needed the money, but the Americans satisfied themselves by studying photographs and experimenting with their own masts.

Spirit of Apricot proved to be truly magnificent. She could reach amazing speeds for a boat her size, doing a steady 32 knots with the outriggers flat on the water. On the 800-mile last leg of the Europe Race in 1989 we went like a train across the Mediterranean to Sardinia and finished eighteen hours in front of the fleet. There was hardly anyone there to meet us, because no one expected a competitor to arrive so early. Among the yachts we beat was *Jet Services*, which then held the record for the fastest crossing of the Atlantic.

Instantly recognisable, *Spirit of Apricot* would attract crowds wherever she went. Enthralled ladies would come up to me carrying baskets of apricots they'd picked from their gardens, or want to tie apricot-coloured ribbons to the stroud. They were glorious days, even Lal would have to admit that. Although she was proud when I won races and would be there at the finish to greet me, she never understood my desire to compete and win.

When *Spirit of Apricot* pitch-poled off the Devon coast in 1989, I think Lal would have been happy if I retired, but she stood by me, as always.

When I regained consciousness after that accident, I saw her sitting beside the bed and, almost delirious, I kept repeating, 'What happened to the wing mast? Is it damaged?'

Lal ignored the questions for about five minutes and then exploded.

'Tony Bullimore, you care more about that bloody boat than you do about your own life.'

'What happened to the wing mast?' I babbled.

'It's gone, okay! Smashed, broken, kaput! If you ask me about it again, I'll ... I'll ...'

She ran out of steam, thank goodness.

When I set my heart on the Vendée Globe, I didn't tell Lal that I expected it to be my last big race. I know better than that. Too many good friends have died at sea on what they declare will be their 'last voyage'.

The initial plan was to have *Exide Challenger* ready for the 1992 race, but she wasn't quite finished in time for qualification because I ran out of money and couldn't get sponsorship. Frustratingly, it was another four years before the next race. In the meantime, I did the Round Britain and Ireland and the Europe Race in *Exide Challenger*, discovering that she lacked speed in light winds. It bothered me, but not unduly. Far stronger winds could be expected on a circum-navigation.

The recession bit hard in the early 1990s. Unemployment and redundancies created a fear of commitment, and companies tightened up on their sponsorship and marketing budgets. I tried everything to get backing, from printing glossy brochures to selling myself door-to-door, but it proved damn near impossible.

When the BOC Challenge came and went in 1994, my last real chance was the next Vendée Globe two years later. Only four weeks before the race, I was still tying up sponsorship and I only made it to the line thanks to the financial support of Exide Batteries, as well as funds from Mitsubishi Electric PC Division and United Overseas Group.

It had been a tremendous struggle that had taxed me for nearly six years. In those frantic last few weeks in Les Sables d'Olonne I relied heavily on my shore crew made up of friends like Wesley Massam, Jim Doxey, my nephew Steve Mulvany and Kevin Pahl, my side-kick who has raced with me for about twelve years – a great guy.

Unfortunately, *Exide Challenger* was never going to be a great boat - she'd proved that already - but in the right conditions she could go like a bat out of hell.

I enjoy the preparation that goes into a long race - readying the boat, studying the charts, weather routing, learning to use new equipment and motivating other people to play their parts. Those final few days are charged with emotion and fed on adrenaline. At the start, I don't try to be the first across the line. I simply want a good position and to get the boat going well.

The part that I enjoy most, however, is when I'm a thousand miles out and the boat is gliding through the water with a whisper, showing off her sails like the plumage of a beautiful bird. I imagine it's the same feeling a conductor gets as he stands before an orchestra, knowing he can alter the volume, cadence and rhythm by simply fluttering his hands.

That's when the boat and the sea start to grow on me. Slowly

I forget about the land and the yacht becomes my world. One morning, I wake up and find myself running my hands over the wheel and almost feeling the heartbeat of the hull beneath my feet. A massive feeling of well-being flows through me and I begin to pamper her and develop a rhythm of checking things and doing particular chores, making sure everything is stowed exactly where it should be. This affinity is so complete that I almost resent intrusions from the outside world.

In the Vendée Globe it had happened as I languished for three days in the Doldrums on the Equator, waiting for a fresh breeze to carry me onwards. I'd lost five days and given a thousand miles head start to competitors half my age sailing faster boats.

The rest of the fleet seemed to fly through the Doldrums, while I had the lightest of breezes. That's the luck of the winds. Hundreds of miles from the nearest land, I didn't wear a stitch of clothing under the blazing sun and occasionally dropped a bucket over the side and doused myself to stay cool. At night, I lay down in my chair, pulled a sheet under my chin and listened to the myriad of small creaks and groans from the boat. She was talking to me.

That's why the loss of the keel hurts so much. It goes far deeper than shattered carbon and crushed foam. *Exide Challenger* had become like a living, breathing entity and I had felt her pain as she battled against the storm. She might not have been a thoroughbred like other boats I've built, but she deserved better than being upside down in the middle of nowhere.

There are certain things on a boat that must not break, and the keel is at the absolute top of the list. If the sails are the lungs of any yacht, then the keel is the beating heart. *Exide Challenger*'s heart had been ripped out of her and she died within seconds. Now she's like some floating carcass being picked at by carrion waves.

I have never felt so wretchedly alone. What on earth was I thinking when I took on this challenge? It seems almost stupid now to pit oneself against something as ageless and unforgiving as the great oceans of the world. It's not as if I can ever leave footsteps in the sand. No matter how deep or quickly

I carve a channel through the water, the seas simply roll back in my wake and leave no trace of the boat's passage.

That's the problem, whenever we start thinking of ourselves as anything loftier or the equal of Mother Nature, she reminds us that she can wear away at continents and create storms that flatten cities. Better and braver sailors than I are now dead and part of a marine food chain.

Should I make one last dive for the life-raft? No. Should I open the hatches beneath the cockpit floor and get some food? No. Should I trigger the last beacon and broadcast another cry for help? No, not yet. Should I swim outside with my flares, fire them into the air in a final act, like the last rocket on Guy Fawkes night? No. I haven't got the strength and the only way I'll live for a few more hours is to stay on this shelf.

The truth is, I've run out of ideas. In total darkness, crammed in a corner full of diesel fumes and rolling grey water, there is no hope. The only warmth I can feel in my body is deep in my chest, but I keep thumping my feet and tapping my fingers.

I've never actually been afraid of dying. I've heard people say that anyone who isn't frightened of death is a fool, but I don't agree. I can't afford to get scared; I have to look at the situation and work out the logistics. That's the only way I'm going to stay alive for a little longer - just in case they're coming.

I've only been truly frightened once in my life, and that was when Lal almost died of an aneurism in December 1985. I remember she'd been having headaches for a long time, terrible pain behind her eyes, and she went to see the doctor on a Tuesday and he said that she had an infection.

On the Thursday I had to judge a yacht design competition in London, and left quite early without waking Lal. She'd tossed and turned all night and needed sleep. In fact, she'd been drifting in and out of consciousness. That morning she was due to go Christmas shopping with a friend, who arrived to pick her up. When Lal didn't answer the door, Novel let herself in with a key and went upstairs.

'What are you still doing in bed, woman? You promised to come shopping with me today,' she said.

'I'm not feeling too well.'

'Let me see.'

Novel pulled back the covers, looked at Lal's face and said, 'Oh, my God.' She ran out of the room and called the doctor. He came straight away and knew immediately that Lal was dying.

When I arrived home that afternoon, there was a note on the kitchen table, saying, 'Taken Lal to hospital.' I drove like a lunatic to the neurological unit. The doctors told me that the brain scan had identified two aneurisms. The surgeon wouldn't operate straight away because he didn't think Lal would survive the night. Next morning, I begged them to try and save her.

They wheeled her to the operating theatre but she started bleeding all over the place so they cancelled the procedure, convinced she wouldn't live through it. That's when I learned how to pray in my own special way. All day and all night I stayed with Lal, telling her to hold on. At one point, I called up her sister, Doreen, who found it hard to understand what I was saying because I was so upset. It had been the greatest year of my life with *Apricot*, but I would happily have traded every victory and moment of joy just to have Lal healthy and well again.

The next morning they did another brain scan and found that, inexplicably, the burst blood vessels had fused themselves and stopped bleeding. The surgeon operated to make sure of the job, clipping one blood vessel and cementing the other.

'Is she going to be all right?' I asked.

'Well, Mr Bullimore, I'm not going to lie to you,' the doctor said. 'The next five days will tell if she has any permanent brain damage. Even if she does survive, there is a chance that she will suffer some form of paralysis in her muscles or limbs.'

My shadow fell across Lal's bed for two days. When she first woke, she saw my face; when she squeezed a hand, it was my hand; and when she first smiled, she smiled for me.

I've never forgotten how scared I was of losing her. Maybe it sounds selfish, but I didn't think I could go on without her. Now it's me who's dying and I'm scared to bits of leaving her alone.

You recovered completely, didn't you Lal, and the doctors

called it a miracle. You liked that. 'Captain Bulldog' is what you like to call me, but I think you might have a bit of bulldog in yourself - what do you think?

God, I wish I could write you a letter. There's so many things that have been left unsaid and they shouldn't be. So where would I start?

Dearest Lal, [that's as good a place as any]

We all make mistakes in life and I've made a few classic ones, but you are, by a million miles, the best thing that ever happened to me.

Do you know what I love most about you? I love the way you move through a room trying to be almost invisible, yet catching glances because you always look so beautiful. I love the softness in your voice and how it gets louder and louder when you're laughing with friends. I love the way you cry at sad movies and how your eyes twinkle when you're happy.

There are so many more things . . . I love the way you look at me when I buy you a present when it's not your birthday or Christmas or an anniversary. Straight away, you know that I want to do another race or build another boat. But you never make me feel guilty, Lal. I love that, because I don't need any help feeling bad about going away, I really don't.

We took the biggest leap of our lives when we married. I hope it didn't cause you too much pain not having a proper wedding with lots of friends. I wish we could do it over again – this time the whole world would know about it.

I've had a lot of time to think, up here on my shelf, and I've had a pretty good life. I've done most of the things I wanted, met some remarkable people and made and lost a couple of fortunes. I don't have any regrets apart from not having children. I know that's going to surprise you after all these years, but it's not just because I'm dying and I want to leave some part of me behind. If we had adopted the twins they offered, when the doctors said we couldn't have our own children, they'd be grown by now and you'd have someone else in your life.

I wish I'd said yes, now. At that time we were working such long hours at the club it didn't seem fair to take on such a big responsibility. I worried that we wouldn't love them like our own, but I know now that isn't true. A magic moment would have come when all of a sudden we loved them as much as any parent can love a child. You would have been a wonderful mother and I might have been at home more often, particularly in the early years.

I know you wanted me at home more, Lal. You couldn't understand what I was searching for, but how do you tell a man to look around the corner when he hasn't reached it yet? I think I've seen around the corner now, but it's too late. If I could, I would hammer on this hull and shout, 'It's over! It's done! Let me out!'

If I had my time over again, Lal, I'd be a lot nicer and more gentle to people. You know I've got a temper and a harsh tongue, but I'd try to change. When things haven't gone my way, I've sometimes taken my frustration out on you. I'm sorry for that. Next time – if there is another life – I'll be more forgiving and considerate.

Do you know what I imagined our future would be like? I've been picturing it for years. I saw us having a little house in Jamaica, not a palace, just a simple wooden affair, not far from where Noël Coward had his cottage. There'd be an air-conditioned room for my computer and I'd spend my days writing. Of an afternoon, I'd wander down the dirt road to the local bar and have a few drinks with the regulars, boring them all stupid with my stories of the sea. Then I'd walk slowly home and sit in a wicker chair in the garden watching the sun dip and the shadows lengthen. I can see you in the garden, Lal, wearing a cotton dress and a wide-brimmed straw hat, surrounded by lilies, bougainvillea, mango trees and hibiscus. There'd even be a little vegetable patch. We'd eat on the porch every night, not needing to talk because we can read each other's thoughts, and preferring to listen to the insects and watch the fireflies.

We almost did it, Lal, didn't we? In 1985 when the City of Birmingham took back the exhibition halls, we were going to move to Jamaica and buy a place not far from your family. I had some good ideas to keep myself busy, and some of them would have benefited Jamaica. I call it one of my 'classic' mistakes not to have gone then. If I look for turning points in my life, then that one could have changed my destiny. Sadly, hindsight is not a compass.

Promise me something, Lal. After the memorial service is over and the insurance has been paid, I want you to sell the house in Bristol. I want you to go back to Jamaica and buy that little house and plant that garden. Make sure it has a view over the sea and a bar down the road and a breeze that blows through the front door and out the back. That's the sort of place I'd like to haunt.

We were together for a long time, Lal, and I know that you'll go on with dignity. You'll cry but don't cry for too long or too often. Think of all the good times and remember that I'll be with you forever and ever.

I'll love you always,

Your old boy – Tony

20

Conditioned by years at sea, Mike Jackson-Calway had become
a creature of habit and began each day with a bowl of muesli, a
piece of toast and an orange. This morning, he was unusually
quiet over breakfast, and his wife Judith sensed something
was wrong. She tried to engage him in conversation, telling
him about a phone call from Susan, their daughter in Sydney,
but could see his mind was elsewhere.

'Do you think he's alive in there?' she finally asked.

Without even looking up, her husband answered: 'I live in
hope.'

Jackson-Calway had always managed to separate himself from the uncertainty felt by families of the missing,
but this time it was different and he didn't know why.
Somehow he had convinced himself that Tony Bullimore was
alive.

He'd overheard the prophets of doom in the canteen and the
corridors. 'Waste of time, waste of money,' they muttered.
Similarly, talkback radio programmes had been dominated
for days by discussion of how much the search was costing
Australian taxpayers. Surely the race organisers should be
footing the bill, many callers argued. Others felt that limits
should be placed on how far south competitors could sail - a
latitude of 40 degrees south, for example.

'Do you know what worries me most?' said Judith.

'What?'

'That after all the hard work and the cost, you'll finish up with two out of three. You rescued Dinelli and you'll rescue Dubois, but not Bullimore. And the sad part is that just saving those two is an incredible feat, but people are going to forget that. They'll just remember the yachtsman who died before you could reach him.'

'That's human nature.'

'Yes, but it's not fair.'

Jackson-Calway smiled for the first time that morning and pecked Judith on the cheek. 'Ah well, we'll know in a few hours,' he said, picking up his car keys.

'What time?'

'The *Adelaide* should reach him by midday.'

'Will you phone me when you know?'

'Of course.'

Turning on the car radio and flicking between stations, he caught the latest news: '*Hopes that British yachtsman Tony Bullimore is alive were raised early today, when an Air Force Orion picked up a tapping sound coming from within the hull of his upturned yacht. The RAAF has confirmed that an underwater microphone monitored the tapping sound for ninety seconds. An hour later, the crew heard a shorter burst of fifty seconds. Experts believe the sound is man-made, strongly suggesting that Bullimore is alive after three days and four nights in his capsized yacht* Exide Challenger. *His fate will be known in five hours when the warship HMAS* Adelaide *arrives in the search area.*'

Jackson-Calway's spirits lifted. Perhaps Tony Bullimore had heard the Orion overhead and started to hammer on the hull. On the dupe file at MRCC, he read the latest sit-rep from 92 Wing and noted that Rescue 258 and Rescue 259 had both picked up a 121.5 signal. This suggested that Bullimore might briefly have turned on his 406 EPIRB beacon to let them know he was alive. However, the sound of 'muffled voices' heard by one crew made it more likely to be a crossed line or radio break through. A 406 MHz beacon has no facility for someone to speak.

Flicking further into the file, Jackson-Calway looked for the latest situation report from HMAS *Adelaide*:

GENTEXT/INTENTIONS/CONTINUE TRANSIT ON SINGLE ENGINE. LAUNCH S70B [SEAHAWK] AT 2100 ZULU WITH AN ESTIMATED 50NM TRANSIT TO DUBOIS LIFE-RAFT. ONCE DUBOIS IS IN AIRCRAFT, TRANSIT TO POSITION OF EXIDE CHALLENGER.

Another INMARSAT-C message reported that the *Sanko Phoenix* was 170 nautical miles from the life-raft, with an ETA of 0200 Zulu, two and a half hours behind the warship.

Glancing at the latest meteorological forecast, Jackson-Calway felt a shudder of trepidation deep in his stomach. A broad area of low pressure was centred to the south-west, moving east at 40 knots: 'Expect winds to tend strong to gale force NW'ly ahead of next front with increasing low cloud and showers. Gusts to 55 knots with cloud-base 100 to 300 feet at times. Expect Strong W/SW winds in wake of front after 0300 on 9 January.'

The same weather pattern which had caused two yachts to capsize now seemed likely to have a final say in the rescue. After a marathon voyage of 2,600km, it had come down to a sprint – the *Adelaide* was racing against a weather front. Having pushed so hard, the frigate had limited fuel and could only afford to spend several hours in the search area before turning back to rendezvous with the *Westralia*. It didn't have the fuel to sit out a storm and then begin a sea search.

Jackson-Calway made himself a mug of tea. The next five hours would be among the most nerve-wracking of his career.

At 7:22 A.M. he received a call from Wesley Massam in Bristol. 'I'm actually with Tony Bullimore's wife at the moment,' said Wesley. 'As soon as you know if Tony is alive or dead or missing, I'd like to know so I can inform his family.'

'Of course,' said Jackson-Calway, who had always known the task would fall to him. This was the part of the job he hated most. Within a few hours he would have to pick up the telephone and tell a wife that her husband was alive, dead, or missing presumed dead.

Meanwhile, more than 6,000km away, Captain Raydon Gates watched the sky begin to lighten from the bridge of HMAS *Adelaide*. The sea emerged a gunmetal grey from behind a morning shower and the wind lifted white veils from the swells.

The warship had closed to within fifty nautical miles of Thierry Dubois' life-raft and the Seahawk helicopter was being readied for take-off on the flight deck. Already the rotor blades sliced through the air, shattering the morning calm. Adjusting his headset, pilot Lieutenant John May gave the thumbs-up and the chopper lifted off the deck and swung low over the waves.

On board, the ship's doctor, Lieutenant Commander David Wright, had prepared for the worst-case scenario of a survivor suffering from severe hypothermia. Before sailing, the *Adelaide* had taken on board equipment designed to slowly warm a patient whose core body temperature had fallen dangerously low. Wright had also briefed the winch crew to keep Dubois as horizontal as possible. If they brought him upright too quickly, his blood pressure could suddenly drop.

Vectored in by Rescue 260, the Seahawk found Dubois, waving frantically from one of two orange life-rafts that he'd lashed together.

'I think he's been expecting us,' said John May.

Dubois had spent the previous three days trying to stay warm, never untying the beacons from around his chest because he feared he might be thrown out of the raft. He had remembered stories of mountaineers and knew that he shouldn't sleep for too long because he risked never waking up. In between short naps, he stayed busy by mopping up and topping up the air in the life-raft.

Lieutenant Commander Arthur Heather opened the sliding side door of the helicopter as it hovered directly over the life-raft. A long line, weighted at the end, was lowered slowly towards Dubois' outstretched hands. Clipping himself to the rope, Lieutenant Hank Scott stepped out the door and Arthur

Heather winched him down towards the raft.

'Are you okay?' he asked Dubois, shouting to be heard above the spinning rotors.

'Yes, yes, thank you.'

'Okay. I'm going to take you up. I want you to relax and stay calm.'

Dubois grinned through his bushy black beard. 'I'm safe, eh?'

'You're safe.'

Spinning slightly in the down-draught, the two men were winched upwards, with Dubois lying horizontally across Scott's chest. As they swung inside, the door shut and the lone sailor sat on the floor, looking remarkably healthy for having been through so much.

David Wright couldn't believe his poise and coolness. The Frenchman very carefully took off his gloves and placed them in the proper pocket of his survival suit. Then he pushed back his hood, unhooked the beacons from around his body and made himself comfortable.

'Request pigeons for mother,' said John May and the Seahawk was given a vector home to HMAS *Adelaide*.

At the same time, a satellite message flashed to Fleet Headquarters and MRCC:

RESTRICTED

SUBJ: OPER ANTARCTIC ONE – RECOVERY

1. RECOVERY OF T. DUBOIS EFFECTED BY ADELAIDE AT 2117Z (8 JANUARY). ETA ON BOARD 2140Z.

2. CONDITION GOOD. IN HIGH SPIRITS.

3. CONTINUING SOUTHERLY TRANSIT AT BEST SPEED TOWARDS YACHT EXIDE CHALLENGER.

As soon as the helicopter had lifted off, the frigate had immediately changed course and headed directly for the last known position of the British yacht. Visibility had fallen to one nautical mile.

Having ferried Dubois to the ship, the Seahawk took off almost immediately for *Exide Challenger*, hoping to hover over the hull and take photographs that would help the RIB crews. The helicopter arrived on top of the hull at 2245Z and forty-five minutes later returned to the *Adelaide*.

Captain Raydon Gates sent the following message to Fleet:

REPORTS INDICATE HULL IN SOUND CONDITION, NEGATIVE KEEL, MAST AND RIGGING STILL ATTACHED. NO SIGN OF LIFE NOR RESPONSE TO HELICOPTER'S PRESENCE . . .

GENTEXT/WEATHER/DETERIORATING RAPIDLY. WHILST SEAS REMAIN MODERATE, EXPECT STORM TO GALE FORCE WINDS WITH RAIN AND REDUCED VISIBILITY. WINDS PRESENTLY 30 KNOTS AND INCREASING. SEA TEMP 2.5 DEG.

Responsibility for the rescue operation now rested solely with Captain Gates. He had to decide if the seas were too rough to launch the RIB. As the *Adelaide* steamed south, he watched the seas build but refused to make up his mind until he saw the stricken yacht.

The previous evening he had contacted the master of the *Sanko Phoenix* to discuss how it might assist in the rescue. The tanker had no sea boats but did have a lifting crane with a capacity of 15 tonnes. Investigating every possibility, no matter how far-fetched, Gates discussed whether the yacht could be secured or hauled up to ensure it stayed afloat while they cut through the hull.

It sounded fine in theory, but in practice it is simply impossible to bring a 90,000-tonne tanker alongside a bobbing yacht in the Southern Ocean. The RIB remained the best option, despite the many problems faced. One crew-member had likened it to putting men with jackhammers on top of an iceblock in a rolling sea and asking them to cut a neat hole.

Rescue 261 had listened to the rescue of Thierry Dubois on HF radio. As soon as they knew he was safe, they flew straight for *Exide Challenger* and, despite the 300-foot cloud base and heavy showers, quickly located the yacht.

Looking at the hull, 'Ajax' Jackson thought it seemed higher in the water than the previous day, when waves had been forcing it under. Now he felt it might be possible to put a Zodiac (inflatable boat) alongside.

With a radio channel open to the bridge, Ajax watched the warship emerge out of the gloom and approach to within half a mile.

'Okay, let's show them where it is,' said Richard Moth. 'Standby, prepare one smoke.'

'Smoke ready.'

'Standby to mark on top of the hull. Drop on my mark. Drop now!'

21

〰️

I'm falling again. The shock of the cold water seems to
blast open my brain and my bowels tighten. Dragging my
body upright, I scream in frustration and kick at the grey
lake in the cuddy, toppling backwards and splashing into it
again.

The waves are picking up outside. Another storm is coming.

A breeze pricks at my cheek. I look upwards to the hole in
the hull and see the night sky. Things are getting worse, not
better. All the different contingencies I tried to put in place,
none of them have worked. I don't have any more ideas.

I've been fighting and fighting, but it feels as if right from
the beginning I've been speeding inevitably towards this
moment. It's almost as if it had been predetermined, like a
deliberate act of vengeance. No matter how I've tried to save
myself, this enemy of mine has stopped me. He dangles hope in
front of a dying man and then snatches it away. I'm a fool to
have thought I could beat this thing. I'm a fool to think anyone's coming to rescue me.

I wish it would give me some way of fighting back. I don't
care how pointless or hopeless it is, I want to die doing something other than lying on a shelf. Let me wrestle with the
helm, or bail out a life-raft, or trek across Antarctica, but
don't let me die like this.

This is maddening. Helplessness is my worst enemy. I need a plan.

I wade into the engine-room and check the water level. For ten minutes I watch the mini-surf roll back and forth in the darkness and decide the hull is lower by about two inches. The watertight compartments are leaking, most likely where the wiring has been threaded through and where the hatches are sealed on the deck. The compartments are tested to withstand high-pressure hoses, but not the weight of water in these waves or being upside down for long periods.

The vacuum effect has started again in the doghouse. I feel it tug at my legs as I wade to the companionway entrance. One moment the water is up to my chin and then it is sucked out again, dropping to my waist. It sounds like an ocean blowhole. Untying the last EPIRB, my numb fingers fumble at the switch as I turn it off and on a few times, making sure it works. I contemplate leaving it on, but a little voice inside my head, says, 'No, Tony, you might need it. What if you free the life-raft? You'll need a beacon.'

I find myself arguing with the voice.

—'But I can't free the life-raft. It's trapped on the cockpit floor.'

'Yes, but the boat might roll over. You might get a few seconds to scramble outside.'

—'It's been four days.'

'Yes, but another storm is coming. Maybe a wave will spin you over.'

—'Or sink the boat completely.'

What if the Argos distress signal has stopped transmitting? How long do the batteries last? A 406 beacon is good for about forty-eight hours, but I think the Argos lasts longer. I hope so. I'm probably drifting at half a knot. If the signal stops for any length of time, I'll have drifted miles away. In the rough seas and mist, they might not find me.

Find me! What am I saying? They're not even bloody looking! They're not going to come all the way down here for me. Even if that was a plane I heard, it hasn't come back. You've bought it this time, Tony. How much longer will you wait before you swim outside? It takes more courage to commit suicide than it does to stay alive.

My mind has been wandering. How long have I been standing here? I can feel the cold creeping into my diaphragm and squeezing my heart. The boat rocks violently as two waves seem to collide from either side. It throws me forwards into the water above the broken window. The suction drags me down. Throwing my arms out, I flail blindly for something to hold. My hands find each side of the frame and the end of my torn finger jams into a sharp edge. The pain swamps me but the heat it generates is almost a relief. I wait for the suction to stop, holding my breath, and then the sea-water surges back through the window, forcing me up.

Exhausted, I stagger to the cuddy and drag myself on to the shelf, nursing my left hand. I lie shivering and watch the white dots dance in front of my closed lids. A voice inside my head keeps saying, 'You're going to die. You're going to die.'

I've only ever prayed once or twice in my life - the first time when Lal almost died. It's not like a normal prayer where you ask for forgiveness and promise to be good. Instead I take a mental journey, concentrating my thoughts and reaching deep inside.

'Come on, Tony, it's time to pray,' the voice says.

—'I can't, I'm too cold.'

'Yes you can. Now concentrate, focus on the journey.'

—'I don't remember how to pray.'

'Yes you do. Wash everything else out of your mind. Concentrate on where you want to go. Can you see the alleyway?'

—'I can't. I'm too tired. I don't have the strength for this.'

'Come on, you pathetic wretch! You're not leaving her alone. Look for the alleyway.'

—'I can see it! I can just see it, but it's not very clear.'

'What do you see?'

—'Little walkways, houses with balconies.'

'Just focus on the journey, Tony. Where are you now?'

—'Turning left and right, going into shade and then light. Something is trying to pull me backwards, I can't see what it is. It won't let me go.'

'Then you fight it! You can do it.'

—'I ... can't ... go ... on.'

'But you're almost there. Just a little further. What do you see?'

—'A door. It's big and heavy, made of wooden planks and iron nails.'

'Keep going.'

—'It's slightly ajar and light is spilling through the gap. I can hear muffled voices coming from inside.'

'Push it open.'

—'It's too heavy.'

'Push it open!'

I lean against the door with all my strength and slowly it opens. Inside there are people sitting around a large wooden table, talking and eating quietly, and others in small groups, deep in discussion. Eventually my eyes lock on the one I have come to see and I walk slowly in his direction. His hand reaches up and rests on my shoulder and I feel at peace. No words pass between us, but everything has been said. For a few moments we smile gently, and then I very slowly turn away and walk towards the door.

Exhausted, I feel myself drifting in and out of consciousness. I keep telling myself that if I fall asleep, I may not wake up. It is now going to take a very special kind of strength to stay alive. I must not give up. I must keep fighting. I must not give up.

My eyes are open, staring into the dark. I have a dream – I can't tell if I'm conscious or not. An Australian warship is coming to rescue me. I can see it churning through the waves, dark against the sky. It's going to lower a small boat over the side and they'll hammer on the hull to see if I'm here. Then I'll swim out and I'll be saved.

One chance, Tony, you're going to get one more chance. Don't mess it up.

22

Wesley says we'll know within four hours. At least I won't have another night of staring at the ceiling or into the garden, wondering if Tony is alive or dead. Sometimes I think that anything would be better than this uncertainty, but that's not right; I'd rather hope for a few more hours, or days, or weeks, than to find out that I've lost him.

I try to think what it must be like, alone in that upturned boat. I imagine being locked in a closet, with no light or fresh air. It's half-filled with freezing water and it spins like a washing machine, constantly tumbling back and forth. I give up because I can never know the true horror.

I didn't cook tonight. I'm too nervous. Instead we ordered takeaways. The house is full of people - friends, nieces, nephews - there must be about fifteen people. Some of the younger ones are sleeping in the spare bedrooms upstairs, while the others wander back and forth between the kitchen and the lounge.

Yvonne brings me a cup of tea. She knows I'm awake.

'Not long to go now, Aunt Lal.' She sits on the edge of the bed. 'Is there anything I can get you?'

'No, thanks.'

'He's going to be all right,' she says. I can't tell if it's a question or a statement.

'I hope so. I still believe that he's alive, but I'm worried about how badly he's injured. I can cope with his body being damaged but not his mind, because he's always had such an active mind. I don't think I could bear to see him brain-damaged, unable to chat or smile or understand what happens around him. I can take care of a damaged body, but not a damaged mind.'

We sit in silence.

'I'll be down in a little while,' I say, and Yvonne knows it's time to leave.

After she's gone, I wonder how many other people are sitting, waiting and wondering whether Tony is inside *Exide Challenger*. They're probably talking about it over the yacht club bars, I think. I wonder what they're saying about him? Nice things, I hope.

Tony didn't have the time to become part of the social scene of yachting. The race became the important thing to him – second best wasn't good enough. That's what you wanted to prove, isn't it, Tony? You wanted to show that a boy who grew up in Bill and Kitty's Café in Southend-on-Sea could compete with anyone in the world. You showed them, didn't you? You had to climb a lot further to reach the top, but that made the victory taste even sweeter.

Look at the trophy cabinet in the front room. It's over-flowing with plaques, mugs, trophies, plates, statuettes and medals. I thought you'd retire in 1985, but you just kept going. It was always a faster boat or a tougher race that captured your imagination. Look where you are now. Have you had enough yet?

At a quarter past twelve we sit around the kitchen table – Joyce, Yvonne, Alan, Anthony, myself, Lois and Jane – seven of us, all holding hands. Steve and Wesley don't join us. They sit in the lounge, talking quietly and watching TV.

We pray out loud, each of us taking turns to say a few words for Tony.

'Please God, help him,' I say, choking back tears. 'Make him safe for a few hours more. He's a good man and I don't want to lose him.'

23

Pete Wicker and the RIB crews gathered for a final briefing in the rec room on HMAS *Adelaide*. Jim Manson went over the plan again.

'If the survivor has battened himself down inside the living compartment he may well be trapped in there. Given the water pressure on the bulkheads immediately aft of him, he may not be able to get out. Which means if he's in there, we're going to have to cut through the hull.

'We have had some information back from Maritime HQ about the construction of the boat. Fleet have been trying different cutting methods and they report that the Broco cutter is effective but also inherently dangerous, given the heat it produces and the toxic gases that are likely to be given off. In addition to this, they tell us that if we can pierce the inner Kevlar and make a hole, then a damage control saw is relatively effective, albeit somewhat slower. It will be a tedious process because the fibres get caught up in the teeth and we'll continually have to bring the saw out.

'What we'll try to do in the first boat is work out the most effective and safest cutting method. We'll also keep an eye on the movement of the boat and the weather conditions, because a decision will have to be made: essentially, whether we go for the fastest means, the Broco, and accept the risks, or whether we have enough time to go for a wood saw cut.

'Cards have been made up to indicate where we are going to make the cut and the layout of the boat. Each crew will have a set of cards.'

Lieutenant Commander Arthur Heather, standing alongside Manson, had just arrived back on the *Adelaide* from photographing *Exide Challenger* from the Seahawk.

'There's not much to hook on to,' he said. 'There's a piece sticking upwards about a foot where the keel snapped. The rest of the hull shows no damage. The underside is very flat-bottomed and almost the whole hull is riding out of the water. Perhaps only the bottom six inches from the deck is underwater.'

Wicker asked about the broken rigging and the best side to approach the hull.

'The rigging lines are to windward, including what's left of the mast,' said Heather. 'A few fragments of sail appear to be acting as drogues.'

'So the leeward side is completely clear?'

'Yes, and if you want to look at securing ropes to the rigging, the wire lines running up to the lower section of the masts are still in place on the windward side.'

Syd Smith had a question. 'How hard will it be for someone to stay on the hull?'

'The sides of the yacht are pretty vertical for the first two feet, but then the bottom of the hull is quite flat.'

As the briefing ended, Wicker called the RIB crew together and went over particular tasks again. Paul Ellul and Chris Smart would have to manoeuvre the boat alongside the hull and keep it there. They would also tend any lines on the boat and retrieve personnel who fell in the water.

Although Fleet had insisted no diver should be put under the hull, Alan Rub knew he might still have to enter the water to check if Tony Bullimore's life-raft had been released from the cockpit sole. Although he had a dry suit, the smallest tear would send freezing water swirling around his body. To protect himself, he would wear a short wetsuit beneath a submariner's jumper and then a full wetsuit over the top with boots, hood and gloves. At best this would give him thirty minutes in the water.

If Bullimore wasn't within the hull and his life-raft had been freed, the search would take on a whole new complexion. He would be assumed to be with his raft and drifting downwind without a beacon to signal his position. With the Orions already having searched extensively downwind without finding any trace of a raft, the most likely conclusion would be that the life-raft had sunk and the yachtsman had perished.

Up on number two deck, the wind chill had pushed the temperature to below zero. Crew-members not on watch began taking up vantage points, searching the whitecaps and deep grey swells. Having come so far, most wanted a good vantage point for the drama about to unfold. The heavy cloud had dropped to 500 feet and the wind blew at 35 to 40 knots.

On the bridge, Raydon Gates leaned back in his large blue chair, letting Ken Burleigh navigate the ship to a rendezvous with *Exide Challenger*. The captain's chair had once rested in the first-class cabin of a Qantas 747, but the airline had donated it to Gates, who spent up to twenty hours a day on the bridge during the voyage.

The radio traffic seemed to be constant.

'Ops to bridge. Can you get a P-3C to vector us in?'

'Roger, over.'

Rescue 261: 'For information, vis [visibility] is about a mile and a half up here.'

'Roger.'

'Weather report from the P-3C, to the south they have a front they hold on radar at about ten miles and there is further weather down to the south-east . . .'

'Ahead 12 knots.'

'Copy.'

The mist seemed to be getting worse, but the real concern for Gates was the approaching weather front. In about two hours they were going to be belted by a fierce storm. Could they get an RIB alongside and cut into the yacht before it arrived?

Thierry Dubois emerged on the bridge from the ship's hospital, his salt-stung face showing the effects of exposure. The 29-year-old was in remarkably good condition, considering his ordeal. He had minor cold damage to his extremities, a laceration on his left index finger, an abrasion to his forehead and mild hypothermia. Although his immersion suit had covered his feet, water had managed to leak inside up to mid-calf and cause damage to his feet.

Dubois borrowed a set of binoculars and scanned the ocean ahead, looking for the upturned hull. More than anyone else, he knew what it took to survive and felt confident. 'Tony designed and built the yacht himself in 1992. He's a good seaman. He can secure the cabin.'

A radio message cut across him. 'This is Rescue 261. We have dropped a white smoke flare.'

'Ahead 18 knots.'

'Copy, 18 knots ahead.'

Rescue 261: 'Smoke about 150 yards away.'

'Roger that. We have the yacht and the smoke visual.'

'Roger.'

'CCS navigator, for information we have the stricken yacht ahead visual. It is currently one half-mile to the south. It is imperative that I get SEC control. I will require manoeuvrability within the next five minutes.'

'Roger that.'

Pete Wicker swung the binoculars towards the stream of white smoke. Through the mist he saw the lonely shape of *Exide Challenger*, one minute riding high out of the water and the next minute covered in wash. About three metres of the yacht could be seen above the water line, depending upon where it rested on the swell.

On the bridge and around the decks there was almost a collective intake of breath. Having travelled in hope, it had taken only one sighting of *Exide Challenger* to convince most watchers that it was a floating coffin rather than a safe haven.

'We've come a hell of a long way to be pulling a body out,' muttered Wicker, under his breath. Until that moment he'd kept an open mind, but now he believed Tony Bullimore to be dead. These same sentiments were etched on the faces of the RIB crew as they prepared to launch the inflatable in the Port Boat Space.

Jim Manson passed on final instructions from the captain. 'Safety is paramount. We are down here to save lives, not lose them. None of you are to put yourselves in personal danger to effect this rescue. I hope I make myself clear.'

This was easier said than done. Everyone involved knew that the moment someone climbed on to the rolling hull and began cutting through, he put himself at risk.

At 0100 hours Zulu time, HMAS *Adelaide* came to within 200 yards of the upturned hull and began to circle slowly, blasting the ship's whistle. Gates and the bridge team went outside, rugged up in pullovers and heavy jackets. Looking around, the captain saw most of the ship's company had gathered on the upper deck, defying the cold to get a glimpse of the yacht.

'I'm going to finish up with dozens of hypothermia cases,' he muttered.

Eight minutes later, Paul Ellul and Chris Smart launched the RIB, both wearing thermal suits because they would be exposed to the elements for longest. Pete Wicker tried to ward off the cold with a submariner's jumper, long-johns, a beanie and leather gloves, but he still shivered as he clambered on board the inflatable.

Thierry Dubois leaned over and shouted advice to him. 'He can be alive. There is air. Maybe you get close and knock, okay? Just knock.'

Grasping the ropes along the sides of the RIB, Wicker heard the engine revs increase and felt the surge of power as the inflatable swung away from the frigate and straight into the teeth of the wind. The RIB roared off the top of the first swell and plunged downwards into a trough. Everything shuddered and shards of freezing spray cut into exposed skin.

The RIB bounced over the swells, cutting the distance quickly, with the hull disappearing and reappearing every ten seconds. The upside-down number '33' stood out dramatically against the white hull, and Wicker was quite surprised at how high the bow of yacht was riding out of the water. The coxswain Ellul timed his approach to surf down a swell that brought them alongside.

'Well done,' yelled Wicker. 'Can you take it back a bit?'

'Behind you,' came a cry.

The next swell threw the RIB on to the hull and then it sucked back into a trough, opening a gap between the two boats. 'You have to get us closer,' yelled Wicker. 'Bring it in again.'

The RIB circled as they searched for the best side to approach. They moved in again and Wicker threw the first grappling hook across the hull, trying to snag it on the far side. His first attempt failed and as he tugged at the rope the grappling hook came barrelling back towards him. Again he tried, having to balance and throw the hook without toppling overboard. Jim Manson managed to snag a piece of rigging on the far side and tied off at the stern. Then Smart threw a 'million to one shot', according to Wicker, and wrapped a grappling hook round the remnants of the keel. It flipped round it twice and then hooked back on itself – a copy-book throw.

With lines now holding the stern and bow of the RIB, it rested hard up against *Exide Challenger*. Wicker glanced across at Syd Smith. 'Here, chuck us a hammer will you, I'll see if he's in there,' he said.

Holding on to the edge of the RIB, he leaned over, reached out and gave three short sharp heavy blows with the hammer. Each impact seemed to bounce off the hull, and he could feel the shock waves shudder up his arm.

Pausing, with the hammer raised, he waited and listened.

24

~~~~~

'BANG!... BANG!... BANG!'

Noise seems to explode into the cuddy. What the hell is that? It can't be rigging, it's too loud. My heart is jammed in my throat. I roll sideways, swinging my legs beneath me as I hit the water.

I can hear an engine, maybe it's a helicopter or a boat. It's coming from the true port side. Christ, they're here; they've come for me. I don't believe it. I have to signal them, I have to hit back. What can I use? Staring madly around the cuddy, I try to find something. The spare beacon! I rip it off the opposite shelf and start hammering on the roof. It has a rubber casing which bounces off without making a sound.

I start punching the roof with fists made useless by the cold.

'I'm in here! I'm in here!' I shout. The sound is soaked up by the walls like water disappearing into sand. I wonder if they can hear me. 'I'm in here! I'm in here!'

They hammer on the hull again. 'Da, da da-ta dah, da! Da!' Funny old bangs. Somebody is doing the banging, that's for sure. I get close to the side of the hull where the banging is coming from and I hear muffled voices.

I keep shouting, 'I'm in here! I'm coming out!' I don't know if anyone can hear me. I'm terrified they might go away again.

Still shouting, I wade through the engine-room with my

chest thumping. No mistakes, Tony. One chance. This is it. The muffled voices are directly above me. A rope snags at my ankle and I fall forwards. Up again, I reach the doghouse but the water feels like quicksand, bogging me down. I pass the broken window and the submerged galley.

At the companionway entrance, I take a deep breath and dive. Cold stabs at my eyes but I need them open. I shoulder the door, slide through and kick off the wall into the dark green. The bubbles rise behind me, floating upwards into an undulating mirror of brightness. I kick once, twice, three times, using my arms to push downwards against the natural buoyancy of the immersion suit. I clear the cowlings and safety rails around the cockpit. Rigging brushes my legs. Deeper, Tony, deeper, you don't want to get tangled – you've come through too much to perish like a fish caught in net.

How far now? What's waiting for me up there? The rest of my life. A beautiful wife. A cottage in Jamaica.

Pressure squeezes my eardrums. One, two, three more kicks. Cold blasts away the cobwebs; I can think clearly now. Up you go, Tony.

I crash out of the water, blinking away the salt and the brightness of the first daylight I've seen in four days. Directly in front of me, filling my entire field of vision, is a warship. It's like one of those pictures they used to put in packets of Woodbine cigarettes. There has never been a more wonderful moment. Absolute, unparalleled elation floods through me, a joy so pure that it actually hurts. Tears mingle with sea-water and run down my unshaven cheeks. I've been given a second chance at life. From a dark, wet and desperately lonely place, I've been reborn.

But where's the rescue boat? I don't know how long I can tread water. I'm exhausted.

I hear voices and turn.

'There he is! There he is!'

'He's in the water!'

A bearded face is peering at me over the upturned hull, looking surprised to see me.

'Can I go that way?' someone cries.

An engine roars and I see someone in black swimming towards me from around the stern of the boat. Three . . . four . . .

five strokes and he's here. The strength in his arms is amazing. He wraps them around my chest and lifts me out of the water like a child.

'Thank you,' I say, but the words choke deep in my throat. I lean back and let my body go limp. It's nice to be someone else's responsibility.

The inflatable boat is coming around the bow of *Exide Challenger*, creating a wash as it turns sharply and heads toward us. The diver is talking to me, his mouth pressed hard against my ear. 'Just stay calm. We'll get you out of here.'

The boat swings alongside us and I see arms stretch out towards me.

'I've got his shoulders,' someone shouts.

'Take his other arm ...'

'Careful, he could be injured.'

The bearded face says, 'On the count of three. One ... two ... three.'

Suddenly, I leave the water and sprawl face-down on top of him. He spins me over and wraps a silver foil blanket around my chest. My head is cradled in his lap. I hold up my hand. 'My finger, my finger,' I say, worried someone might grab my hand.

The swells are hitting the RIB from the side, making it roll and I can feel the wind tug at the blanket, but the world seems like such a beautiful place after four days in a black hole. As the engine roars, every beat of the propeller reverberates through the solid deck. Surfing off the first swell, the boat becomes airborne and slams down into a trough. Everything jars. The coxswain slows down and weaves between the waves.

'I thought it time to make an appearance,' I say, trying to smile. They all look so worried. What's wrong?

'Just stay down. Keep still. We'll have you on board in a jiffy.'

'Oh God, this is wonderful,' I say. 'If you didn't have a beard I'd kiss you.'

He grins. 'Don't let that stop you.'

I reach up, grab his face with my numb hands and plant a kiss on his cheek. Then I clutch the diver and give him a bear hug. I want to kiss them all.

'Just stay down. You could be injured. Don't move.'

The radio crackles and buzzes in the background. People are talking about medical teams and blood pressure. The warship looms over me, the steep sides curling upwards, stark against the low clouds. Shouting above the engine, I ask, 'What's the name of the ship? Where do you come from?'

The bearded face answers, 'I'm Pete Wicker and this is the Royal Australian Navy frigate the *Adelaide*.'

'Australian?'

'Yeah.'

'I knew it. I had a dream ...'

'What happened to your finger?' asks the diver.

'I lost it when the hatch slammed shut.'

'It looks painful.'

'To be honest, I can't feel a bloody thing.'

I can hear the radio again and one of the crew says to me, 'We're not going to lift you out, we're going to lift the whole RIB and take you out on deck. It's the safest way.'

So I lie as still as possible, as the cables take the strain and a winch begins lifting the boat upwards. About two-thirds of the way up, I notice the faces - dozens and dozens of them, peering over the railings and taking up every vantage point. There are curious eyes, fascinated stares, anxious looks and disbelief. These people don't know me, I've never even been to their country, yet I have the overwhelming feeling that we belong to one another; at that precise moment we see life as one.

The RIB swings into a saddle on deck and I say to someone, 'Are we on board? Did you get a picture of my boat?'

A large plane screams overhead. Where did that come from?

Orders are being shouted and people crowd around me, lifting me on to a stretcher. Through the tangle of arms, a hand grasps mine. It's Thierry Dubois.

'Hello, Thierry, what are you doing here?'

'It's a long story.' He smiles. 'We'll have lots of time to talk later.'

Four people whip me across the deck into the ship, metal doors clang shut behind us. The corridors are narrow and it's difficult to negotiate with a stretcher. Cameras flash all about me.

'Spare hands,' shouts the doctor. He looks at me. 'Now just

relax and let us take hold of you. Okay, on three – one . . . two . . . three.'

They lift me on to an examination table.

'I'm going to cut the suit off you, is that okay?'

'Do what you have to.'

I watch big scissors go to work and a drip being slid into my arm. They wrap a sheet around me and then the silver foil. A special heater pipes hot air on to my body and the gentle heat seeps into me. Those parts of my body that aren't damaged warm up beautifully, but I still can't feel my hands or feet.

The doctor puts an oxygen mask over my mouth and nose.

'Can you move your toes for me? . . . Now your legs . . . Let's try your fingers. Can you feel this? . . . How about this? . . . How do you feel?'

'Okay, I guess.'

'We're getting a core body temperature.'

I need to ask him something. He pulls back the plastic mask. 'Am I going to lose any fingers or toes? I mean, apart from this.' I hold up my pinkie.

'It's too early to say.'

He's not going to say any more, but I press him.

'You're actually in better condition than I expected. You have some minor frostbite, but most of the injuries to your feet are non-freezing injuries – what they called "trenchfoot" during the First World War. You should be okay.'

A man arrives at my bedside. Others seem to clear a path for him, so I know he must be important.

'Hello, Tony, I'm pleased you're safe. My name is Captain Raydon Gates and I would like you to welcome you on board the HMAS *Adelaide*.'

'Thank you, sir.' I shake his hand.

'We're very pleased that you're alive.'

'So am I. So am I.'

'We also have Thierry on board.'

'I know. What happened to him?'

'He capsized in the same storm.'

Raydon Gates has very intense eyes, and he stares at me as if wanting to make absolutely sure I'm real. Later he tells me that every time he sees Thierry or me walking around the ship, he thinks, 'They shouldn't really be here. They shouldn't be alive.'

Lying on the examination table, feeling the tiny jets of warm air massage my skin, I wonder about Lal. I know someone would have phoned her with the news, but I want to talk to her and tell her I'm okay. The doctor says I have to wait until my feet are bandaged, and he runs more tests.

'There are journalists outside, threatening to kick down the door.'

'What do they want?'

'You.'

He tells me how big a story I've become, but it doesn't sink in. Why would anyone be interested in me?

Some of the media get inside and start asking me questions. Once I start talking, I can't stop. I sound like a demented chipmunk.

'... It was fabulous, absolutely fabulous. When I heard the banging on the side of the hull I had to think about it for a few seconds because the continuous banging from the rigging and the other noises had been quite excruciating ... When I heard the illogical banging, it was like heaven, I actually heard a voice outside and I started to shout, "I'm coming, I'm coming."

'And boy, when I saw this ship sitting there and the plane going over the top and a couple of guys peering over the upturned hull it was heaven. Absolute heaven. I really, really never thought I would reach that far. I was starting to look back over my life and started to think, "Well, I've had a good one. I've done most of the things that I wanted to do. I had a good wife." I don't mind telling the world – I've become more human. In these last six days I've become a different person. I won't be so rude to people. Not that I was, but I'll be much more of a gentleman and I'll listen to people more.'

25

~~~~~

SOUTHERN OCEAN
Thursday, 9 January 1997

Pete Wicker accepted the congratulations of crewmates and wrapped his hands around a steaming mug of tea. Salt spray still dripped from his beard and dried on his cheeks. People pressed close, asking him questions. Everyone seemed to be smiling and joking.

'So, Pete, you knocked on the hull and yelled, "Avon calling!"'

'Yeah, otherwise he might have thought you were collecting money.'

'Did he give you the secret password?'

Wicker grinned broadly. His sense of excitement made him feel twenty years younger. All the worries of the previous few days had been blown aside by the sound of one man's voice and the sight of his grey head bobbing beside the upturned hull.

Having hit the hull three times, he had paused with the hammer in mid-air, waiting for a response. The RIB crew heard it together - a tapping sound and then a muffled cry. They looked at each other.

'Christ, he's alive!'

'Shhhhh!'

Then the shouting came through more clearly. 'I'm in here! I'm in here!'

Wicker hammered an acknowledgment, changing the tune

to funny knocks. 'Da, da da-ta dah, da! Da!'

Jim Manson picked up the radio and yelled into the receiver, 'He's alive! He's alive!' The message went straight back to the bridge.

'Are you all right? Can you get out?' screamed Wicker, as loud as he could.

The muffled reply was incomprehensible.

'What did he say?' asked Manson.

'It sounded like "No!",' said Wicker. He grabbed hold of an axe and dragged himself higher on to the hull. Swinging it hard, it sank easily into the foam.

Thumbing the radio handset, Manson radioed the bridge, 'We have made contact with the survivor who has indicated that he is trapped inside. RIB crew effecting rescue. Over.'

As Wicker raised the axe again, he heard the muffled voice going further and further aft in the boat.

'Where the bloody hell is he going?' he muttered. 'He must be right back there, calling up through the remnants of the keel.'

The voice kept moving and then stopped. Wicker buried the axe into the hull, punching a ragged hole the size of a fist through the outer layer.

As clear as crystal, a voice rang out, 'Ahoy! I'm here. I'm here.'

Wicker looked around. Unable to pick up the direction, but knowing it was very close. The radio blared a message from the bridge. 'There he is! There he is! He's in the water!'

Tony Bullimore had surfaced on the opposite side of the hull near the stern. Wicker peered over the top and saw a head bobbing in the water. The face turned and looked imploringly towards him. Immediately, he slashed the forward ropes with a blow from the axe and Maxwell cast off at the stern.

'Can I go that way?' cried Rub to Manson, who didn't get a chance to reply. The diver was already in motion, plunging into the water and rounding the bow with powerful strokes. The RIB went the opposite way, the nose arcing upwards as the engine surged.

Bullimore could be exhausted or badly injured; he could drown before they reached him, thought Wicker. As the boat rounded the hull he saw the yachtsman's face. He had the hollow-eyed, almost haunted look of someone who had been right to the edge. At the same time, his face revealed utter relief and exhaustion.

The diver reached Bullimore several seconds before the RIB. Wicker took the survivor's shoulders, Manson had one arm and Rub pushed from underneath. Two good heaves and he slid into the boat on top of Wicker, who rolled him over.

'I thought it time to make an appearance,' said Bullimore.

Wicker had been briefed by the ship's doctor to keep the survivor as horizontal as possible. In advance stages of hypothermia, a sudden movement such as sitting upright can be fatal.

He nursed the yachtsman's head in his lap.

'If you didn't have that beard I'd kiss you.'

'Don't let that stop you ...'

The crew laughed as Wicker recounted the story. 'And that's when he planted one on me.'

'Yeah, you got to watch those Poms,' Syd Smith joked.

'He has to be desperate to kiss a big ugly git like you,' someone shot back.

Wicker had never been so thrilled. It had been the most satisfying moment of his naval career. Never before had he been given the chance to give someone back his life. It was a feeling shared by the entire ship's company. No one present would ever forget that moment.

Thirty thousand feet above them, the crew of Rescue 261 celebrated with a soft drink, toasting their success.

'To be part of one rescue is amazing, but two in the same day is breathtaking,' said Squadron Leader Richard Moth.

'And to think we almost missed it,' said Ajax. 'He didn't waste any time coming out.'

After vectoring the *Adelaide* to the upturned hull, the Orion had plugged out above the clouds, shutting down one engine to conserve fuel. From altitude, using radar, it could track the approaching weather front which had now moved to within five miles. The cockpit crew assumed HMAS *Adelaide* would circle the hull and appraise the situation before beginning any rescue attempt.

In the co-pilot's seat, Ajax had radioed the bridge, 'Rescue 261 to *Adelaide*. How long before you plan to launch?'

'The Zodiac is in the water now,' came the reply.

Moth and Ajax looked at each other. 'Let's get back down there.'

Nosing into a shallow dive, the Orion descended to 300 feet and flew directly over *Exide Challenger* as the RIB pulled alongside it. Ajax watched the grappling hooks being thrown over the hull as the crew tried to find a tethering point. Within seconds the Orion had screamed past and Moth came back round on a race-track pattern. At the furthermost point in the turn, they had a message from the bridge.

'Rescue 261, this is *Adelaide*.'

'Go ahead, *Adelaide*.'

'For your information, contact has been made with Mr Bullimore. He is alive inside the vessel. We are launching a rescue plan.'

Hollers and whoops rang out through the aircraft.

'Well, I'll be ... What a canny old bastard,' cried Sean Corkhill.

'The wily old fox owes us a beer then,' said Ajax. 'Air Force Sydney, this is Rescue 261. Please pass to 92 Wing operations that Mr Bullimore is alive inside the vessel.'

The Orion swept back overhead and Ajax could see the white hull and dark RIB alongside. 'How the hell are they gonna get him out?' he wondered out loud.

As they passed directly above, he looked down to see a bobbing grey head near the stern.

'He's in the water! He's in the water!'

At the same instant the words were echoed back through the radio from the *Adelaide*. A diver was in the water, swimming towards the survivor. He wrapped his arms around the figure and held him until the RIB arrived.

When the Orion swept overhead again, the inflatable was racing over the swells towards the *Adelaide*. Lying within, Tony Bullimore lay wrapped in a silver foil blanket, with only his grizzled, unshaven face visible.

'We're looking at the luckiest son-of-a-bitch alive,' said Moth.

Ajax nodded. 'And I think he knows it.'

SAVED

*

At Perth International Airport, Vic Lewkowski didn't have an office and had been controlling the SAR ground operation using mobile phones. At 9.30 A.M., local time, a call came through from the air operations communications centre in Sydney – Tony Bullimore had been rescued.

Lewkowski ran across the tarmac towards the Orions where maintenance crews continued working in the sweltering heat. Yelling to be heard over the Auxiliary Power Unit, he shouted, 'He's alive! He's alive!'

Cheers rang out and bottles of drinking water were poured over heads and sprayed in a celebratory water fight. The twelve-hour shifts in horrendous heat had been worthwhile: a man's life had been saved. It didn't matter that they worked in the background, or that the P-3C crews always grabbed the media attention – every one of them had played a role in an astonishing rescue.

Larry Smith and his crew had flown the last mission on Wednesday night, arriving back in Perth in the early hours of Thursday morning. The crew got their heads down at the Great Eastern Motor Lodge and other nearby hotels, agreeing to meet later in the morning for news of the rescues.

By the time Smith woke and turned on the television, Dubois had been picked up safely by the Seahawk. He ran from room to room, saying, 'He's okay. He's okay.'

HMAS *Adelaide* was still an hour away from *Exide Challenger*, so they agreed to meet for breakfast at a nearby coffee shop, a few minutes walk up the road. Someone stayed behind to wait for the call. The crew had just ordered a second round of toast and more coffee when the messenger arrived out of breath.

'He's alive! He's okay.'

They dashed back to the hotel and all crowded into one room to watch the first reports from the *Adelaide*.

Smith, like Phil Buckley, had always appeared confident of success, but the sense of relief and elation he felt at Tony Bullimore's rescue told him that he had 'hoped' far more than 'believed' the yachtsman could survive.

'I've read books about shipwrecks and stories of survival and that kept my hopes up,' he admitted afterwards. 'We search for worst case and hope for the best case, looking as hard as we can. We looked until our eyes hurt. We searched those tracks until the PLE came up. It's not a good feeling when you have to set power, climb out and go home.

'But this is great. This makes it all worthwhile. The old heart was pumping towards the end. You feel responsible for the people down there and no one wanted to lose them.'

At MRCC headquarters in Canberra, the staff had been taking bets on when they'd hear something. Mike Jackson-Calway had nominated 0145 Zulu – 12:45 P.M. local time. The office seemed to be crowded with spectators, but it was nothing compared to the footpath outside, which had been taken over by TV cameras, reporters, photographers and journalists.

Jackson-Calway sat at his desk, with Rick Burleigh next to him. David Gray, the Press Officer, hovered in the background, drafting various statements in his head, one for each outcome.

The telephone rang and the whole room seemed to stop, as if someone had freeze-framed a video. Only Jackson-Calway moved as he picked up the receiver.

'This is HMAS *Adelaide*. Please be advised, at 0143 Zulu, Tony Bullimore was safely picked up. *Adelaide* circled the vessel, blowing its whistle but got no response. It launched a boat which knocked on the upturned hull and Tony swam out.'

Jackson-Calway very calmly took a note and said thank you. Then he turned to Rick Burleigh. 'They've got him. He's alive!'

The room erupted in cheers and David Gray almost danced a little jig near the printer.

'How? How?' The questions had started.

'They knocked on the hull and he swam out. Just like that!'

Laughter echoed off the low ceilings. They'd done it! Three out of three! The largest search-and-rescue operation undertaken by the Australian defence forces in peace-time had succeeded spectacularly.

But amid the euphoria and congratulations, Jackson-Calway picked up the telephone.

26

BRISTOL, ENGLAND
2:00 A.M., Thursday, 9 January 1997

Wesley answers on the second ring but I can't look up from the kitchen table. Lois and Anthony give my hands a squeeze.

Turning his back to the table, Wesley stares out the window into the darkened garden. For a long while he just listens. Then he says, 'Will you please confirm what you just said.'

After a pause that lasts forever, he says it again: 'I'm sorry, will you please confirm what you just told me.'

In the absolute silence a large fat tear rolls down my cheek. Oh God, Tony, where are you? Please be all right. Please don't be dead.

'Are you sure?' says Wesley.

He raises his fist in the air and I know. I scream and suddenly people are embracing me and crying. It's almost as if a part of me has left my body and I'm floating in the air. The burden has gone and it feels lovely. We hug, we kiss, we jump, we dance, we open a bottle of champagne and we shout, 'He's alive! He's alive!'

An hour later, a young female photographer knocks on the door, carrying a bottle of champagne. It's two o'clock in the morning but her editor has sent her to get a picture of me. I feel sorry for her and invite her inside, where she takes the first pictures of the party in full swing. Later, she brings along photographs of Tony after the rescue. He's wrapped in a silver blanket, with a haunted look in his eyes. I can see his mouth open and his hands raised a few inches above his chest.

'He's all right,' I say to Wesley. 'He's talking.'

I manage to get a few hours' sleep and then wake to see the morning TV news coverage. Tony's eyes are almost hollow, they're so sunken, and his face is bruised and bloodied but he's talking, rattling on at a hundred miles an hour. He doesn't know where to begin and end, he just wants to thank people.

They keep talking about 'heroic yachtsman, Tony Bullimore' and using words like courageous, remarkable, astonishing ... and they're talking about my Tony.

'He'll be trying to call you,' says Jane as we sip mugs of tea on the sofa.

'Yes.'

Steve puts his head around the door. 'When do want to do these TV interviews? They're waiting outside.'

'Let me have a shower and get changed first.'

Upstairs, under the stream of water, I think of how many tears have been washed away over the past few days.

'You don't know what you put me through, Tony Bullimore,' I say out loud.

'I'm sorry, Lal.' He sounds contrite, but I know he's smiling.

'I told you that boat was coming for you.'

'You did.'

'They thought you were dead, but I knew better.'

'You did.'

On the doorstep, a journalist asks me if I will ever let Tony sail in such a race again.

'I wouldn't like him to do it again,' I say, 'because it's too much for me to have to sit and wonder what is going on. But I will not make his mind up for him. He has got to do it for himself. He has his own mind. Tony is stubborn. If he makes up his mind to do something he'll do it. He is courageous, he is honest, he is genuine. He is ever such a nice bloke. He is like a bulldog, a great, big beautiful bulldog.'

At 7:50 A.M. Tony calls from the ship and I run to the phone. His first words are 'I love you'. Then he asks if I'm all right.

'Of course I'm all right. How about you?'

'Yes, you know me. Nothing keeps me down.'

'You're a very, very naughty boy. You nearly killed us here,' I chide him.

'What about me then?' he professes. It's the same old Tony, but I can hear a quiver in his voice.

'So tell me, are you all in one piece?'

'I lost a little bit of one finger and my feet are pretty wrecked, but the doctor says they'll be okay. I've had a nice shower and I'm being looked after.'

He says that he's sorry for having me put through the last four days and promises not to do any more long-distance voyages without my permission. I keep thinking, 'Oh, yes. I wish I had a tape of this call, Tony.'

We didn't even mention my flying out to Perth to meet him. He knew that I'd be there even if I had to swim all the way.

27

〰〰

SOUTHERN OCEAN
Thursday, 9 January 1997

What joy! A bunk with a mattress, wonderful soft sheets and a cotton blanket. I lie in the darkness, close my eyes and tell myself, 'I'm saved. I'm on an Australian warship.'

I still can't quite believe it. A part of my mind is still rolling inside that floating tomb. It's as if I've left a bit of myself behind inside the cuddy, drifting aimlessly and living in hope. What will become of *Exide Challenger*, I wonder. She'll become waterlogged and sink eventually, I suppose. Until then she'll keep drifting eastwards, past Macquarie Island and South Georgia, slowly circling Antarctica. She'll be no danger to shipping, because there are so few ships down there.

Mercifully, sleep comes quickly, and for the first time in months I have a complete night's rest. There are no sails to trim, or charts to read, I can just sink into that soft mattress, smell the freshly laundered pillow slip and plan the rest of my life one day at a time.

The sense of disbelief stays with me because everything seems like an incredibly vivid dream. So much so that the next morning, as I stand on the flight deck having a cigarette - it's the only place on the *Adelaide* where you can smoke - I turn to a young leading seaman beside me and I stare at him for a long time.

'Is everything okay?' he asks, growing uncomfortable.

'You're in the Australian navy, aren't you? This is an Australian warship?'

He laughs and in a wonderful Aussie drawl says, 'Yeah, too right, mate. No worries.'

The medical report from the ship's doctor says that I was in the first stages of hypothermia. My core temperature had fallen to 36.1°C (normal core temperature 38°C). Both my feet have been badly damaged by constant immersion in water. I have frostbite on the tip of my left index finger and forehead, a broken tooth, moderate dehydration and multiple abrasions to both hands. My severed finger will have to be 'tidied up' by surgery when I reach the mainland.

The doctor wants me to stay off my feet and keep them raised on a chair, but I'm like a kid on the first day of summer break. Life has too much to offer. Every cup of tea, every conversation, every ten-minute ciggie break on the flight deck is a bonus. I remember Dave Mathieson having a heart bypass, and afterwards he told me about colours being richer and smells more intense. Now I know what he means.

Because I can only hobble around, people tend to visit me in the Petty Officers' Mess. They all ask me about what happened and I'm happy to talk. Maybe if I keep retelling the story, I can transfer some of the bad memories and someone else can share the load. This afternoon I had twenty young seamen around me on the flight deck, all asking questions and offering me a cup of tea or a smoke. These are wonderful people.

I'm getting five-star treatment in the POs' Mess, with Mark 'Knocker' White making sure I have a real cowboy's breakfast every morning and Vaughn 'Jock' Heath, Garry 'Gazza' Mason and all the other POs in the Mess really looking after me. At night, when the watch comes off duty, I get mugs of tea and hot buttered toast. It is all bloody fantastic.

Thierry and I have lots of invitations for dinner in the CPOs' and the Officers' Ward Room. We're guests of honour at a formal dinner held by Captain Gates. Sometimes, it's all too much and I look forward to slipping out on to the flight deck. What better way to end an evening than to glance over the stern of the *Adelaide* as she pounds along at 25 knots, leaving the Southern Ocean in her wake.

From the bridge of HMAS *Adelaide*, the news of my rescue had flashed around the world, relayed by the MRCC in Canberra. At the Vendée Globe headquarters in Paris, the following message arrived:

SOUTHERN OCEAN YACHTS IN DISTRESS
SITREP SEVEN 0153Z, 9 JAN 97
1.   MR THIERRY DUBOIS RESCUED BY HMAS ADELAIDE AT 2117Z BY HELICOPTER AND SECOND SURVIVOR MR BULLIMORE RESCUED AT APPROX 0115Z AND BOTH SURVIVORS BEING GIVEN MEDICAL TREATMENT ON BOARD HMAS ADELAIDE.
2.   FURTHER DETAILS WILL BE RELEASED IN LATER SITREPS.

The MRCC sent a message of thanks to HMAS *Adelaide* and also to the master of the *Sanko Phoenix,* who had gone so far out of his way to take the tanker to the search area. The delay had cost the shipping company £40,000: 'IN WHAT MUST BE ONE OF THE LONGEST RANGE RESCUES IN HISTORY THE PROFESSIONALISM AND WILLINGNESS SHOWN BY ALL PARTICIPANTS IS GREATLY APPRECIATED ... YES, MIRACLES DO HAPPEN AND ITS NICE TO PART OF THEM.'

Further congratulations arrived from Australia's Maritime Commander, Rear Admiral Chris Oxenbould:

THE RESCUE OF THE TWO VENDÉE GLOBE YACHTSMEN DUBOIS AND BULLIMORE WAS A MAGNIFICENT ACHIEVEMENT IN THE MOST DIFFICULT OF CIRCUMSTANCES AND ONE WHICH REFLECTS PLANNING AND CO-OPERATION OF THE HIGHEST CALIBRE ... YOUR ROLE IN THE OPERATION WAS CRUCIAL TO ITS SUCCESS AND THROUGH YOUR PROFESSIONALISM YOU HAVE BROUGHT YOURSELVES GREAT CREDIT WHICH, IN THIS CASE PARTICULARLY, REFLECTS UPON AUSTRALIA AS WELL. PLEASE ACCEPT MY SINCERE THANKS AND CONGRATULATIONS AS WELL AS THE HEARTFELT APPRECIATION OF THE INTERNATIONAL YACHTING COMMUNITY.

The rescue centre in Canberra received congratulations from the French government, Vendée Globe organisers and maritime rescue organisations in Japan, France and Britain. The Queen sent a message describing it as 'an extraordinary feat of survival' and praising Australia's defence forces on 'their dramatic rescue'. The British Prime Minister, John Major, broke from his tour of India to express his delight. 'It is an extraordinary story. It is quite wonderful news.'

Suddenly, I begin to realise just how much had been invested in rescuing Thierry and myself. Not just in terms of men, women and machines, but the enormous amount of goodwill and the prayers that were offered for our safety. For all the optimism that surrounded the search, the universal sense of relief and disbelief shows that very few people expected such a happy outcome. Raydon Gates summed it up: 'Like the chaplain, I'm starting to believe in miracles. We were working on hope rather than confidence. When he bobbed up alongside the yacht it was a tremendously exciting feeling.'

Thierry and I have become public property, and the journalists on board want interviews, exclusives and photo opportunities. They ask a thousand questions. How did I survive? How did the darkness affect me? Did I realise the Australian defence forces were on their way to rescue me?

The truth is, I don't know all the answers. I'm sure that experience counts for a lot. I tell them, 'I'm not a big lad, I'm not that tough. Just a little bloke in a black hole. I owe my life to the brave people who came out looking for me. I wasn't brave. It was a horrific, traumatic experience. It was a case of praying and hoping that there was something happening above the water. It was sheer determination, a little water, a little chocolate and hanging on in there, believing something might happen.

'Think about it. This is the ultimate thing that I've ever done, I really mean that. I've been dead lucky because a bunch of people said, "Go for it!" and they came down and looked for me.'

This instant fame is quite amusing until I hear some of the stories emerging from the newspapers. Some have confused me with Pete Goss and called me a former Royal Marine; others have listed my former occupations to include everything from an undertaker to a bookmaker. What rubbish!

A British paper claims that I've been approaching rival chocolate companies asking for £20,000 to 'remember' which brand of chocolate I ate to stay alive. This upsets me until I discover that it's a misunderstanding created by a sports marketing company which had tried to get me sponsorship for the Vendée Globe. I set the record straight by telling reporters that any money from endorsements will go to charity.

Meanwhile, my real concern is for Gerry Roufs, a French Canadian who is missing in the South Pacific. Gerry had apparently been coming second in the Vendée Globe when he radioed race headquarters on 8 January, giving his position as two-thirds of the way to Cape Horn. Since then, there's been radio silence.

Isabelle Autissier on *PRB* has turned back to try to find him, and three other boats are being redirected to go past his last recorded location. What a race this has been! First Raphael Dinelli, then Thierry and myself, now Gerry Roufs. The remainder of the fleet is stretched over 5,500 nautical miles in four oceans.

Meanwhile, the *Adelaide* is heading back to the Australian mainland. It will take four days. The tanker *Westralia* is coming to meet us on Saturday morning to refuel the frigate at sea. By the time we dock, the warship will have used 600,000 litres of fuel. 'If only you could rig up a sail,' I joke.

I haven't seen much of Thierry, I think he's taking things easy and contemplating what happened. It's nice to hear him say that he'll be back for the next Vendée Globe - the sport needs dedicated people like Thierry and I'm sure that he will conquer the oceans.

I haven't even thought about my future - that can wait. For now, I just want to mend and rebuild my strength, while enjoying the simple things like drinking a cold beer and listening to the constant stream of jokes coming from 'Jock' Heath, 'Gazza' Mason and the other guys in the Mess. My feet are starting to hurt, but the doctor says that's a good sign. The numbness is wearing off and the nerves are coming back as the blood circulates in the tiny capillaries. A couple of weeks in the Australian sunshine will do them the world of good.

On Saturday morning, there's a thirty-minute thanksgiving service on the flight deck. 'Their very presence here with us is miraculous,' says the ship's Chaplain, Barrie Yesberg. 'Miracle' is a pretty good word to describe it. He's standing at an altar fashioned from a card table and covered with a blue cloth captioned, 'Protect Men where so'er they go.'

I've never been a very religious person. I'm not an atheist, but nor am I a deep believer, yet I have never doubted the power of prayer or the ability of religion to bring people comfort. I know a lot of people around the world were asking for my salvation, including entire congregations in places as far away as the Caribbean and in Europe, North America, Australia and Britain. I owe them my thanks and perhaps my life.

We arrive in Fremantle on Monday morning and the reception is incredible. Ten thousand people line the dockside. Klaxons blare, car horns sound, balloons, flags and streamers fly in the breeze. Young children are held above heads, trying to recognise their fathers and mothers among the crew lining the railings.

More than forty dignitaries, including Federal and State politicians, have turned up, along with the High Commissioners of Britain and France and about a hundred and fifty journalists. The Australian TV networks are crossing live to broadcast the event.

Lal couldn't get an earlier flight and won't be in Perth for a few more hours. What a shame she missed this. They want to take me down the gangway in a wheelchair but I tell them, 'Not in a million years. I'm going to walk.'

My feet are spongy and painful, wrapped in bandages, covered with socks and sandals. I manage to hobble down the narrow ramp, with the help of a few steadying hands. Someone calls for three cheers from the crew and the sound makes the tears well up. What a reception!

Hobbling to the podium, I face the crowd with HMAS *Adelaide* as a backdrop. 'If it wasn't for the professionalism, the dedication, the in-built spirit of Australia, I am positive - absolutely positive - that I wouldn't be here now. I am slightly emotional about this, all I am going to say is thank you to everyone on the *Adelaide*, I'm going to turn around ...'

I turn slowly and raise my fists in a salute. The crowd erupts.

'Let me say one last thing. Thank you Australia for giving back my life. Thank you very much.'

Thierry makes a lovely speech in broken English. 'A lot of people are using the word hero, but in fact if you want to speak about heroes I think Australia has a lot of heroes and I think some of them, the aircraft crews, the ship's crew, a lot of heroes. We are not heroes, me and not Tony, we owe everything to these guys and the air crews and to the Australians.'

Captain Gates is totally unperturbed by all the razzmatazz. Rising to his feet, he tells the crowd, 'Compared to them I certainly don't stand here as a hero, but I do stand here as a very proud Australian and a very proud naval officer.'

Afterwards, Thierry is reunited with his mother Bridgette and his girlfriend Murielle Dehoue. We hold a brief press conference and someone asks me if I'm considering trauma counselling.

'What would you sooner do, have a beer in the pub or be counselled?' I ask.

Amid the laughter, another journalist questions the huge bill for the rescue, which will fall upon Australian taxpayers.

'There is something a little absurd about the tremendous cost of rescuing people who attempt difficult challenges,' I admit. 'I have thought about it very deeply and I don't know whether we have the right to lean on society, communities or countries to say, "Well, here we are, come and rescue us."

'At the same time, people walk to the South Pole, they sail the oceans of the world, they go up as high as they can ... whatever. If all these things were taken away, it would be a little bit like the taming of mankind.'

The Federal Defence Minister, Ian McLachlan, says there is no question of the Australian government asking for any refund. 'This is experience you cannot buy. The costs would have been run up anyway, probably practising somewhere else. The knowledge we will get out of this is irreplaceable.'

These same sentiments are echoed to me later when Squadron Leader Alf Jonas, an Orion pilot, told me about the 75th Anniversary of the RAAF the previous year. Apparently, a budget of several million had been spent in advertising the celebration. 'Afterwards, you could have asked anyone in the street and I doubt if one person in a hundred could have told you about the anniversary,' said Jonas. 'Yet this last week has done more for our international standing and prestige than any number of displays or open days.'

After the emotional welcome, Thierry and I are driven to Fremantle Hospital. The sun shines down through the trees, casting shadows across the neatly trimmed parks and gardens. There's a warm wind and I can smell freshly cut grass and eucalyptus trees. This feels like home, yet I've never been here before.

Isn't it amazing how our lives can turn on a fraction of a second or a casual connection? Fate can be measured in degrees of luck and coincidence. On a glorious summer morning with the sun burning down from an endless blue sky, it hardly seems fathomable that I could have been so close to dying in a dark freezing hull. What unknown factor has made me different from Gerry Roufs? Why have I been spared, while hopes for him are fading? There are no rational arguments or answers.

Dr Harry Oxer chats to me at the hospital and examines my feet. He's a consultant in diving and hyperbaric medicine – the main man when it comes to treating divers who have the bends and injuries related to frostbite and trenchfoot.

He wants me to keep off my feet and forego any partying until my body can repair blood-deprived extremities. I'm supposed to spend two hours every day in a hyperbaric chamber, to increase the oxygenation of my blood and accelerate the healing process. The chamber looks like a coffin.

Harry seems like a nice guy and his staff are really friendly. I could get used to all this tender loving care.

28

PERTH, AUSTRALIA
Monday, 13 January 1997

I'm so excited about seeing Tony, I barely sleep on the plane.
The last few days have been hectic and the phone hasn't stopped ringing from well-wishers, journalists, agents, publishers
and film-makers. I feel like telling them, 'He's mine. You can't
have him. Let him rest.'

Jane, Wesley, Steve and Dave are with me because I'll need
help getting Tony to and from his treatment each day in a
wheelchair. I've never packed in such a hurry and probably
brought all the wrong clothes for the weather in Perth. I don't
care; I just want to see Tony.

The TV cameras are waiting at the airport, along with a car
from the British Consul General's office. The warship had
arrived at 8:00 A.M., seven hours ago. We are whisked off to the
residence of Anthony Abbott, the Consul General, and his wife
Margaret, a lovely house in a leafy suburb, surrounded by
gardens.

I try to imagine what I'm going to say to Tony when I see
him. What words are there? 'Just be strong,' I tell myself.
'You've spilled enough tears.' But when I see him my hand
flies up and covers my mouth. 'Oh dear. Oh my God,' I cry. He
looks like a ghost. He's lost so much weight he's disappearing
into his clothes. There are bruises all over his face and
bandages on his feet and hands.

We fall into each other's arms and weep. I can feel his shoulders shaking as I put my arms around him. 'Oh-oh,' he says, 'oh-oh'; it's almost like the sound a child makes when they're hurting. Then he puts on his happy face and is typically ebullient, chatty and charming. He squeezes my hand, turns to a journalist and says, 'You see why I fought so hard to stay alive?'

'How are you?' I ask.

'My toes are hanging off a bit ... and my fingers,' he laughs and holds up his hand, showing me the missing digit.

'It wouldn't make any different to me if you came back on peg legs. I'd still have you and I won't let you go.'

Tony can't stand still and I feel him shuffle from side to side. 'When I go sailing again,' he announces in a big loud voice.

'Oh, don't, please,' I whisper.

He's teasing me. 'No, it'll be all right next time. Nice and easy, you know.'

Afterwards, when the TV cameras have gone, I ask him a few questions about the accident but I can see he doesn't want to talk. He keeps changing the subject and asking me about how everything is at home. Is Yvonne still staying at the house? Has Lois finished her law exams? The tiniest details seem to matter to him, even if it's about nuisance pigeons nesting in the eaves.

Unfortunately, we can't be together on our first night. Tony has surgery on his frostbitten left hand and stays overnight at the St John of God Hospital. Next morning I pick him up and take him to the hyperbaric unit for his session in the decompression chamber. When we arrive, Tony flirts with the nurses and chats away.

'We're ready for you now, Mr Bullimore,' says the sister.

'How about a cup of tea first?' says Tony. Then he slips out the side door for a cigarette.

'Ready now, Mr Bullimore?'

I get the impression Tony is delaying things, but I can't understand why.

'Which chamber is it?' I ask.

'That one.' The nurse points to a rather small metal chamber, built for one person. My heart goes out to Tony.

'You can't put him in there,' I say. 'He'll think he's still under the boat.'

Without any discussion, Tony is switched to a bigger chamber, where other people are being treated at the same time. Tony can sit inside and chat to his heart's content, swapping stories, discussing ailments and not having to think about the cold, dark hull.

I'm very protective of him and I look for the slightest sign of trauma or delayed shock. When I mention the possibility of counselling, he just smiles and says he doesn't need that kind of help.

'Just talk to someone who knows the right questions to ask,' I say, but Tony shakes his head. He just keeps talking, all the time talking. At first it worries me. What happens when he finally stops talking about what happened, I wonder. Will the true horror then dawn on him? Will the demons come out? Then I decide that as long as he keeps talking to people he'll be all right.

The listeners are everywhere. When he's wheeled along the street, tourists wave and want to take have their photograph taken beside his wheelchair. Even when he's supposed to be resting at the Burswood Hotel, I find him chatting away to other guests, visitors, the management, bellhops and waiters.

The only person he won't talk to is me. He's never told me what happened down there in that dark hole, I've had to read about it in newspapers and magazines. On about the third morning in Perth, I finally ask him.

'But you know what happened,' he says.

'I've read things and seen interviews, but I want to hear it from you.'

'Where do you want me to start?'

'The beginning is a good place.'

He tells me about Heard Island and the little birds he tried to rescue. Then the storm and the rogue waves. I listen and stare out of the window at the beautiful Swan River meandering through gardens, past the Perth city skyline, on its journey to the sea. Such serenity makes it hard to picture the wretchedness of the Southern Ocean.

Tony falls silent and I turn around.

'What's wrong?'

He shakes his head.
'Can't you tell me what happened?'
He shakes his head again.
I don't know why he can't tell me. Maybe he thinks he won't be able to stop once he begins and it frightens him. Or perhaps he thinks that if I hear it from other people it won't scare me so much. That's why he finds it easier to talk to strangers.

Tony is very brave and strong to have lasted as long as he did. He lost two and a half stone and still feels pain all over his body from what he went through. I feel very sad for him to see him go through all this. I just want to scoop him up and take him home and look after him. I want to wrap him up in cotton wool ... for five minutes at least.

Postscript

Although I do not have nightmares, I don't sleep as well as I once did. I often get up in the early hours and go downstairs, where I make myself a cup of tea, sit in an old armchair and drift back to the Southern Ocean. I'm not sure what I'm looking for.

A few weeks ago I went on a discussion programme hosted by Esther Ranzen, on post-traumatic stress. There were quite a few people who talked about the problems they'd faced after terrible experiences, but I didn't have anything to contribute. I think Esther Ranzen grew slightly impatient with me because she wanted me to talk about having nightmares and emotional fallout.

I couldn't help her. I know it's flippant to say that a few beers down the pub with mates is better than any counselling, but I grew up in a tough school where people had to deal with setbacks and bereavement very quickly and get on with their lives. Back then, counselling consisted of an extra spoonful of sugar in your tea.

Occasionally, Lal asks me about what happened, but I can't tell her. I've always tried to shield her from the hurt in the world and I don't want her to know how bad it really was. Lal says that she won't read this book because she doesn't want to be reminded of those days. I'm pleased about that; I don't want her to be hurt any more or to have nightmares.

The public reaction to my rescue has been truly amazing. I've received more than 20,000 letters from around the world. Some of them are brief postcards saying simply, 'Glad to see you're alive,' while others are long heartfelt letters from people who followed every up and down and twist and turn of the search. They tell of being in tears as they knelt in front of their televisions watching me emerge from the hull.

Pensioners write and describe their problems; churchgoers recount how they prayed for me; blind people say that I must now have an inkling of what it's like to live in permanent darkness. One young schoolgirl put on the envelope 'The Upside-Down Sailor' and nothing else, but her letter still reached me.

I've accepted awards for bravery, opened fund-raising appeals for charities, drawn the National Lottery and been honoured with an invitation for Lal and I to visit Buckingham Palace and have an audience with the Queen. The list could go on and on. It all seems so unreal and far removed from the black hole in the Southern Ocean.

I can't explain why my rescue should generate such a response. Perhaps Tony Wright, a journalist for the *Sydney Morning Herald*, summed it up in a feature he wrote on the day HMAS *Adelaide* arrived in Fremantle.

He wrote of the heroic efforts of the RAAF fliers in their Orions, skimming above the giant waves in winds that rarely dropped below 45 knots. And of the *Adelaide*, with its crew of 143, knifing through the ever-colder waters on a voyage unparalleled in Australian naval history. Then there were the men and women bunkered down twenty-four hours a day in the Maritime Rescue Co-ordination Centre in Canberra, holding together all the threads of the operation.

'But central to it all was the spectre of one man freezing or starving or suffocating on the high seas,' wrote Wright. 'It is just possible that when Bullimore swam out of his tomb, he and all his rescuers did millions of people a favour. For a while there, it seemed everyone wore a smile and stepped just a little lighter.'

What does the future hold for 'the upside-down sailor'? I don't know. For a brief moment down in the dark hole, I thought of promising that I'd never set foot on a boat again. It's easy to make pacts with yourself or with God when things are looking bleak. But I've come to the conclusion that I really do this for love. Sailing is more than a hobby or a profession to me - it's a grand passion and a way of life. I can't let go.

Maybe in a few years' time I'll retire from ocean racing and have a nice little boat so I can pull a few ropes and go cruising. I can see myself doing that until I'm too old to climb over the side of a boat.

Six years ago I set myself the challenge of sailing single-handed around the globe in the toughest yacht race in the world. I didn't succeed. Perhaps if I'd completed the Vendée it would have been different, but now it feels like unfinished business.

When I mention this to Lal over a bottle of wine and a meal, she looks away in disgust. 'If you do this race again, don't expect any support from me,' she says. 'I can't go through that again.'

I understand completely. I love her desperately and the hardest part of this is the thought of leaving her for any length of time. Now, I'm beginning to sense that she's weakening. She knows that I won't be happy if I leave this dream unfulfilled, and she always says, 'At our age in life it's important to be happy.'

'Just one more,' I say. 'I promise this is the last time.'

'And what happens then?'

'Then we get our little cottage in Jamaica, like the one Noël Coward had, with a vegetable patch and a garden full of bougainvillea and mango trees. You'll wear cotton dresses and a straw hat and I'll have old trousers, a baggy shirt and a Panama hat. We'll sit in our wicker chairs, overlooking the ocean, sipping long cool drinks and thinking, "Oh, what a wonderful life it's been." And do you know what we'll do then?'

'What will we do then, Tony Bullimore?'

'We'll live happily ever after.'